A Special Scar

Second edition

Every 85 minutes someone in the UK takes their own life, but what happens to those left behind? In a society where suicide is often viewed with fear or disapproval, it can be difficult for those personally affected by a suicide death to some to terms with their loss and seek help and support.

A Special Scar looks in detail at the stigma surrounding suicide and offers practical help for survivors, relatives and friends of people who have taken their own life. Fifty bereaved people tell their own stories, showing us that, by not hiding the truth from themselves and others, they have been able to learn to live with the suicide, offering hope to others facing this traumatic loss. This new, revised edition includes new material on:

- Counselling survivors of suicide
- Group work with survivors.

The new edition incorporates the latest research findings which have added significantly to our understanding of the impact of suicide, an area which the UK Government has targetted for action in the mental health arena. This new edition will continue to be an invaluable resource for survivors of suicide as well as for all those who are in contact with them, including police and coroner's officers, bereavement services, self-help organisations for survivors, mental health professionals, social workers, GPs, counsellors and therapists.

Alison Wertheimer has been working as a freelance writer and researcher since 1987, after working in the voluntary sector for twenty years. She has a private counselling practice, is a supervisor with a bereavement counselling service and runs workshops on the impact of suicide bereavement.

A Special Scar

The experiences of people bereaved by
suicide

Second edition

Alison Wertheimer

First edition published 1991 by Routledge
Second edition published 2001 by Brunner-Routledge
27 Church Road, Hove, East Sussex BN3 2FA

Simultaneously published in the USA and Canada
by Taylor & Francis Inc.
325 Chestnut Street, Philadelphia, PA 19106

Brunner-Routledge is an imprint of the Taylor & Francis Group

Typeset in Times by Mayhew Typesetting, Rhayader, Powys
Cover design by Jim Wilkie
Printed and bound in Great Britain by Biddles Ltd, Guildford and King's Lynn

British Library Cataloguing in Publication Data
A catalogue record for this book is available from the British Library

Library of Congress Cataloging-in-Publication Data
Wertheimer, Alison.
    A special scar : the experiences of people bereaved by suicide / Alison
Wertheimer.–
    2nd ed.
        p. cm.
        Includes bibliographical references and index.
    ISBN 0-415-22026-2 – ISBN 0-415-22027-0 (pbk.)
        1. Suicide–Great Britain. 2. Bereavement. 3. Suicide victims–Great Britain–
    Family relationships. I. Title.

    HV6548.G7 W47 2001
    362.28'3'0941–dc21
                                                                    00-068862
ISBN 0-415-22026-2 (hbk)
ISBN 0-415-22027-0 (pbk)

For Anna Rosamunde
15 August 1942–26 February 1979

Clinical diagnoses are important . . . but they do not help the patient. . . . The crucial thing is the story. For it alone shows the human background and the human suffering
Memories, Dreams, Reflections

C.G. Jung

Contents

Foreword

The first edition of this important book opened our eyes to the special needs of people bereaved by suicide. Since that time the author and others have increased our understanding of these needs and have helped to develop services to meet them. In this second edition she has drawn on this knowledge and experience to augment and enhance the foundation which she laid.

Why should it matter so much how people die? Surely what really matters is how they lived? Yet the way to death *does* matter. One of the saddest things about suicide is the fact that it may become the only thing that is remembered about a person, and remembered with fear. Part of the reason for this is the difficulty which we, the survivors (for we are all survivors), have in making sense of anything so senseless. Suicide calls into question the priority which we give to life, it outrages our basic assumptions. When life is all we know, how can anyone be anti-life?

This book is written by a survivor of suicide. Alison Wertheimer lost her own sister by suicide, but she has not made the mistake of assuming that this makes her an expert on the subject. Her expertise comes from very wide reading and from the systematic interviews she has carried out with fifty other people who have been bereaved by suicide. In fact she is very self-effacing and she avoids pontificating, theorising, and offering simple answers to complex problems. In much of the book she allows the survivors to speak for themselves, elsewhere she quotes the opinions of others, but they are always opinions offered for our consideration rather than holy writ. And because she shows us bereavement through the eyes of the bereaved, what we see is often direct and painful, but not without hope. Her witnesses are coming through one of the most painful and complicated types of bereavement. Little by little, in their own ways, they are picking up the pieces and assembling a new model of the world. Often, one feels, it is a stronger and more mature set of assumptions which is emerging and we, the readers, are privileged to share in this process of maturation.

There are, of course, many kinds of suicide and many different reactions to suicide which may be appropriate. There are suicides which come unexpectedly, as a bolt from the blue when some acute mental illness or aberration, which might have been transient, leads to a consequence that is anything but transient. Such suicides are a major trauma to the survivors.

Then, there are suicides that come at the end of a long and painful struggle, whose final outcome was never much in doubt. Some mental illness can be just as malignant as cancer and cause relentless pain, not only to the sufferer, but to the family as a whole. When, despite every effort to mitigate the pain, the illness ends fatally, we should hardly be surprised if our immediate reaction is one of relief. Our grief, when it comes, is more for the misery that preceded the death than for the death itself.

Occasionally a suicide can be a kind of triumph over death as when someone willingly lays down their life for the sake of others. To those of us who benefit from this largesse our gratitude is not unmixed with guilt. Do we deserve to benefit from the death of another, no matter how freely chosen this was? Yet if we refuse to benefit do we negate the very meaning of the gift?

Many bereavements are so painful that the survivors feel as if they are being punished. When the bereavement results from suicide, the imputation is much greater. Why did he (or she) do this to me? What have I done to deserve it? The fact that in most instances the lost person was only seeking their own quietus is of little account.

By its very essence suicide is an act against the self, and even those suicidal people who blame others may be simply seeking a vent for their own distress. How often do we find that people, in the extremes of misery, hit out at those they love; perhaps they too felt that they were being punished.

In this, as in many other ways, the survivors have something in common with the dead. Does this mean that we are all potential suicides? In the vast majority of cases the answer is 'no'. Suicide remains a very rare act. For every person who commits suicide there are 8,000 who don't and there is certainly no reason to regard a family as 'doomed' simply because one member has chosen to end his or her own life.

Even so, suicide does strike at the very nature of a family. Every family is a network of individuals who share a common need to protect and support each other. They do this by means of a complex set of rules, alliances, and assumptions which allow each to contribute to and benefit from the shared commitment of the whole. Family structure and functioning are always changed by bereavements, but bereavement by suicide is often seen as a rejection of this central supportive function. Leadership is undermined, alliances broken or devalued, and faith in the family as a source of love and security is called into doubt. People who normally communicate with each other and trust each other may find themselves unable to do so. Small wonder that suicide is sometimes seen as the skeleton in the family closet.

The people who have assisted with this book have not been afraid to face the facts of suicide. They show us what has harmed them and what has helped them. They show us that, far from being destroyed by speaking of the unspeakable, a family which chooses to face the facts of loss can achieve a new, firmer identity.

Alison Wertheimer is to be congratulated on drawing all these strands together into a volume which will be of value to members of caring professions, counsellors and other bereavement service providers. She ended the first edition of her book with a challenge to all of us who care about those affected by bereavement to improve the services which we offer. Ten years later some have taken up this challenge and skilled help is now available to many of those who need it.

Whether or not such expert support is needed, her book will also help the friends and families of those bereaved by suicide as well as bereaved survivors themselves to understand and to cope with one of the worst misfortunes which life has to offer.

Colin Murray Parkes OBE MD FRCPsych
November 2000

Preface to the second edition

Reviewing what I had written over ten years ago and preparing this new edition has felt, at times, not unlike the process of bereavement – though less painful. I had to think about what could be retained, about what needed to be discarded, and what was new that needed to be incorporated?

A Special Scar was written partly because of my only sister's suicide and of course I am still a survivor of her suicide, although it is now more than twenty years since she took her own life. That event changed my life and the effects of Rosamunde's suicide will always remain with me. Nevertheless, being a suicide survivor does not form a major part of my present identity, my sense of who I am. So I am writing now from a different place, and inevitably with altered perspectives. I hope that this has not been detrimental to the process of writing. Because of the years which have elapsed it feels as though this second edition is really two books in one. If the result is an occasional unevenness, I hope that readers will understand the reasons for this.

The first edition was written with a wide-ranging readership in mind. It was written for survivors as well as their relatives and friends. I also envisaged that it would be read by people who, whether in a voluntary or professional capacity, care for, assist, support or counsel those bereaved by suicide: general practitioners, social workers, psychologists, psychiatrists and other mental health professionals, befrienders, counsellors and therapists, members of the clergy, police, coroners and coroner's officers. I hope that remains the case.

Material from interviewing fifty survivors formed the main part of the original edition and their stories remain as the 'heart' of the book (though some of the original accompanying references have been updated). Listening to people who have been more recently bereaved by suicide, I am aware of how often the narratives remain unchanged. Each person's grief will be different, but there are also common threads in shared experiences, feelings and thoughts. I hope therefore that the book will continue to speak to survivors, as well as informing those who have a helping role.

Since writing the first edition, I started working as a psychodynamic counsellor. Some of the people I see are survivors of suicide, and they have offered many fresh perspectives on grieving the self-inflicted death of someone close. Counselling for people bereaved by suicide tends to be addressed relatively briefly within the general bereavement counselling literature, perhaps in a chapter on sudden death or 'difficult' losses, and I hope the chapter on counselling will prove to be a useful addition to what others have written. Deciding how to approach the chapter on counselling was not easy. I am aware that many of my fellow counsellors work from a person-centred or integrative perspective. However, in the end I concluded that I could only write from my own understanding and experience. To do otherwise would, to borrow a person-centred term, have lacked 'genuineness', but I have attempted to make the chapter accessible to counsellors and therapists who may work in very different ways.

The past decade has seen a welcome increase in the UK in the number of support and self-help groups for survivors of suicide and a new chapter on groups for people bereaved by suicide reflects the experiences and learning of some of the people who have been running these groups. I have not come across any published accounts of the work of survivor groups in the UK, so this chapter was written partly to fill that gap, however inadequately.

Since the late 1980s, a growing body of research has added significantly to our understanding of the impact of suicide on those left behind. Comparative studies suggest that suicide deaths are not always the most difficult losses to grieve and in some families the death is experienced as a relief after many difficult years. With other suicides, however, we know that the death occurs within a family which is already struggling to cope. We need to use that knowledge to identify and offer help to those families of survivors who are particularly vulnerable and who are at risk of unresolved grieving.

Researchers have also identified some of the particular reactions to suicide deaths including guilt, blame, shame and the need to know why the death occurred. Although these can all be experienced by other bereaved people, they are more prevalent amongst those bereaved by suicide.

There is increasing recognition that, for many survivors, suicide bereavement can be a traumatic loss. Survivors may experience similar reactions to the survivors of collective disasters – anxiety, guilt, sleep disturbance, flashbacks and so on. The 'personal disaster' of suicide can sometimes have the same devastating effects as a major and more public disaster.

With this knowledge at our disposal, we should be able to meet the needs of suicide survivors more effectively than at present. We have a long way to go before those who are newly bereaved are routinely offered good quality, appropriate and timely help and support.

Suicide is slowly moving up the public agenda. The Department of Health's commitment to reducing the annual suicide rate is welcome, though it cannot be left solely to our health services to ensure that this happens. Suicide prevention requires 'joined up' inter-Departmental thinking at national government level.

Better inter-agency collaboration is also needed at local level, not only to reduce the number of suicide deaths, but to provide a more effective and co-ordinated response in the aftermath of a suicide. The police, ambulance services, accident and emergency departments, Samaritans, coroner's officers, bereavement services, and counselling and advice services. Many survivors are too traumatised to seek help, and services need to adopt a proactive response.

Reaching out to survivors of suicide, however, is not solely the duty or responsibility of agencies and organisations, whether voluntary or professional. As Colin Murray Parkes reminds us, care of the bereaved is a communal responsibility. We do not always find this easy. It stirs up painful feelings, bringing us, as it does, face to face with the pain of loss. With suicide deaths, we are forcibly reminded that we cannot always succeed in keeping people alive. Yet the survivor *is* alive and needs more than the comfort of strangers. At least one in five people in the UK has been personally affected by a suicide death. Given that figure, supporting the suicide bereaved has to be everyone's business.

Alison Wertheimer
October 2000

Acknowledgements

I would like to thank the following: the King Edward's Hospital Fund for London who provided financial support to meet the interviewing costs, and the Nuffield Foundation whose grant financed the transcription of the interview tapes; my agent, Gloria Ferris, for her encouragement in the early stages of this project; Gill Davies and Edwina Welham of Routledge; CRUSE, The Compassionate Friends and the Editor of *New Society* for putting me in touch with people willing to talk about their experiences as suicide survivors; Douglas Chambers, Phil Clements, Libby Insall, Colin Murray Parkes, Barbara Porter and Susan Wallbank for their advice on particular issues; and John Costello who helped me stay on the journey.

A legacy from my father, who died while I was researching this book, enabled me to take time off from other work and write this book without interruption. For that I wish to thank him.

Above all, I owe an enormous debt of gratitude to the survivors who shared their stories with me. I am grateful for their openness, their willingness to share thoughts and feelings which were often painful and difficult to talk about.

I would also like to thank the following for their help with this new edition. The counsellors and group leaders whose ideas and experiences were invaluable in preparing the new chapters; they are too numerous to name, but I hope that they will recognise their contributions. My clients who, in very different ways, have taught me so much over the years. And lastly, my editor, Kate Hawes, for her patience when I begged for yet another postponed deadline.

Acknowledgement is due to the following for permission to quote from 'The Guide' by U.A. Fanthorpe: Peterloo Poets (*Standing To* 1982) and King Penguin (*Selected Poems* 1986).

Part 1

Introduction

Chapter 1

Suicide: an introduction

The act of suicide, which represents both personal unhappiness and the implied belief that the victim's fellow-men are powerless to remedy his condition, can never be viewed with indifference.

(Carstairs 1973: 7)

Suicides are a significant cause of early death, and are responsible each year for nearly half a million years of life lost in those aged 75 and under.

(Department of Health 1998)

The idea that a person chooses to die creates in us a profound sense of unease. Suicide challenges some of our most deeply held beliefs. It defies the cherished notion that all human life is sacred; it challenges the value of life itself, and places a question mark over the taboos against the taking of life. The suicide of another person forces us to question the value and meaning not only of life in general but of our own individual lives.

For many people, the contemplation of apparently self-chosen death hardly bears thinking about and yet, over the centuries, they have found it impossible to ignore the subject. There have been persistent attempts to categorise and compartmentalise suicide and, in doing so, perhaps we have been trying to make ourselves a bit more comfortable with it. Suicide has been examined from many angles. Lawyers, doctors, novelists, poets, philosophers and theologians have all contributed to the debate.

But the fruits of that continuing quest for understanding are not only to be found in the pages of legal, medical and philosophical journals. We have inherited a collection of images of suicide, and our reactions to the act of suicide do not occur in a vacuum. Historical images have helped to shape society's attitudes and psychological reactions towards those who take their own lives, and towards the survivors of suicide – family and friends who are bequeathed what is usually such a painful legacy.

Suicide is a complex and multi-faceted act shaped by many different factors. It is also replete with paradoxes. In most cases, suicide is a solitary event and yet it has often far-reaching repercussions for many others. It is rather like throwing a stone into a pond; the ripples spread and spread. The act of suicide is often carried out in secret, hidden from the gaze of others, and yet it becomes the subject of public scrutiny. The person who died and their family become involved with the police, emergency services, coroners and the media. The suicide is a personal and private tragedy for the bereaved, but enters the public domain. The person who dies may be regarded as a victim for whom death is the only option, but it is often those left behind who feel they are the true victims of another person's act. Those bereaved by suicide (like others experiencing loss) must face a host of conflicting feelings: anger mixed with sadness; love and hate for the person who died; guilt often alternating with angry blaming of others.

The next part of this chapter provides a factual introduction to suicide (numbers, gender differences, at-risk groups, etc.). The remainder discusses society's attitudes towards suicide; the role of the media; and the language of suicide. The following chapter focuses on the survivors – those bereaved by suicide. These two chapters form the backcloth to Part 2 of the book, which describes the experiences of fifty individuals bereaved by suicide.

Facts and figures

National and international suicide rates

Every 85 minutes someone in the UK dies by suicide, each leaving behind an average of six people who will suffer intense grief (McIntosh 1987a). Seventy per cent more people die by suicide each year than are killed in road accidents. Worldwide there are an estimated one million suicide deaths a year (Clark and Goldney 2000: 20) and at least six million more new survivors. In many countries today, suicide is one of the ten leading causes of death.

It is virtually impossible to make valid comparisons between national suicide rates of individual countries, as methods of collecting information about the causes of death vary. The official statistics are also likely to be affected by whether or not a country has religious sanctions against suicide. A recent analysis of data from 49 countries found that average reported suicide rates were lower in countries with religious sanctions than in those without (Kelleher et al. 1998). This suggests that procedures for recording and reporting possible suicides may be affected by religious beliefs which condemn or do not support the practice of suicide.

Despite the unreliability of international statistics, suicide appears to be more common in affluent, industrialised countries, which tend to have comparatively high rates (Stengel 1973). Suicide is not necessarily an escape from material poverty, and wealth does not act as an insurance policy against suicide.

In the UK, it has been suggested that the official mortality statistics do not provide an accurate picture of suicide deaths (Stengel 1973; Chambers and Harvey 1989), a position echoed in the USA (McIntosh 1987a).

It is not always clear whether the person actually intended to commit suicide. In the case of a suspected suicide, an inquest will be held, but there must be clear proof that the person who died intended to take their own life. According to a former coroner, 'The common-sense or balance of probabilities approach will get short judicial shrift' (Chambers 1989: 181). In the absence of any clear proof of intent, the verdict is likely to be 'accidental death', 'death by misadventure', or an 'open verdict' (see Chapter 7). The legal system, in England and Wales, in particular, has a significant impact on the classification of death as published by the Office for National Statistics. As Hill points out, 'Shrinkage in official suicide statistics can be traced to the way in which deaths are classified' (1995: 14).

Some coroners may be less inclined than others to pass verdicts of suicide (Keir 1986) and they will seek to protect relatives from what is sometimes considered to be a distressing and unwelcome verdict. In certain circumstances, the evidence must be heard before a jury, and juries, like some coroners, can be reluctant to return a verdict of suicide. An examination of inquests in Inner North London found that juries hearing cases of deaths on the London Underground returned suicide verdicts in only some 40% of these cases, despite the fact that 'the common assumption must be that all such deaths are suicidal' (Chambers and Harvey 1989: 184).

In some instances, a verdict of suicide may not even be considered. Take the case of a car in which the driver is the sole occupant. On an empty road, in apparently good weather conditions, the car leaves the road, and the driver is killed. There are no witnesses to offer possible explanations, and faced with an apparently inexplicable event, the verdict will almost certainly be 'accidental death'.

Various attempts have been made to estimate the true rate of suicide in Britain. Estimates have included: double the official published figures (Chambers and Harvey 1989); and 25–50% more than the official statistics (Alvarez 1974), between a quarter and a half as many again. More recently, the under-reporting of suicides has been challenged by the Samaritans who include 'deaths by undetermined causes' in their calculation of the total numbers of suicide deaths. This is on the basis that a significant proportion of these 'undetermined' deaths are widely considered to be cases where individuals have deliberately taken their life so their inclusion provides a more accurate picture of all possible suicides (Samaritans 2000). (These combined figures will be referred to as 'suicides' below.)

There were 6,182 suicides in the UK in 1998, a decrease of 10% since 1987. However, that figure masks considerable variations between individual countries: there was a 13% decrease in England and Wales and an 18% decrease in Northern Ireland but this contrasts with a 13% *increase* in

suicide deaths in Scotland, which has seen a significant increase in suicides
of young males. There are also variations in the suicide rates for different
age groups, an issue which is discussed below.

Gender-related issues

Three-quarters of all suicide deaths involve males, and that proportion
increases to four-fifths for 25–34-year-olds.

In England and Wales, female suicides have declined from 8 to 6 per
100,000 population over the last eleven years, but Northern Ireland has had
a slightly smaller decrease and the rate for Scotland has remained more or
less the same at 10 deaths per 100,000.

Male suicide rates in the UK as a whole have remained fairly steady and
over the last six years have stayed at around 19 or 20 per 100,000 population. However, Scotland and Northern Ireland have had fluctuating rates
which stood at 32 and 18 per 100,000 in 1998.

There are some significant differences in the methods men and women
use to commit suicide. Women tend to opt for less violent methods and
nearly half die as the result of self-poisoning or overdosing, compared with
less than a quarter of male suicides. Forty-five per cent of males die by
violent means such as hanging/suffocation, shooting, cutting/stabbing or
jumping/falling, whereas less than three out of ten female suicides use one
of these methods.

Age-related issues

During the 1980s and 1990s there was great concern over the increase in
suicide among young males aged 15–24 and although suicide deaths have
decreased from 760 in 1998 to 571 in 1998, the rate was still 16 per 100,000
compared with a national rate overall of 13 per 100,000. Suicides among
25–34-year-old men are also cause for concern with 1,316 deaths in this age
group in 1998, compared with 932 in 1988.

A number of different factors are thought to be linked to suicide and
attempted suicide in young people, notably: alcohol and drug abuse; growing up in families where there is parental unemployment, mental illness,
addiction, divorce, separation or death; experience of physical and/or sexual
abuse; and being held in custody (Samaritans 2000: 24).

Suicide rates for older men and women have declined since the 1950s,
although they still have relatively high rates compared with the population
as a whole, a fact which has been rather overshadowed by the recent
concerns about suicide and young people. A total of 938 people over 65
took their own lives in 1998, which is roughly 15% of all suicides for that
year. Suicide in older people has been found to be strongly associated with

one or more of the following: depression, physical pain or illness, living alone, and feelings of hopelessness and guilt.

Seasonal and other factors

Suicide could be thought to be associated with winter, with its bad weather and long hours of darkness. In fact, seasonal patterns of suicide suggest a different picture, although in many societies, there is a belief that the weather can influence both physical and emotional states (Barker et al. 1994). Researchers have identified seasonal variations in rates of completed suicides, with a peak in late spring and early summer, an argument which is given added weight by the fact that suicide rates in the southern hemisphere tend to follow the same seasonal patterns (Stengel 1973). As Barker and colleagues suggest, this possibly occurs 'because of seasonal changes in the occurrence of episodes of affective disorder and/or the discrepancy noticed by depressed persons viewing the external world bursting into life when their internal world is lifeless' (1994: 375). The contrast between inner and outer worlds may be experienced as unbearable.

Suicide also has weekly patterns: more people kill themselves at weekends or immediately afterwards than on other days. For some people, going out to work during the week may offer some respite from isolation and depression. Weekends remove that protection, as can holiday periods such as Christmas or Easter.

Regardless of seasonal patterns, for some people there will be times when they are more at risk of committing suicide: these may be anniversaries, whether they commemorate seemingly happy occasions such as weddings or birthdays, or sadder events such as death or divorce. As one young woman said, after making a serious suicide attempt on the anniversary of her father's death: 'It was the time when all the hurts came out' (Shneidman 1982).

At-risk occupational groups

Research studies, including statistical analysis, point to an increased risk of suicide among certain occupational groups and 'It is commonly accepted that high stress, together with easy access to means, are important factors which put people in certain occupations at greater risk of dying by suicide' (Samaritans 2000: 28).

A study of *farmers* in England and Wales found that they have an elevated risk of suicide. Between 1991 and 1996, there was a farming suicide every 11 days. The reasons are complex, but may include easy availability of firearms, work-related stress, financial difficulties and family problems (Malmberg et al. 1997). Most often there was a mental disorder, compounded by occupational, financial, legal, health or relationship problems.

Nurses, and female nurses in particular, are also a high-risk group. Between 1991 and 1996, a female nurse died by suicide every nine days. This increased risk of suicide among female nurses was borne out by a literature review of suicide in nurses (Hawton and Vislisel 1999), although the authors were unable to pinpoint evidence about contributory factors other than an association with smoking. Male *medical and dental practitioners* also have above average suicide rates.

The number of suicide deaths among *prisoners* doubled between 1994 and 1998, and despite a package of measures designed to prevent self-harm in prisons, including the Samaritans Prisoner Befriending Schemes, self-inflicted deaths in 2000 are predicted to exceed the 91 suicides in the previous year (*The Guardian* 2000). Continuing concern led to an official enquiry being set up which, in addition to proposing further preventative measures, criticised the often inhumane and insensitive treatment of families of suicide victims (HMIP 1999).

Copycat suicides

There are many examples in history of imitative or 'copycat' suicides which have, on occasions, reached epidemic proportions, as occurred in Budapest in 1928 when, in the space of two months, over 150 people deliberately drowned themselves in the Danube. The authorities finally sent out a patrol boat to drag would-be suicides from the river, thus putting an end to that particular epidemic (Chesser 1967). More recently, there have been reports from the USA of apparent 'cluster suicides' involving young people from the same town (Lukas and Seiden 1987).

The unprecedented and continuing growth in mass media means that information about suicide is widely available, in factual and fictional form, raising the issue of whether this coverage can lead to imitative suicides. Two recent studies of the potential effects of dramatic portrayals of self-poisoning in popular drama series have proved inconclusive. The first study (Simkin et al. 1995) found no evidence that two television drama broadcasts depicting paracetamol self-poisoning had significantly affected the rate of paracetamol overdoses. The second (Hawton et al. 1999), which also studied a portrayal of self-poisoning in a popular TV drama, found an associated short-lived increase in patients presenting at hospital with self-poisoning. The researchers also concluded that media portrayals could influence the method people used.

From these and other studies, it would appear that teenagers and young adults are particularly vulnerable to imitative acts. On the other hand, the media does have a potentially positive role to play in education and prevention. It may also serve to destigmatise the issue of suicide (Samaritans 1997).

Little research has been undertaken in the UK about whether factual reporting on suicide can act as a catalyst for imitative behaviour, although there is evidence from elsewhere (Sonneck et al. 1992) that reporting which avoids dramatic or sensational coverage can have a positive effect in terms of reducing the likelihood of copycat suicides.

The media play an increasingly important part in all our lives and its portrayals of suicide can have far-reaching effects, an issue to which we now turn.

Suicide and the media

As Simon Armson, Chief Executive of The Samaritans, acknowledges: 'Any suicide is a newsworthy event. The fact that an individual has chosen to end their life, quite deliberately and prematurely, attracts the attention of the public' (Samaritans 1997: 2).

Media coverage ranges from the sensational to the somewhat more reticent. Reports of real-life suicides are often accompanied by dramatic headlines such as: 'Fireball suicide of lovesick businessman' or 'Would-be MP leapt to his death'. Sometimes, reporting goes to the other extreme. Common euphemisms for possible suicides include: 'foul play is not suspected', 'tablets were found near the body' and 'no one is being interviewed'. It is still comparatively rare to read in the death notices that someone 'died by his own hand' (*The Guardian* 3 October 1986); instead people die 'tragically' or 'suddenly and tragically', although the fact that a person took their own life does seem to be acknowledged more often in obituaries of well-known figures than was previously the case.

The media often present selective images because reporting, at a national level at least, focuses on a tiny proportion of suicides – the more sensational or bizarre, the more public suicides, and the suicides of the famous. Inevitably this distorts, providing only a partial picture of suicide.

Issues such as suicide which can provoke extreme discomfort are also the subject of humour in the media, and it is something which those bereaved by suicide have to learn to live with. A recent example of this 'sick humour' was the series of fictional articles in a major Sunday newspaper which concluded with a no-details-spared description of the author's 'suicide' (*The Observer* 1999).

Just as those bereaved by suicide can often become obsessed by the need to discover why the person took their own life, so society in general also wants, or even needs, to know why suicides occur. It is as though if society can come up with the answers, the act of suicide will become less threatening and will feel more under our control. Perhaps something apparently so incomprehensible will become understandable. It is not surprising when the media steps in at this point to offer some answers, or at least some clues, even though reporting can be overly simplistic about the causes of suicide.

Perhaps inevitably, the media will offer simple answers to why people take their own lives even though we know that suicide is a multi-determined act. Psychological, socio-economic, familial, interpersonal and genetic factors can all play a part (Hawton 1998). Something may be the precipitating factor or the 'final straw', whether it is the ending of a relationship, redundancy or failing an exam, but that is rarely if ever the whole story. Recent newspaper stories have suggested, for example, that the National Lottery, Ofsted, memory problems, Barclay's Bank, listening to folk music and wealth have led people to take their own lives.

While in the past, people bereaved by suicide have described their experiences through visual art, drama, film and literature, some are now moving from the fictional and the disguised to the autobiographical. Writing about what he describes as a 'new way of telling true-life stories', O'Hagan suggests that while people have always written novels about real happenings, there is now a newer form of memoir (1996: 14), reflected in an upsurge of books about major illnesses, death and dying. Tim Lott's book about his own suicidal depression and his mother's death by suicide is part of this new genre, written in order 'to work through some conclusions that I consider to be firm' (1997: 269), perhaps a way of making sense of his own and his mother's experiences, though he assures the reader that he did not undertake this work as therapy.

For Charles Glass, on the other hand, although it was many years since his mother's suicide when he was in his teens, researching and writing about it *was* a kind of therapy: 'I never saw a psychiatrist, underwent therapy or attended a group . . . Since deciding to write about other people's experiences almost everyone I interviewed asked me – why are you writing about this? This is not a story so much as therapy by journalism' (1995: 24).

Similar messages can be heard from Dan Perceval, whose mother also commited suicide when he was a teenager. Introducing the film he made about the experiences of suicide bereavement, he had this to say: 'Producing this film and booklet is part of my need to confront a subject that everyone would prefer to avoid . . . I still have a long way to go in dealing with my mother's death but it has helped me to break the taboo of silence' (1994: 3).

Suicide will continue to feature in the media, whether in factual or dramatic contexts. In response to this, the Samaritans have produced media guidelines on the portrayal of suicide (1997) for journalists and broadcasters. As well as offering basic factual information, the guidelines address common myths and misconceptions about suicide, discuss copycat suicides in the context of media reporting (see above), and set out a series of recommendations on appropriate terminology, together with suggested approaches to factual reporting and dramatic portrayal.

Reporters and photographers often have to tread a fine line with survivors of suicide. Contact with the media can be experienced as intrusive, but it can also give a voice to relatives and friends or their spokesperson and enable them to say what they want to about the person who died. Sensitive reporting, Clark and Goldney suggest, can 'prevent contagion and educate the community' (2000: 23). We return to this issue in Chapter 7, which discusses the experiences of individual survivors in relation to media reporting of inquests.

Attitudes towards suicide

Unlike politics, the weather or the latest football results, suicide does not crop up that often as a topic of conversation. Even thinking about the fact that some people apparently choose to end their lives can leave other people feeling deeply uneasy. They avoid the subject because it can arouse such powerful emotions. 'We do not, in truth, really want to know', Keir suggests, because 'contemplation of the deed itself, the manner of its execution – the overdose, the drowning, the hanging – fills us with horror' (1986: 13). If the subject is raised, people may take the opportunity to express condemnatory and punitive attitudes. They may distance them-selves, claiming a total inability to understand how 'someone could ever do such a thing'. Or they may, as Alvarez suggests, 'dismiss suicide in horror as a moral crime or sickness beyond discussion' (1974: 14).

As James Hillman writes in *Suicide and the Soul*:

> Going into questions of death and suicide means breaking open taboos . . . opennesss about suicide is not easily gained . . . The law has found it criminal, religion calls it a sin, and society turns away from it. It has long been the habit to hush it up or excuse it . . . as if it were the primary anti-social aberration.
>
> (1976: prefatory note to 1964 edn, 17)

People have taken their own lives throughout recorded history. Suicide is a universal phenomenon, occurring in every culture and society, and a number of writers have examined historical and present-day religious, social and philosophical attitudes towards suicide (e.g. Stengel 1973; Alvarez 1974; Keir 1986; Pritchard 1995).

Religious attitudes

Twelve suicides are recorded in the Old and New Testaments, but there is no specific injunction against suicide in the Bible and none of these deaths are overtly condemned or judged in any way (Barraclough 1990). However, by the fourth century AD, the Christian Church had come to regard suicide as a mortal sin. It was seen as failure to uphold the sanctity of life, a refusal of God's grace, providing the victim 'with a one-way ticket to damnation'

(Alvarez 1974: 70). The twentieth century, on the whole, saw more tolerant and sympathetic attitudes emerging, perhaps as the result of our increased understanding of the reasons which may lead people to commit suicide. The Roman Catholic Church still views it as a cardinal sin (Pritchard 1995: 11), but Christian funeral rites and burials are no longer withheld from those who take their own lives.

Judaism has always emphasised the importance of preserving life, although neither the Old Testament nor the Talmud include any specific sanctions against suicide. Present-day Judaic thought distinguishes between premeditated or 'wilful' acts of suicide, which are considered unacceptable, and those carried out when a person is of 'unsound mind' or under extreme physical or mental stress (Keir 1986). In doing so, a judgement is made as to whether the person who takes their own life, does so rationally with conscious intent, a theme which recurs in debates about the rights and wrongs of self-inflicted death.

Islam is one of the few world religions which has always unequivocally condemned the act of suicide. Several specific sanctions can be found in the Koran and is one likely reason for the very low rates of reported suicide deaths in certain Islamic countries today (Pritchard 1995).

Hinduism, on the other hand, has never rigorously proscribed suicide, although the different views in respect of gender reflect a certain ambivalence. While there is a taboo against male suicides, the Hindu faith has seen it as acceptable for bereaved women to commit suicide, for example (Keir 1986; Pritchard 1995).

In the Buddhist tradition, attitudes towards suicide are equivocal and have varied between sects, an uncertainty reflected in some of the accounts of religion and suicide. According to Keir (1986), Buddhism forbids suicide, while Stengel (1973) suggests that suicide is tolerated or even encouraged under certain conditions.

Today's society is frequently characterised as an increasingly secular society but, particularly in the latter decades, religious practice has become an important element in more people's lives. This phenomenon, together with the multi-ethnic nature of Britain's population today, has implications not only in the field of suicide prevention but in terms of the support offered to families bereaved by suicide.

Legislation and suicide

Historically one of the ways in which society has dealt with its collective fear and hostility towards suicide has been to criminalise it (Stengel 1973; Alvarez 1974; Hillman 1976) and although religious beliefs have played a part, religious considerations are not the sole reason why legislation was introduced (Stengel 1973). As in many other countries, suicide was equated with the homicide. Self-murder was viewed as the unlawful taking of life and both suicide and attempted suicide became criminal offences in England in the mid-sixteenth century.

As recently as the 1950s, people attempting suicide were having to stand trial and although they represented only a small fraction of total attempters, the majority of those ending up in court were found guilty. Sentencing could result in imprisonment, imposition of a fine, or being put on probation. In the majority of suicides, however, coroners frequently passed a verdict of suicide 'while the balance of mind was disturbed', thus avoiding the pronouncement of a felony (Stengel 1973).

Compared with the rest of Europe, England was slow to repeal its anti-suicide legislation – nearly two hundred years after France and more than a century after Austria, for example. Campaigning by the medical profession, as well as by magistrates and the clergy, led to the eventual repeal of existing legislation and the passing of the Suicide Act (1961). Although the Act decriminalised suicide and attempted suicide, it introduced a new criminal offence: aiding, abetting, counselling or procuring the suicide of another person carries a penalty of up to fourteen years' imprisonment.

Laws change over time and legislation, past and present, reflects our ambivalent and often conflicting attitudes towards those who take their own lives – or attempt to do so.

Current attitudes towards suicide

Attitudes have changed and we would doubtless like to think that we are more tolerant of people who take their own lives or attempt to do so. While acknowledging the understandable fear of suicide, Hill suggests that 'Nowadays self-destruction evokes pity as often as outrage . . . suicide may now be acceptable in some circumstances . . . Judgements about suicide now tend to be relative to its circumstances and consequences' (1995: 152, 153). However, as Pritchard points out, 'former attitudes still reverberate, creating confused and ambivalent echoes which continue to plague modern humanity' (1995: 9). This should not surprise us. Confronted with the issue of death, whether their own or that of others, human beings have tended to react with fear, hostility, denial or ambivalence. The fact of death is a painful reminder that we are not omnipotent, that it is inescapable.

As the Samaritans have recognised, our attitudes towards suicide and people who are suicidal are a matter of some importance, not least because they affect the way we react to emotional distress in others. If we respond by distancing ourselves or trying to distract the person, their distress may turn into suicidal despair. It was a concern about our reactions to suicide and to people who are suicidal which led the Samaritans to commission two major surveys in the 1990s.

The first of these enquiries, *Challenging the Taboo* (1996), was a telephone survey which questioned 1,000 adults. They were asked whether they had been directly affected by suicide and what their views were on suicide and depression. The results suggest that while some people are sympathetic towards those who are suicidal, others are rather hostile.

- Although just over half the sample believed that 'people who are depressed should pull themselves together and get on with life', over a third disagreed with this statement.
- More than a third of the sample agreed with the statement that 'people who attempt suicide are only thinking of themselves'.
- While roughly 40% of respondents said that people who attempt suicide deserve more sympathy than they get, 20% disagreed with this.
- While 60% of the sample agreed with the statement that 'suicide is not an easy way out', about a third felt that it was.

Perhaps rather surprisingly, older people tended to be more accepting of people who took their own lives or felt suicidal. Younger people were less sympathetic compared to the rest of the population, though as they form part of a high-risk age group, perhaps being asked to think about suicide was more threatening.

The second Samaritans telephone survey, *Listen Up* (1998), questioned people about how they would respond to a series of hypothetical scenarios where a friend was emotionally distressed. Their findings revealed that the majority of people were good listeners and would be broadly sympathetic, although there were significant gender differences.

- Men were more likely to offer practical advice, tell the person to snap out of it, try to distract them, crack jokes, change the subject or pretend they hadn't noticed.
- Women were more likely to encourage the person to seek professional help, listen whenever the person needed to talk, stay with them and encourage them to talk about their feelings.

As the report pointed out, helping someone close who is in despair is not easy, though 'the ability to listen in a crisis can make the difference between life and death' (Samaritans 1998: 2). The differing responses of men and women described above are of particular concern, given the continuing high suicide rates among young males and the fact that many do not share their problems with peers.

Both these surveys give some cause for concern, but they also provide useful information about where suicide prevention initiatives need to be targetted and the issues which need to be addressed in reaching out to suicidal people.

The language of suicide

Finding the words to talk about suicide can be difficult, particularly for those who have been bereaved by suicide:

> I couldn't say 'suicide' for years. I always said 'taken her life'. It's awful isn't it? (Pam)

> I usually say 'she took her own life' . . . because that gives her the dignity of having made a decision and taken the action herself and I think she needs that – I need her to need that anyway; it's my need I suppose. (Francesca)

> 'Killing oneself' is pretty raw and 'committing suicide' I don't like because you commit sins and crimes. (Bridget)

It can be difficult to find an acceptable language for the act of suicide. Too often the words carry messages about committing crime. 'Killing oneself' has echoes of 'self-murder', but attempts to find an alternative vocabulary can result in equally harsh or distressing messages. 'She took her own life' may seem preferable to 'she committed suicide', but although it perhaps 'decriminalises' the act, it then implies a degree of conscious choice, and hence a conscious rejection of other people.

People who attempt suicide are often referred to as having 'failed', the implication being that those who die are 'successful'. But as Dunne points out, 'From the perspective of suicidologists, the person who completes suicide is considered "successful" . . . From the perspective of family members and friends, the suicide itself represents failure' (Dunne 1987a: xii).

How does one describe people who die by suicide? The Samaritans have recently produced media guidelines which suggest that phrases like 'suicide victim' and 'commit suicide' should be avoided. Instead, they propose, terms such as 'died by suicide' and 'a suicide' should be used. The first edition of this book used the term 'victim' for people who died by suicide. I chose to do so partly on the basis that dictionary definitions include the following: 'somebody that is adversely affected by a force or agent' and a person 'made to suffer'. Although suicide may sometimes be a rational conscious act, I think that many people who die by suicide are victims in the sense that self-inflicted death is not a conscious choice and people who take their own lives are frequently powerless to halt the drive towards annihilation and self-destruction. In this edition, I have used the terms 'victims', 'the deceased', 'people who died by suicide' and 'people who kill themselves' interchangeably.

I continue to use the term 'survivor' in this edition, although its use has been questioned in some quarters. My original decision to use this term was partly due to the fact that it was widely used in the USA, where more attention has been focused on the needs of those bereaved by suicide. In addition, *Survivors of Suicide* (Cain 1972) was the title of one of the first published works on this subject. But the word 'survivor' was also in recognition of the fact that survivors of suicide have affinities with survivors of other disasters. This is discussed further in Chapter 2 (pp. 21–22). In this edition I have continued to write about 'survivors' but also 'people bereaved by suicide'.

One further point about language. We live with increasingly diverse structures and patterns of family relationships, and some have created 'families of choice' including same-sex partners and close friends. Perhaps this creates linguistic difficulties for bereavement researchers who not infrequently (particularly in the North American literature) refer to people who have died as 'loved ones'. It is a term I have avoided, partly because relationships between the person who dies by suicide and those left behind have often been characterised by ambivalence or hate as much as by love. As a booklet written to help children bereaved by suicide points out, 'Not everyone who dies is loved by everyone all the time', but 'Whether we loved a person or disliked them we will grieve over their death, as long as in some way we felt attached to them' (Winston's Wish 2001: 23).

As the survivors' quotations make clear, people whose lives have been touched in a very direct way by suicide often have strong views about the language used. They also struggle to find words that they are comfortable with, maybe partly because suicide is so dis-comforting. Professionals can also find it difficult to agree among themselves about an appropriate terminology. There is no 'right' or 'wrong' language, and I am aware that sometimes the terminology I use may offend. Finding a language to talk and write about suicide is not easy, but perhaps as we talk more about people who take their own lives and those bereaved by suicide, we shall find that we have the right words. When suicide is less of a taboo, perhaps we will be able to reach a shared language and an agreed terminology.

Chapter 2

Survivors of suicide

The emergence of the survivor

Until the 1960s, people bereaved by suicide were a largely hidden group. The attention of researchers, clinicians and policy-makers was focused almost exclusively on people who attempted suicide or took their own lives and efforts were directed mainly towards suicide prevention. Survivors were isolated from one another, little was known about them and about their circumstances, and they received little or no help in coming to terms with their loss. Interest in survivors and awareness of their situation began to emerge in rather roundabout ways.

The development of what became known as 'psychological autopsies' drew attention to the needs of suicide survivors. These autopsies began in the late 1950s, when staff at the Los Angeles Suicide Prevention Center were asked to study a series of equivocal deaths where the coroner had not been able to certify the mode of death. Relatives, friends, employers and others who had known the deceased were interviewed in order to reconstruct the person's background, personal relationships, personality traits and character (Shneidman 1993: 191). During the course of these interviews, it became apparent that survivors wanted to talk about their grief, their guilt and anger, and often their own suicidal feelings. 'It was usually the first time [they] had been given the opportunity to talk about the suicide' (Colt 1987: 14).

Although the psychological autopsy has certain limitations as a research tool, a number of researchers who have used this methodology, have also drawn attention to its therapeutic value for interviewees (Colt 1987; Asgard and Carlsson-Bergstrom 1991; Shneidman 1993; Hawton et al. 1998). Asgard and Carlsson-Bergstrom, for example, found that 65% of their informants reported experiencing a positive effect on their emotional balance and 34% thought it had shed new light on the suicide (1991: 26). Litman and colleagues (1970) also found that the experience could help to lessen the survivor's guilt and make acceptance of the death easier.

Alongside the psychological autopsies, a number of mental health professionals with an interest in this area began to explore the impact of suicide on families and friends. Some of their findings were published in *Survivors of Suicide* (Cain 1972), the first major work to describe the experiences of suicide survivors. In the following year, Shneidman (co-founder of the Los Angeles Suicide Prevention Center) suggested that in the case of suicide, the largest public health problem was not suicide prevention or the management of attempted suicide, but how to alleviate the effects of suicide on those left behind (1973, quoted in Barrett and Scott 1990: 1–2).

Cain and his colleagues (1972) reported that relatives and friends of suicide victims experienced major problems. However, they were mainly writing about survivors who had been receiving specialist professional help, which suggests that they were experiencing particular difficulties with their bereavement. There were also no comparisons of suicide survivors with other bereaved groups. More recent research has presented a more optimistic picture (see below) of the outcomes for survivors. Nevertheless, the work of Cain and others was instrumental in drawing attention to the needs of those bereaved by suicide.

More publications about suicide survivors began to appear. A bibliography published in the mid-1980s listed over a hundred books and articles (McIntosh, 1985–6). At the same time, support groups and other forms of assistance for survivors were also being developed in the USA, McIntosh (1985–6) reporting over 150 such groups.

In the UK, meanwhile, clinicians and researchers continued to pay little attention to the needs of suicide survivors with the notable exception of Barraclough and Shepherd (e.g. 1976, 1977, 1978). A literature review published by CRUSE Bereavement Care (Henley 1984) drew almost exclusively on articles and books published in the USA. Although generalist bereavement services were seeing some survivors, there was only a handful of local suicide bereavement support groups. Although there is now a growing awareness of the particular needs of survivors (see Chapter 15), the UK still lags far behind the USA in terms of research and support services.

Who are the survivors?

Various attempts have been made to estimate how many people are affected by each suicide death, focusing mainly on family members. Shneidman (1969) suggested that for every death, six people would suffer intense grief; Bernhardt and Praeger (1983) estimated that each suicide would involve, on average, a minimum of five family members or 'significant others'; and McIntosh (1987a) considered that at least six other people will be affected. More recently Campbell (1997) has suggested that an overly narrow definition of 'survivor' has led us to underestimate the numbers of people directly affected. In a review of referrals to the Crisis Intervention Center,

Louisiana, Campbell found that while the overwhelming majority of people asking for help had experienced the suicide of a parent, child, spouse or sibling, others had lost grandchildren, grandparents, stepchildren, stepparents and others.

In the UK, a recent survey (Samaritans 1996) asked participants if they knew anyone who had died by suicide. What they discovered was that just over one in four personally knew of someone who had died by suicide and nearly one in five have experienced the suicide of someone to whom they were close:

- immediate family: 15%;
- another relative: 21%;
- friend: 29%;
- acquaintance: 15%;
- work colleague: 11%;
- other relationships: 5%;
- did not want to answer: 7%.
  (Note: the categories are not exclusive.)

The central part of this book (Chapters 3–14) describes the experiences of people bereaved by the suicide of a family member but as this survey suggests, suicide can affect a wide circle of people. 'Suicide appears to be the most personal action an individual can take yet . . . it has a profound social impact' (Stengel 1973: 13).

Take the case of a young man who dies from carbon monoxide poisoning, after driving the family car to local woods. His death will have a major impact on his immediate family, his parents, brothers and sisters, as well as other relatives: grandparents, aunts, uncles, cousins, perhaps nephews and nieces. Then there were the neighbours who had known him since childhood; friends who had been around since primary school; other more recent friends; the girlfriend he split up from recently; the garage owner who gave him a job; the GP who had been treating him for depression. Suicide can also affect total strangers: the children who found the car; the policewoman who was called to the scene and had to inform the young man's parents; the coroner's officer; and the pathologist and the local reporter sent to cover the inquest.

There is increasing recognition of the many different 'secondary survivors' of suicide deaths, some of whom, without support, may be at risk of developing anxiety, depression, or symptoms of post-traumatic stress disorder (PTSD). Even if they do not go on to develop problems, 'groups ranging from the resuscitation team to the deceased's school, club or workplace may be affected' (Clark and Goldney 2000: 22). Even the suicide of a prominent public figure can affect people, the impact on young people of the suicide of a pop star being a case in point.

A study of adolescent witnesses of a peer suicide found that 29% had developed anxiety disorders, PTSD and major depression within six months of the event (Brent et al. 1993a). Young people are a vulnerable group in mental health terms as they negotiate the transition to adulthood. This, combined with the fact that young males have an above-average suicide rate, makes it imperative that their peers are offered support following a suicide death.

Survivors may be complete strangers. They may have found the body while out walking, or they may be drivers whose car or train 'killed' the person. They may only need short-term support, but 'such support is important, if the long-term effects of post-traumatic stress disorder are to be minimised' (King 1997: 5). An American study found that in one of five cases, a stranger discovered the victim's body, and in one in twenty cases, the actual suicide was carried out in front of a complete stranger (Andress and Corey 1978).

Suicide deaths on the national rail network and the London Underground create many secondary survivors. Train drivers who have been involved in suicides have reported a range of subsequent problems including insomnia, sexual difficulties, recurrent nightmares, and heightened stress and anxiety (Finney 1988). There are 100–150 suicides on the London Underground each year and around 170 people take their lives on the rail network – including a disproportionate number on the East Coast Mainline. In response to this, a collaborative research project involving the NHS and Railtrack has been set up, the aims of which include assessing the effects of these suicides on families, but also on railway and emergency service staff, and bystanders.

The impact of suicide deaths on mental health nurses, psychiatrists, psychologists and psychotherapists and GPs has been the subject of a number of recent studies and articles (Brown 1987; Boakes 1993; Valente 1994; Holmes 1995; Grad 1996; Grad et al. 1997). While professionals report many typical responses to suicide such as a sense of loss, shock, sadness, anger, fear and relief, there are also feelings of professional failure and concern about their reputation amongst colleagues. Grad and her colleagues (1997) also found significant gender differences, with women experiencing more guilt, shame and professional self-doubt. Writing about this sense of failure, Boakes suggests that:

> Death by suicide is a rejection of the central supportive and healing intent of the services. It strikes at the very *raison d'etre* of the health care professional . . . As healers and helpers, members of a caring profession, [the suicide] shows us to have failed. It challenges our omnipotent fantasies, our beliefs in our capacity to help, to cure, to save.
>
> (1993: 74, 76)

Rather less attention has been paid to the patients of therapists who die by suicide, despite the fact that this loss occurs during what is often a time of critical growth and change for the patient. A study which examined the reactions of patients to their therapist's suicide (Reynolds et al. 1997) found that while these paralleled the reactions of other survivors, there were particular features which are cause for concern. Some of these patients continued to deny that the death was suicide, most were reluctant to re-enter therapy and this, combined with the fact that the majority saw suicide as an acceptable solution to some problems, suggest that they are at risk of developing pathological grieving.

Other survivors, whose relationship to the person who died is not publicly recognised or socially sanctioned, may suffer from 'disenfranchised grief' (Doka 1999) where their status as a mourner is unacknowledged. 'Hidden survivors', Doka suggests may include lovers, neighbours, fellow residents in care homes, foster parents and other caregivers. Because they are cut off from potential sources of support, these 'hidden mourners' may be at risk of incomplete or arrested grieving.

Survivors – or victims?

The previous chapter questioned whether 'survivor' is the most appropriate term to describe people bereaved by suicide, an issue which is also discussed in relation to counselling (see pp. 15–16). It merits further brief consideration here, not least because terms, descriptions or labels often matter a great deal to people personally affected by suicide. The manner of death affects their core identity, their sense of self and how they feel others perceive them, and this may be reflected in language too.

People bereaved by suicide may be uncertain as to whether they feel they are survivors or whether they are really victims; this is one of the many ambiguities surrounding suicide. Grad (1996: 37) describes one survivor who argued that rather than calling her deceased spouse 'a victim of suicide', it was she herself who felt like the victim – of her husband's unexpected death.

People bereaved by suicide sometimes shun the term 'victim' because it implies powerlessness and being at someone else's mercy. It can be hard to admit that the person who took their own life can leave others feeling helpless. We don't like to think of ourselves as victims. Writing about the Holocaust, Karpf suggests that the word '"victim" today has become so stigmatised a concept, such a term of abuse, [it is] as if we can't bear the notion that people might find themselves in positions of helplessness . . . victims challenge our belief in the infinite power of volition' (1997: 251–2).

Some writers use the term 'survivor-victim' (e.g. Shneidman 1993: 165), suggesting that both terms are relevant, though they may appear contradictory. Writing about people who have experienced collective trauma and disaster, Menzies Lyth asserts that 'their own and other people's views of them are fraught with apparent contradictions. The survivor is a victim – as much, though differently, as those who perish' (1989: 249).

Opinions are divided about the use of the term 'survivor', but one of the arguments for retaining this term for people bereaved by suicide is that there are many commonalities between survivors of suicide and survivors of other traumatic collective disasters. As Shneidman points out:

> A case can be made for viewing [a suicide death] as a *disaster* and, using the verbal bridge provided by that concept, learning from the professional literature on conventionally recognised disasters – those sudden unexpected events . . . that cause a large number of deaths and have widespread effects.
>
> (1993: 166)

Lifton, in his seminal study of a group of survivors of Hiroshima, described the survivor as 'one who has come into contact with death in some bodily or psychic fashion and has himself remained alive' (1969: 479), pointing to the similarities between the reactions of the *hibakusha* of Hiroshima and survivors of other individual and collective forms of disaster. The reactions described by Lifton are common experiences of people bereaved by suicide including: feelings of guilt, anxiety, a sense of victimisation, a heightened awareness of one's own mortality and attempts to block out painful feelings (psychic numbing). Like the *hibakusha*, who bore physical scars, survivors of suicide can also feel they carry permanent, if less visible, scars.

Similar reactions are described by Menzies Lyth (1989), writing about survival and loss in the aftermath of collective traumatic events such as the sinking of the *Herald of Free Enterprise* and the Aberfan disaster. As she suggests, when disasters occur, 'one cannot draw a rigid distinction between the survivor and the bereaved' (1989: 248).

Studies of the impact of suicide

Studies published in the 1970s and 1980s were important in drawing attention to the needs of people bereaved by suicide, although, as Barrett and Scott point out, they were 'based, in large part, on clinical observation, intellectual conjecture and theoretical speculation' (1990: 2). Studies comparing survivors' experiences with those of people bereaved by other deaths were few and far between.

A decade later, when Clark and Goldney (2000) undertook an overview of the impact of suicide from research and clinical perspectives, they were able to draw on a larger number of studies, many based on more rigorous methodologies. Larger groups were being studied, more research involved the use of control groups, and there were more comparative studies (see below); one or two longitudinal studies had also been undertaken, providing valuable information about the longer-term outcomes for survivors. Most of the research cited by Clark and Goldney has been undertaken in the USA and Australia. Although studies have also been undertaken in Europe, Clark and Goldney do not cite any UK research.

There is now a substantial research literature focusing on particular groups of survivors:

- parents: Seguin et al. (1995a); Brent et al. (1996a); Nelson and Frantz (1996);
- adolescents: Valente and Saunders (1993);
- siblings: Brent et al. (1996a); Nelson and Frantz (1996);
- spouses: Barrett and Scott (1990); Farberow et al. (1992); Smith et al. (1995); Cleiren et al. (1996);
- families: Van Dongen (1993);
- friends (of younger people): Brent et al. (1993b);
- college students: Range and Niss (1990); McIntosh and Kelly (1992); Silverman et al. (1994–5);
- psychotherapy patients: Reynolds et al. (1997);
- psychotherapists and other mental health professionals: Valente (1994); Grad et al. (1997); Grad and Zavasnik (1998).

Bereavement by suicide has traditionally been associated with a particularly difficult grief process compared to other losses. Individuals were considered to be particularly vulnerable to severe grief and an increased risk of taking their own lives. However, these assumptions were often based on clinical experience and individual case studies and there was little clinical or research evidence to support an alternative view (Ness and Pfeffer 1990).

This viewpoint has been challenged by a number of comparative studies:

- suicide and other deaths: Barrett and Scott (1990); Thompson and Range (1992);
- suicide and natural deaths: Farberow et al. (1992);
- suicide and accidental deaths: Seguin et al. (1995a); Cleiren et al. (1996);
- suicide, accidents and natural deaths: McIntosh and Kelly (1992);
- suicide, homicide and natural deaths: Range and Niss (1990).

These studies have explored a number of variables including: timescales of recovery; the bereaved person's history of separation and loss; family dynamics; culture; gender; age of the bereaved; age of the deceased; relationship with the deceased; and specific reactions such as blame, guilt and the need to understand why the death occurred.

Although there is, of course, individual variability in grief, recent research findings and clinical experience have enabled us to revise and reframe some of our previous assumptions about suicide bereavement and its outcomes.

> There are more similarities than differences in morbidity between those bereaved by suicide and through other causes, and the specific mode of death itself creates few if any quantitative differences in bereavement outcome after a suicide . . . However, differences in the themes of grief are common findings, but . . . may not be exclusive to suicide.
>
> (Clark and Goldney 2000: 4–5)

These common characteristic themes include shock, horror, disbelief, shame, rejection, guilt, blame, anger, and the need to know why (Clark and Goldney 2000) – themes which are discussed in Parts 2 and 3.

Although it appears that the mode of death itself does not play a significant part in determining the survivor's mental well-being, recent studies suggest that there are other reasons why some people bereaved by suicide may be particularly vulnerable in terms of their grief and recovery. Research into factors which can have an adverse effect on the way in which an individual copes with a bereavement suggest that the following are relevant:

- the bereaved person's history of attachments and losses, particularly any early losses;
- the relationship to the deceased (e.g. parent; spouse), and the quality of that relationship (e.g. overly dependent or hostile);
- the age of the deceased;
- whether or not the loss was expected;
- pre-loss stresses;
- attitudes towards the loss;
- the prevalence of psychiatric illness in the family;
- disturbed family dynamics;
- the availability of support following the death;
- the severity of grief in the early months.

These 'predictors', it would appear, occur more frequently amongst people bereaved by suicide. Studies comparing people bereaved by suicide with people bereaved by other deaths found that amongst the former:

- there were more losses and separations in the life cycle (Seguin et al. 1995b);
- less support was available within the family (Seguin et al. 1995a);
- the relationship with the deceased was more often marked by conflict or extreme dependence (Seguin et al. 1995a; Cleiren et al. 1996);

- there was a higher incidence of depressive illness, alcohol dependence and schizophrenia in the family (Seguin et al. 1995a);
- a disturbed family background was more common (Cleiren et al. 1996);
- there were more feelings of guilt, shame and rejection (Reed and Greenwald 1991);
- life events after the suicide appeared to increase stress and reinforce isolation (Seguin et al. 1995a).

This suggests that people bereaved by suicide *may* be more at risk because they are already vulnerable. Suicide may be 'added to an already problem laden background [so] it is not unexpected that some families bereaved by suicide may experience extreme difficulty' (Clark and Goldney 2000: 6). This 'vulnerability model' has implications for identifying and offering support to at-risk individuals and families (see Chapter 15).

Features of suicide bereavement

In considering the common themes of suicide bereavement, we need to bear in mind that 'an individual's grief is as unique as their fingerprint' (Clark and Goldney 2000: 6) so that we avoid falling into the trap of assuming that there are universal responses. Nevertheless, as the discussion of clinical and research findings in this chapter and the experiences of survivors described in Part 2 suggest, there *are* commonalities. A group of American survivors meeting to share their experiences in the early 1980s discovered that their

> reactions were not universal, nor did they describe any one person's experience all the time. Yet there seemed to be enough to suggest a syndrome of sorts – a set of behaviours, attitudes and emotional reactions which both typified us in our responses to the world and separated us from it.
>
> (Dunne and Dunne-Maxim 1987: xiv)

This final part of the chapter provides a brief introduction to the chapters in Part 2, which describe the experiences of fifty people who have experienced the suicide of someone close to them. Their stories will, hopefully, illustrate some of the more theoretical discussion in this chapter.

The suicide (Chapter 4)

The survivor of suicide is faced with a death which is, more often than not, unexpected, untimely, and possibly violent. Survivors who witness the suicide or find the body have to come to terms with that experience. Memories of the scene can remain with the survivor for many years; they may fade, but they may never disappear completely. Even when a person has not actually discovered the body, being told about the circumstances of the suicide can leave the survivor with horrific images of the scene of the death (Shneidman 1982). Where the victim died in a violent manner, this reaction is likely to be intensified. Survivors may relive feelings and smells associated with the scene (Clark and Goldney 2000: 7).

Even if the deceased has made overt threats about taking their own life, when the suicide occurs it is often experienced as a traumatic event. A recent study of widows and widowers found that two months after the death, a third of those bereaved by suicide or accidental death were experiencing symptoms of post-traumatic stress disorder (Zisook et al. 1998).

Where the suicide was completely unexpected, feelings of disbelief about the manner of death are not uncommon. Survivors often receive news of the death from complete strangers and the death may have occurred many miles away, both these factors increasing the likelihood of survivors experiencing feelings of disbelief or denial (Bowlby 1985). Denial may persist, particularly in the case of children, but adults also may cling to other explanations (Clark and Goldney 2000).

The immediate and direct involvement of the emergency services creates an additional source of stress. An intensely personal event is, at the same time, a matter for public scrutiny with the involvement of the police, the coroner's officer, and possibly the media.

Britain has virtually no cultural guidelines for viewing the dead except among certain religious and/or ethnic communities. In the absence of any norms, deciding whether or not to view the body may be even more difficult. Survivors are often advised not to visit the mortuary or the undertakers. However, not only does this deny them the opportunity to confront the reality of the death, but it can leave them with disturbing fantasies about the state of the body – fantasies which may be much worse than the reality.

Events leading up to the death (Chapter 5)

Some suicides are totally unexpected, but in other cases, the death occurs after months or years of stress (Hauser 1987; Clark and Goldney 2000). The deceased may have made repeated threats or attempted suicide on more than one occasion. As Hill points out: 'Clues, warnings and threats are commonly given by those who are suicidal to people close to them' (1995: 141).

For some families, the suicide may have seemed inevitable and the death may come as a relief; but for others the suicide will create disaster, either because the suicide occurred in a family which had seen itself as 'normal' and the death therefore comes totally out of the blue, or because there are significant pre-existing problems within the family, making it difficult for survivors to grieve in a healthy way (Seguin et al. 1995a).

The relationship between the deceased and the survivor may have been difficult; it may have been stormy and conflict-ridden, or very close and mutually dependent (Seguin et al. 1995a). Communication in the time leading up to the death may have been fraught or non-existent, leaving considerable unfinished business between the survivor and the person who died (Clark and Goldney 2000).

Faced with overt threats of suicide, some survivors will become caught up in a power struggle, the suicidal person determined to die and the survivor equally determined to prevent that happening (Lake 1984). For other survivors the thought of suicide is too horrifying to contemplate and they may attempt to deny the possibility, while not always succeeding completely. As one person realised after the suicide had occurred: 'I knew that she meant it, I just never thought she'd do it.'

The search for understanding (Chapter 6)

Suicide can seem a meaningless act triggering an endless search for why (Hauser 1987). The death of an elderly person (and even perhaps the death of a younger person from a disease like cancer) may cause great anguish to the bereaved, but timely death or death from a physical illness can often be more easily accepted and understood. Suicide, on the other hand, can seem like a self-chosen death and the survivor will almost invariably want to know why the victim made that choice. Trying to understand why can preoccupy survivors for months and even years although, as Stengel reminds us, the most important informant can no longer be questioned' (1973: 46).

Survivors will seek to answer the question 'why' in many different ways; they may go over and over again the days and weeks leading up to the suicide, searching for clues that they feel they missed at the time; their own relationship to the victim will almost certainly come under the microscope; the actions of others may be scrutinised; where a note was left, it may be endlessly read and re-read in the hope of discovering fresh clues or further answers; survivors will often scour books on suicide in the hope that these will yield the answers.

Suicide and the law (Chapter 7)

Suicide was decriminalised in 1961, but all violent, unnatural or sudden unexplained deaths have to be reported to the local coroner. If the death was unnatural, the coroner is then obliged to hold an inquest in public to establish: the identity of the deceased person; when and where the death occurred; the medical cause of death; the circumstances surrounding the death; and the identity and intent of the person who inflicted the fatal act (King 1997: 6).

Evidence must be gathered for the coroner; photographs may be taken and personal items belonging to the victim may be removed. The suicide note will also be taken away as evidence although in some instances, survivors are given photocopies and the original is returned. These are necessary procedures but for the survivors they can feel extremely intrusive at a time when they are highly vulnerable.

The coroner's court is open to the public and anyone who wishes may attend the inquest, including representatives of the media. This is often a source of considerable distress to relatives (Hill 1995; Biddle 1998) who feel that their private grief is exposed to public scrutiny.

The inquest is not a 'trial' in the legal sense, but the way the process is conducted and the language and setting of the court can often leave the survivors feeling as if they, or the person who died, is on trial.

Funerals (Chapter 8)

Even if they hold no formal religious beliefs, survivors may still be concerned as to whether the suicide was a sin and how that will be viewed by religious officiants when it comes to the funeral. They may wonder whether or not the person is 'at peace'. Some people may question their belief in God and an after-life, wondering about their future and the spiritual state of the person who died (van der Wal 1989).

Members of the clergy are often in contact with a bereaved family immediately after the death so are potentially a valuable source of support. Like anyone else, though, religious officiants will almost certainly have their own views and feelings about suicide which may colour their response to survivors.

Parkes' suggestion that 'the funeral is usually regarded as a last gift to the dead' (1998: 167) may be particularly meaningful for some survivors. They may have felt helpless to prevent the suicide occurring, but thoughtful planning of a 'good' funeral is something they *can* do for the deceased.

The funeral has other important functions: it can bring together a network of people to express their support for the bereaved relatives (Worden 1991) and acknowledge their own sense of loss; it allows the bereaved to experience the full reality of the death (Parkes 1998); and the ritual of the funeral enacts a separation of the living from the dead (Raphael 1985). All these functions are important for survivors of suicide. Where survivors have not seen the body, apart from the inquest, the funeral also may be the only time they come face to face with the reality of death by seeing the coffin, and hearing public words of farewell.

Facing suicide as a family (Chapters 9 and 10)

As the discussion of recent research above demonstrates, the impact of suicide on individual family members and on the family as a whole will depend on a number of factors including the family dynamics and history, whether the suicide had been anticipated and perhaps regarded as inevitable, and the degree of disturbance present in the family.

Nevertheless, suicide will severely tax even those families who have generally healthy or adequate coping strategies. As many of the survivors whose experiences are described in Part 2 discovered, bereavement by suicide raised particular difficulties which, while not unique to suicide, were characteristic of this type of bereavement.

Support from family and close friends can play a major and consistent role in alleviating anxiety, feelings of rejection and depression amongst those who are suddenly bereaved (Reed 1998: 295). However, some survivors may be too deeply preoccupied with their own grief to support others in the family, or they may refrain from openly displaying their feelings in case they overwhelm other family members.

According to Bowlby, 'the tendency to apportion blame is likely to be enormously increased' (1985: 184); there may be silent accusations about who was thought to be responsible for the death; sometimes family members will openly point the finger of blame at each other. Parents-in-law may blame the surviving spouse, adding to existing feelings of rejection and stigma.

Family members often respond very differently and men and women commonly have very different coping strategies (Stroebe 1994). One person may weep openly while another may only cry on their own – or be unable to cry at all. The process of grieving is highly individual, but differences within the family can become a source of friction.

In some instances, the family may seek to avoid distress by refusing to acknowledge the manner of death. After a brief interval, the dead person may no longer even be spoken about. Family myths or 'secrets' may be created where the truth becomes denied or distorted as families attempt to avoid their feelings of guilt and the pain of their loss (Pincus and Dare 1978). This is particularly likely to happen where the survivors include children, and when communication in the family often becomes distorted as attempts are made to hide the truth from them (Worden 1991).

Facing the world: other people's reactions (Chapter 11)

Social support can make a significant contribution to a healthy recovery from bereavement, but earlier studies of suicide survivors (cited in Van Dongen 1993) have frequently reported stigmatisation, social isolation and strained relationships. Suicide has been described as not being a socially acceptable way to die under any circumstances, and without the special rituals and ceremonies which could mobilise support (Wallace 1977).

Recent studies, including comparisons with support after other types of bereavement, highlight some particular issues relating to the social support offered to survivors of suicide and how that is experienced.

Range and Niss (1990) found that suicide survivors may have less social support in the early stages, but over time this becomes similar to support received by people bereaved from other causes, challenging the view that suicide survivors necessarily receive less help than other bereaved people. However, survivors may be reluctant to avail themselves of support. Van Dongen found that despite the availability of strong support, many survivors did not access potential support and

> tended to withdraw during the months after the suicide. It is possible that social isolation may be a coping strategy to conserve energy and provide the [survivor of suicide] with time for grief work. This suggests that social isolation may be more self-imposed than due to rejection by others.
>
> (1993: 137)

This may also have something to do with the type of support offered.

> Friends and relatives are often helpful after a suicide but . . . social support too often consists of food, shelter and concrete aid (what might be called tangible assistance), or clarification and information about resources, but less often emotional support: being listened to, cared for and valued.
>
> (Rudestam 1992: 43)

Other people perhaps feel more comfortable offering practical help, but the upshot may be that survivors feel that they lack emotional support. Uncertainties about support are, doubtless, often mutual. Difficulty in offering emotional support may stem from uncertainty and discomfort, but survivors too often feel uncertain about their role, about whether they should mention the person who died when encountering other people (Van Dongen 1993). They may face the added burden of having to 'educate' their friends about the nature and causes of suicide and about how to behave towards them (Clark and Goldney 2000: 12).

Looking for support (Chapter 12)

Some survivors will find all the support they need from family and friends but others may also look for help outside their immediate circle. The survivor may have assumed the role of 'coper' – the one who tried to support the suicidal person and held everyone else together. Acknowledging the need for help and support in this case can be difficult. Furthermore, if survivors believe that they were in some measure responsible for the death, guilt, shame and stigma may leave them feeling undeserving of help or support.

Some people who take their own lives will have been seen by their GP or by mental health professionals shortly before they died. Asking for help can be difficult, if the survivor feels that these professionals failed the deceased by 'allowing' them to die (Dunne 1987a: 183). There may be considerable anger and resentment towards the 'helping' professions if the survivor believes that they failed to 'help'.

The experiences of survivors described in Chapter 12 may have been different if they had been seeking help now. The addition of new chapters (see pp. 196–236) reflects the growing awareness of the needs of survivors. There has been a modest increase in specialist support services since the first edition of this book appeared and a growing awareness amongst some generalist health professionals that suicide survivors constitute an at-risk group, some of whom may need assistance to recover from their bereavement. But there is still a long way to go.

The reactions of survivors (Chapter 13)

The earlier chapters in Part 2 mainly focus on the survivor's experiences of coping with the external world – family members, friends, neighbours and colleagues, the police and other emergency services, coroners, clergy, GPs, members of the press. Chapter 13 turns to the survivor's inner world, the feelings survivors will often face on their own. As Storr reminds us: 'the loss of a loved one . . . can only partially be shared . . . the work of mourning is by its very nature something which takes place in the watches of the night and in the solitary recesses of the mind' (1989: 31–2).

Any attempt to describe these reactions can fall into the trap of becoming a rather mechanistic exercise, reducing the complex and often difficult process of grieving to a formal checklist. Nevertheless it is important to address this. Many of the survivors whose experiences are described in Part 2 of this book had felt their reactions to be highly abnormal, signs of illness, or even insanity, rather than part of a healthy grieving process. For some, it was only after meeting and talking with other survivors that they could begin to understand that their thoughts and feelings were typical reactions to suicide.

Particular reactions are characteristic of suicide bereavement, even though they are not unique to survivors of this type of loss (see pp. 24–25 above). Recognising that survivors may be particularly susceptible to reactions such as shock and horror, guilt and blame, anger, rejection and shame is important for anyone in a supportive role, but also, of course, for the survivors themselves.

Surviving suicide bereavement (Chapter 14)

For the survivors in Part 2 finding a way through was often a difficult journey, though it could also become an enriching experience from which they emerged feeling stronger. What had seemed unbearable at first, could become bearable. Some were able to find meaning in what had previously seemed meaningless.

Whatever the outcome for individuals, the lives of people bereaved by suicide will be altered irrevocably for as Parkes reminds us, 'the old environment must be given up, the new accepted' (1998: 11). The person who took their own life may have done so believing that their only choice lay in death, but the survivor has other choices. As Jean, a survivor of her daughter's suicide, realised:

> Life will never be the same again. I accept that and I look on that as a challenge. Life is all I have, and life is what my Anna didn't want. So, in a way, I will live to the full for both of us.

Part 2

Aspects of suicide bereavement

Chapter 3

Meeting the survivors

When planning this book, I hoped to be able to interview between forty and fifty people, although several people had expressed doubts as to whether that number of people would be willing to talk about such a difficult issue as suicide. In fact, nearly a hundred people contacted me; there seemed to be no shortage of people wanting to talk about their bereavement. In the event, I saw fifty of them, and it is their stories which are told here.

I have used the word 'stories' deliberately. Although I set out with a tape-recorder and notebook, I decided that, as far as possible, I wanted people to be free to relate their stories in the way that they felt most comfortable. I had a subject guide to hand, but even this was frequently discarded as people began to tell their stories – on some occasions for the first time. I saw my role as listener rather than interviewer, and my decision not to undertake formal, structured interviews reflected Cain's comment that, 'given the clamorous needs of many survivors for psychological assistance, survivor research will often acquire a strong action research flavour' (1972: 24).

Contact was made with survivors through a number of different channels. The single largest group contacted me as the result of letters circulated by two national organisations: CRUSE Bereavement Care; and The Compassionate Friends, a self-help organisation of bereaved parents. Other survivors responded to a letter in the now-defunct weekly magazine *New Society*. The remainder were identified through personal contacts, and through other survivors.

It was not my intention to conduct a formal and methodologically rigorous research study and the fifty people interviewed were not selected in any systematic way, so how representative are they of survivors in general? Do they represent a range of survivors in terms of their circumstances, reactions and coping abilities, or are they a group with particular problems? Only a small proportion had used specialist sources of help and unlike some of the groups of survivors studied by Cain (1972) and his colleagues, they were not part of a clinical group, identified through a hospital or other treatment setting. The common denominator was a wish, maybe even a need, to talk to someone – to tell their story – and this is the opportunity I offered.

Perhaps this need to talk is one of the reasons why, although I also suggested that some people might prefer to write about their experiences, only one person chose to do so. However, one or two people who were interviewed did also share poems, letters or diaries they had written around the time of the suicide.

The interviews were confidential. Only first names have been used, and just over a third of people asked to have their name changed. For some, this guarantee of anonymity was very important, reflecting the continuing need of many survivors to maintain confidentiality.

The length of interviews varied between one and three hours, the average length being about one and a half hours. With three exceptions, the interviews were conducted in the survivors' own homes.

Background to the survivors

The fifty people interviewed comprised fourteen men and thirty-six women. The fact that fewer men than women were prepared to be interviewed matches the experiences of Lukas and Seiden (1987). They found that men were generally less willing to talk to them, and speculated that this was possibly because they thought they had less need to talk to other people. It may also have been a reflection of the different coping strategies of women and men, with the former being more 'emotion-focused', concentrating on their feelings and expressing their emotions (Archer 1999: 241).

The ages of the survivors at the time of the suicide varied widely. The youngest person had been four when the death occurred and the oldest was sixty-eight. Almost half had been in their thirties and forties, many of them being the parents of young adults who had taken their own lives.

At the time of the interviews (carried out between February 1988 and February 1989), seven people had been bereaved for less than a year, and a further twenty people for between one and four years. Six people had been bereaved over twenty years previously, all except one of these being adults who had experienced the suicide of a parent during their childhood.

The biggest single group of survivors consisted of parents (21), followed by almost equal numbers of siblings (10), children (9) and spouses (9). One person had lost a former lover. Two people had been bereaved twice by suicides in their family.

The survivors included doctors, teachers, social workers, civil servants, journalists, nurses, factory workers, shop assistants, clerical workers, students, housewives; others were currently unemployed or had retired from full-time employment.

The people who had died by suicide

The fifty survivors had experienced a total of forty-five suicides: twenty-three men and twenty-two women. (There are fewer suicide victims than survivors because in some cases more than one family member was interviewed.)

The youngest person who had died by suicide was eighteen and the oldest seventy-five. By far the biggest single group (13) comprised young people aged twenty to twenty-five. Just under half the deceased were under thirty, and less than 7% were over sixty.

Almost half the victims had left some sort of note behind – a far higher proportion reported in other studies (see Chapter 6).

The single most common method used was overdosing on pills (13), sometimes in combination with alcohol. Information on the method used was only available in forty-one of the forty-five cases, but of these forty-one victims, twenty had used a method which could be described as 'violent' (jumping or lying in front of a train, jumping from a tall building, using a shotgun, self-immolation or hanging).

Appendix 2 summarises the information on individual survivors and victims.

The survivors' reasons for being interviewed

Survivors were asked why they had agreed to talk about their experiences, and a number of different reasons emerged. Some related to the survivors' own needs: they thought that talking to another person might help them in some way.

Liz, whose brother had died four years previously, was someone who felt that the interview might be personally helpful. She hoped it would provide a means of overcoming her inability to talk about Tony, and before we met she wrote:

> it will be of therapeutic value to me as I've never talked about it . . . Although other members of the family refer to him in conversation, I cannot. I suppose partly for selfish reasons I thought maybe it would help me to talk about it.

In some instances, people had not even been aware that they still needed to talk about the suicide. Hilary, who was eighteen when her mother committed suicide thirty-five years previously, was surprised to find herself crying during the interview. Afterwards she wrote: '[the interview] helped me, even though I didn't know I needed helping'.

For other survivors, the interview provided a welcome chance to talk about the person who had died; as Heather admitted: 'I guess I just like talking about Alastair'. Survivors often had little or no opportunity to talk about the person they had lost. After a time, even their name seemed to be banished from conversation by friends or more distant relatives.

Suicide can seem a very senseless act, and for some survivors, sharing their experiences with a wider audience was seen as a way of injecting some meaning and purpose into what could otherwise feel meaningless. Peter, for example, felt that by being prepared to talk about his sister's suicide, perhaps the subject would become less of a taboo, and that suicide would begin to carry less stigma.

For Kevin, who was ten when he discovered his mother's body, the interview was a chance to talk about the person who he was only now, twenty-five years later, beginning to understand and cherish. He talked of wanting to honour her memory, but, like Peter, he also saw it as an opportunity to help counteract some of society's more negative attitudes towards suicide.

So as well as meeting their own needs, many survivors hoped that by taking part in the interviews they would also be helping to lessen the taboos which surround those who take their own lives and those left behind. Denise, whose father hanged himself when she was four, hoped that contributing to the book would help lessen the isolation of 'people who live in their own little hell, trying to sort it all out for themselves'.

It was encouraging that so many of the survivors said that they had found the interview helpful. I had been concerned that people would find it too distressing or that the experience would be negative or even harmful. My anxieties were somewhat allayed by learning of the experiences of other researchers in this field (Shepherd and Barraclough 1979; Solomon 1981) who reported that survivors had found it helpful to talk openly and at length to a non-judgemental and uninvolved person. Researchers conducting psychological autopsies have also reported similarly (Asgard and Carlsson-Bergstrom 1991).

The fact that people knew they were talking to someone who had personal experience of suicide bereavement was particularly important to some survivors. Several people made it clear when we met that they had only agreed to be interviewed because they had been told in the introductory letter that I was also a survivor of suicide. As Miriam said: 'I feel strongly that such a study should only be undertaken by a researcher who has shared the experience.'

Finally, after the suicide, many survivors had scoured their local libraries and bookshops, searching for information on suicide and trying to find out how to cope with being a survivor. Having found nothing that could really meet their needs, they were eager to contribute to a book which they felt could perhaps help other survivors in the future.

Chapter 4

When the suicide happens

Even now what I can't really bear to think about is how he must have felt when he was taking the aspirin, what despair he must have been in, those awful thoughts he must have had. (Suzy)

It was just the worst day of my life. (Jennifer)

Finding out

Whatever has gone before, it seems that nothing can prepare the survivor for the suicide when it happens:

It was 3rd December, the day my son died. [A friend] dropped me off at the bottom of the road. It was quite dark. As I walked up the road I saw a figure standing at our gate; it walked towards me and I saw it was [her husband]. He took hold of my arm and I could feel waves of shock coming from him. 'You'll have to prepare yourself', he said, 'Jon is dead'. I stumbled into the house and then I screamed 'No! No! No!' (Carole)

Like Carole, most of the survivors I met had been told the news by other people. But those who had actually discovered the body still had vivid memories of an event which, in some instances, had taken place many years before. The memory of what was seen can remain with the survivor for a lifetime (Lukas and Seiden 1987). It was over twenty-five years since four-year-old Denise and her mother came home from shopping one day:

[My mother] sensed there was something wrong. She went whipping through the house and got to the foot of the stairs and started to scream and then ran out; and so I followed to see what she was screaming at – and he'd hung himself on the staircase; and I do remember quite vividly; I remember standing there looking; I haven't blotted it out. I haven't been told that either . . . it's a memory that's always been with me.

It is not unknown for the person to actually commit suicide when other people are in the house. Betty sat watching television one evening unaware that, in an upstairs bedroom, her son lay dying from an overdose; he had even waved the bottle of pills at her as he left the room – but she had not understood the significance of this, nor had she understood the reason why, earlier that day, he had quite uncharacteristically hugged her and told her how much he loved her. That afternoon she had watched him writing letters, not realising that they were suicide notes. Now she is left with the distressing feeling that she was virtually a witness to his suicide – albeit an innocent witness.

Even when survivors hear the news from other people, they will often retain clear memories of the circumstances. Bad news has a way of etching itself permanently on to the mind. Fifty-two years after her brother died, Ann could still clearly picture herself standing on the staircase of the office where she worked, and being told that Giles had taken his own life.

However, the fact that the death was suicide does not always emerge straight away; survivors are sometimes left uncertain as to the exact circumstances of the death. When the local police came round to tell Jennifer her brother was dead, all they had was a message from the police in another part of the county who had been called to the scene of Tim's death. They told her that Tim had been killed on a railway line, and the possibility of suicide did not even enter her mind at that point: 'It didn't register that he could possibly have done it himself. I thought it must have been an accident. It was only later that day', she says, 'that it started to click that he'd done it himself.' She believes that even if the police were not sure what had happened, they should have mentioned the possibility of suicide. As it was, having begun to take on board the fact that Tim had been killed in an accident, a few hours later she then had to readjust to the fact that he had taken his own life.

Some people intending to take their own lives disappear without trace, perhaps wanting to protect relatives from the shock of finding the body, perhaps wanting to guard against the possibility of being found to be still alive. For the survivors though, this can mean days or even weeks of not knowing, or at least not being sure, what has happened. Tony's body was eventually found in a pond which had frozen over in an unusually cold spell, and it was seven weeks after his disappearance before the family finally knew what had happened to him. Others may not have to wait quite so long, but it can still be a distressing time for relatives. Richard's body was discovered after nine days, but although Susan felt sure she knew what had happened, and told the police she suspected suicide, she still had to face comments from the police that her husband had probably gone off with another woman. The police, as the saying goes, 'have to keep an open mind', which can be hard for survivors who, because of what they know about the missing person, are more or less certain of what has happened. They may feel the police are not listening to them.

Sometimes the survivor will seem to know instinctively that the other person is no longer alive, even when there is still no proof. After her son disappeared, Lois reported him missing to the police but knowing, at the same time, that Simon was already dead:

> Everyone said, 'Oh, don't worry, he'll turn up', but something went inside me, and I just knew and it wasn't because of all these threats [of suicide], I hadn't really believed them, but it was just something inside me went; I no longer had that closeness.

Not everyone will be so sure. Sometimes, when the body is not discovered immediately, the survivors will be uncertain when the death actually occurred. Janice's elderly mother had lived alone and her body was not discovered for several days. The fact that she does not even know which day her mother died is something which Janice has found particularly upsetting. For other survivors, anniversaries are made more difficult than usual because the death has been registered with a date which the survivor knows to be wrong. When talking about her husband's death, Susan several times made the point that the police insisted Richard's death had occurred on the date he was found, a date which she knew to be wrong; but, as she said, 'you're in such a state of shock that it seemed irrelevant at the time to make a fuss and I just let it go'. Fifteen years after Richard's death, though, this was still something she felt strongly about.

A person will sometimes kill themselves when those closest to them are away from home. When this happens, survivors may wonder whether this was a deliberate choice – were they doing it to protect people they knew would be upset, or did they decide to wait until there was no one around who might stop them? Whatever the reason, it can leave survivors like Carol with inevitable 'if onlys'. A single parent, she had organised a weekend away, but had made arrangements for her ex-husband to be around. Alan's brother was also living at home. When Alan's father came round on Sunday morning, he discovered that Alan had hanged himself. Now Carol is left wondering – 'had I been there, I feel Alan wouldn't actually have died that weekend . . . [but] I'm not sure whether that would have been putting off what would have happened anyway'.

Jean was on holiday when her daughter walked out of the psychiatric unit where she had been admitted as an in-patient and killed herself. Jean knows she badly needed the holiday to recharge her own batteries and in order to cope with looking after Anna when she came out of hospital; but despite this, she still felt guilty when she had to tell the coroner she had been away at the time of Anna's death, particularly when she was not able to explain why she had needed that break.

First reactions

A sense of numbness, of bluntness of feeling is common among bereaved people (Parkes 1998), and can serve to protect them from feelings which may be too overwhelming to face immediately (Kast 1988). The shock of hearing about the suicide can be so great that survivors may find it impossible to believe what they have been told. A vague sense of disbelief can turn into denial. Three days after his wife's disappearance, John still felt sure that Averil would return home at some point. When her body was eventually washed ashore the coroner's officer gave him the news, and asked if he would identify her from clothes and jewellery found on the body: 'I still couldn't believe it, and I said "Yes, I'll be over; I'll show you that it's nothing to do with Averil".'

The fact that John was advised not to see his wife's body, well-meaning advice which he accepted at the time, only added to his sense of disbelief. He began to think:

> perhaps it's someone else's body. He [the pathologist] . . . said don't look, didn't he? She could have changed her clothes with someone – she was a very generous person – and all the while nobody has officially told you, except for this bit of paper, that that's your wife.

Where the survivor has been in contact with the deceased only hours before, and everything had seemed to be perfectly normal, news of the death can seem totally unbelievable. When Joan was woken by the phone one night, and told that her sister had been found dead in bed she couldn't believe it: 'I'd only just been talking on the phone. I just thought, I'm still dreaming, and I said out loud, "You're just pulling my leg".'

The numbness experienced by many survivors in the first few hours can last for days. Pat remembers waking up the morning after her daughter had died, 'trying to believe, trying to accept. You don't; you can't. It's like someone giving you a pill that's big and saying "swallow that". It's impossible, it won't go down. You've got to chip away a bit at a time.' This numbness persisted; even after the funeral when everyone came back to the house and Pat found she was able to chat to everyone without breaking down or even crying. As she subsequently realised, it took some time for the reality of Caroline's death to sink in.

The period immediately after a death is often a busy one for families; other relatives and friends have to be informed, and funeral arrangements made. In cases of possible suicide, there will also have to be a post-mortem and preliminary inquest before the body can be released for burial or cremation. Numbness helps some survivors to deal with these tasks more or less automatically, but it can leave people incapable of doing even that. This state of immobility was vividly described by Leonard Woolf, writing of the days following Virginia Woolf's suicide:

> the long drawn out horror of the previous weeks had produced in me a kind of inert anaesthesia; it was as if I had been so battered and beaten that I was like some hunted animal which, exhausted, can only instinctively drag itself into a hole or lair.
>
> (Woolf 1969: 95)

Nichols has suggested (1981) that families should have a 'no decision' period of up to thirty-six hours after a sudden death, an idea which would seem to have many advantages. Survivors often talked of having made decisions immediately after the death which they subsequently regretted, including the decision not to see the victim's body (see pp. 50–51).

The involvement of strangers

When a death occurs, Parkes suggests that the bereaved person 'needs time and protection from intruders' (1998: 166). But when someone is thought to have committed suicide, and particularly if the death occurs in the family home, survivors surrender the right to any such privacy, as Carole found after her son's body was discovered at the family's home. Their doctor came round, she remembers, but 'then the police came, and the CID, and the photographers, and an undertaker'; suddenly their house was filled with strangers.

After Janice's mother committed suicide, strangers had entered the house before Janice arrived; the police had had to break in, and when Janice and her sister reached the bungalow, their mother's body had already been taken away. The body cannot be handed back to relatives until the coroner has issued a burial order, and for survivors, it can feel as though other people – strangers to boot – have completely taken over. Anne Downey described what happened after her son's body had been found: 'Two strangers in black took you away . . . people filled the house . . . then someone took the note away and talked about inquests and evidence' (1987: 13).

Survivors of suicide may have little chance of nursing their wounds in private, as Victoria Alexander, an American survivor, discovered when her mother took her own life: 'I was angry at my exposure, at having my open wounds and those of my family available for inspection by the police, by the medical examiner, neighbours and passers-by. *Their spectacle was my nightmare*' (1987: 110; my italics).

Conley (1987) has suggested that 'first responders' such as the police and the coroner's officer have three main areas of responsibility to fulfil: to satisfy the requirements of the law, to meet the needs of the survivors, and to secure the dignity of the dead person. It can be hard to meet all these requirements simultaneously. For example, the need to carry out a legal investigation can cut across the need to support relatives.

It is highly unlikely that survivors will have had to face this sort of situation before, and, in a state of shock, they are unlikely to realise that the police need to rule out any suspicion of foul play. Being subjected to what one survivor described as 'quite a grilling' by the police is an unpleasant experience at the best of times, but survivors might find it easier if the reasons for this and other necessary procedures were explained to them.

Clark and Goldney suggest that the doctor who certifies the death at the site of the suicide could explain to relatives the reasons why the emergency services did or did not attempt resuscitation and why the police and coroner's officer needed to be there (2000: 476).

Some survivors did comment positively on their dealings with the police: 'very very sweet; couldn't have been nicer' (Eileen); 'helpful, kind, and compassionate' (Robert). But not everyone had found the police so helpful. Maureen came home after hearing that her son had shot himself to find not only that her house was full of strangers but that she was not allowed back into her own home, and no one would tell her why:

> No one would tell me anything, see? And that was the hardest thing. If someone had just got hold of me, brought me in here, and sat me down and said, 'Look, Paul's shot himself, he's still upstairs, we can't move him yet', I would have known.

As it was, no one would tell her where Paul's body was. Sitting in a neighbour's house, she could hear the police, as she says, 'banging about' in *her* house. And all the police would say was that they were 'just tidying up'. It was some time before the police even confirmed officially that Paul was dead. As Maureen commented: 'they don't know how to tell you your son's killed himself, [but] they should come out with it just the same'.

As Maureen realised afterwards, the police were probably trying to protect her from the mess; Paul's bedding, his clothes, and the carpet all had to be burnt because of the blood. But not being told anything, not having anything explained, can leave survivors with fantasies which may be worse than reality. When Alastair's body was found in the local forest his parents wanted to go over there immediately, but were told by the police not to. 'So we didn't go', Heather recalls, 'but maybe that sowed the seed of "this is too horrid".'

Giving people bad news is never an easy task, but some survivors had been on the receiving end of considerable insensitivity. Mark described how: 'the police blundered in and did their blundering thing'. When a policewoman came to interview his wife about their daughter's suicide, Francesca, who is a trained counsellor, found that:

> instead of interviewing me, she . . . sat down at my feet, took her hat off, and told me how she understood because this had happened to her close relative and she started to tell me all about this, using me as a counsellor and I was sitting thinking . . . what exactly is this all about, what's happening to me? I'm being made to listen to this policewoman who needs some help and I'm a helper – I'm not a helper in this situation and can't be, so I just sat . . . and eventually she went. It was quite bizarre.

Several survivors commented on how young the police were who had been sent round to see them, and how awkwardly they behaved. Delivering news of death is never going to be easy for the police. Like Francesca, Susan found herself in the anomalous situation of being the one who ended up doing the looking after:

> [They sent] the youngest policeman in the [local] police force . . . together with the youngest policewoman. They hadn't the faintest idea what to do. They were really frightened. I found myself trying to mother them . . . and they gave me the phone number of the police station [in the area where her husband's body had been found] and they didn't even help me find the code. It sounds incredible to tell you that fifteen years later, but it really stands out in my mind.

Jane's experience was not dissimilar: '[There were] two of them. They both looked about fourteen years old and incredibly embarrassed.' Age does not automatically confer greater sensitivity or ability to handle difficult situations, but perhaps more experienced members of the police force would be more comfortable in this sort of situation and more able to support relatives. Training could also place greater emphasis on talking to relatives. The behaviour of the police and other emergency services at the time of the suicide is a matter of considerable importance, as these examples show; survivors will often remember how they were treated for a long time afterwards.

Unlike the police and the coroner's officer, ambulance crews are not there in an investigatory capacity, which may make their job somewhat easier; some survivors were particularly appreciative of the way that the ambulance staff behaved. Carol described the ambulance crew who took Alan's body away as 'superb', and she was particularly touched to receive a card from them the next day saying how sorry they were about his death. In contrast to the way the police behaved, Francesca found the ambulance crew who came to the house particularly kind and sensitive. Not only did they take the trouble to explain to her why it was not possible to try and re-start Patricia's heart, but when they arrived at the hospital she was allowed to remain in the ambulance alone with the body and say goodbye to her daughter in private.

Farewells

Sudden death leaves the survivor no opportunity to deal with any unfinished business in the relationship, and no chance to say a proper goodbye (Clark and Goldney 1995). Indeed, what subsequently turns out to have been the last conversation between them will often seem quite normal to the unsuspecting survivor. Pat talked to her daughter only hours before Caroline jumped from the top of a multi-storey car park, and heard her say, 'I'm fine'; in Pauline's case her son went off 'happy as a sandboy', she remembers, saying 'Cheerio, and see you next week'.

But not all survivors have such apparently normal partings. Some people were left with memories of an angry farewell exchange and having to come to terms with that. Melanie was living apart from her husband and had recently applied for a legal separation. Ian's last words to her before killing himself were 'You'll have blood on your hands.' That was seven years before the interview. She still cannot forget those words, but she has reached the point of being able to acknowledge that she was not responsible for his death; at the time she felt less sure.

Facing the horror

As some of the initial numbness begins to wear off, survivors will often experience overwhelming feelings of horror, thinking about how the person actually died, and wondering what they went through at the end (Clark and Goldney 2000). Lois, whose son killed himself with a knife, found that particularly shattering:

> the horror of a loved one choosing to murder themselves is quite horrendous . . . I thought if he would do such a thing, he'd go for a walk along the river, that's what I thought – that he would just slip away; but he chose a very dramatic death really.

Sometimes, the thought of such violence makes it almost impossible fully to accept the manner of death – let alone talk about it – however hard the survivor tries. Marie, whose husband Oliver died on the railway line near their home, has found that although 'it's something you talk about, work through, come to terms with . . . I think there's a limit to what you can talk about accepting'.

While some people manage to push any thoughts about the actual death to the back of their minds, others may find themselves unable to do so. Two months after her daughter died on the London Underground, Jean found she was becoming totally obsessed with thoughts of how Anna had died:

> I just spent the whole time thinking about the death . . . the whole time. I thought, you're going to get totally obsessed like Anna, you've got to stop this . . . that's all I thought about – her jumping and her looking, and how she looked in the funeral parlour. I just went over and over it, and how she felt and whether it hurt. I was in a terrible state . . . so yes [a year after her death], I am still very obsessed with the way she died.

Wondering what the person was going through at the time they died preoccupies many survivors, though being given information by other people about what is likely to have happened can help to lessen that preoccupation. For several days after Tim's body had been discovered on the railway line, Jennifer found that all she could think about was how violently he had died, and so she was glad to hear from the coroner that Tim would almost certainly not have felt anything. Heather, too, was helped by discovering that the way her son had chosen to end his life would almost certainly have meant a painless death.

Not having been there when the suicide happened, and realising that the person had died alone, can be a cause of considerable anguish to survivors like Phyllis whose daughter, Julie, died of an overdose. Nearly four years later she still asked herself: 'Why didn't I ring her? Why didn't she phone me? Could I have done anything? Was she scared? Was she frightened? When she was dying, did she call out? It's awful.'

Survivors can blame themselves for not having realised how bad the deceased must have been feeling. They may feel that they should have known what was going on, even when the person had not shown any particular signs of distress. As a mother, Pat found that particularly hard:

> I find it hard [to live] with the knowledge that she was going through all this dreadful pain and I didn't know. And that's the overriding thing that's painful to me. I mean she killed herself and she's dead and she's gone and that is a dreadful pain but the worst thing for me to cope with is the knowledge that before she died she was in such terrible pain and going through such torment and I didn't know . . . To think that we were here for those two days before she died . . . and I'm her Mum and I didn't even know and I couldn't help.

This sort of questioning may also be the survivor's way of trying to understand what led the other person to take the final step. Tim's death left Jennifer with many questions:

What must you be thinking that minute before you do it? If you're going to do something like that, what must you be thinking, what must you be doing? You wonder all kinds of things: whether he sat there a long time . . . thinking, whether he experimented with something on the line to see how fast the trains were going, or if he cried.

Trying to understand why the person committed suicide is an extremely common reaction among survivors (see Chapter 6), but one of the greatest puzzles can be – what happened at the very end, what was the final trigger? Things may have been going badly wrong for the person for some time, but why that day, what was it that finally tipped the balance? This is a question which the survivor may never be able to answer.

Viewing the body

It has been suggested that viewing the body is important because by seeing the deceased, the bereaved come face to face with the reality of the death, can begin to accept what has happened and acknowledge that they will not see that person alive again (Raphael 1985; Staudacher 1988). This is echoed by Clark and Goldney who suggest that:

> Opportunity should be offered to view the body, but if it is mutilated the alternative of maintaining vigil over the covered body may be preferred. Families may be angry if this opportunity is denied. If a decision is taken not to view the body, negotiations should be made with a family member or the funeral director to take photos of the body in case of future need. These may be useful later to avoid fantasies of misidentification.
>
> (2000: 476, 478)

For Maureen, going to see Paul's body at the undertakers did help her towards acceptance.

> If I hadn't gone, I would never have believed he was dead. I had to go to prove to me that it was Paul [or] I'd have been out looking for him . . . I had to see that he was actually at peace.

Even Irene, who described her dead husband's face as being 'so full of pain you could almost touch it', still feels glad that she was able to see him. For some of the survivors, there had been a desperate need to touch and hold the person, a need that they were sometimes denied. Pat and Robert were told by a policeman that they couldn't see Caroline's body straight away.

Like any mother, Pat badly wanted to hold her daughter at that moment. She feels she has been left with a dreadful gap and wishes she had insisted, but as she now says, over a year later: 'I didn't really know that I had the right to; perhaps if I had I would have insisted'. At moments of crisis like this, though, when survivors are in shock, standing up for their rights may be the last thing they feel able to do.

By the time the body has reached the undertakers and has been placed in a coffin, the chance to hold the body for the last time may have passed, something which Jean still regrets. Having been told by her brother that Anna's body was 'viewable' she went to the undertakers, and although she was relieved that Anna's face was unmarked,

> what really distressed me about it was that I couldn't hold her. They'd done her up, I suppose because of the post-mortem; it was just her face and she was all done up in a kind of white parcel . . . like a cardboard box . . . when you've had your own child, you need to hold them, and I needed to see her body . . . [I] wanted to see Anna's hands but I thought I had just better not look.

Because her brother had told her, Jean knew that Anna would look all right, but survivors may need more specific information. It is possible that Jean could have seen and touched Anna's hands, but she refrained from doing what she instinctively wanted to do because she did not know what to expect.

Where survivors have no information about the state of the body, what they are left with are fantasies which may be so horrendous that the survivor decides they could not possibly bring themselves to see the body. But fantasies can be much worse than reality (Raphael 1985), as David discovered when he went to see Paul after his son had shot himself: 'When I saw him, he was so perfect and so normal I was sort of quite relieved.'

Not all survivors will want to see the body, of course, but sometimes they may not even feel that they had any choice in the matter. Other well-meaning family members may put pressure on the survivor, with comments like 'best to remember her as she was'. As Raphael points out, being able to remember the person when they were alive is important, but the bereaved need to acknowledge them as dead too:

> The experience of seeing . . . the dead person as a dead person makes it possible for the bereaved to develop an image of the person as dead . . . different and altered from the living image. This image may then be held alongside the living image in the processes of separation and mourning.
>
> (1985: 36)

Other people will often feel they are being helpful by suggesting to relatives that they should not see the body. Nancy, who was abroad when her daughter died, was advised by her vicar not to see Clare: 'He said "Don't; better remember her as she was", and I thought, well [he] knows what he's doing and I abided by that. But I've regretted it ever since.'

Sometimes survivors have to face not only discouragement but outright disapproval. When Suzy's father committed suicide, she knew that going to see his body was something she both wanted and needed to do, but other people in the family did not see things in the same way:

> I'd already decided I'd go and see my father; my mother was very shocked at that and my sister thought it was revolting . . . I felt it was important. I wanted to say goodbye . . . I hadn't seen him the day before [when he had died].

Janice was faced not only with her sister's disapproval, but with being strongly advised by the undertaker not to see her mother's body. Fortunately, though, she was able to talk this through with a therapist and looking back, is glad that she did in fact go to see her mother at the undertakers, despite pressure being placed on her not to do so.

Having someone to talk things over with can help survivors sort out what it is they want to do and can help them reach a decision which is based on their own feelings, rather than on the wishes of others. When Christine's husband took his own life, she recalls how 'everyone – the police, my parents, the undertakers' tried to stop her seeing Graham's body, which had been badly damaged and, after three weeks, was also decomposed. Only the bereavement counsellor who she had started seeing understood her need to go and accompanied her to the undertakers.

In many cases, survivors will not see the body until it reaches the undertakers, but several people said how much they had wanted to see the body before that. Not being sure what to expect, not knowing what is 'allowed', and not having things explained can prevent survivors from doing what their instincts are telling them is right. Heather did not see her son Alastair, when his body was in the hospital mortuary but admits: 'I wish I had gone. I had visions of bodies in drawers and I didn't want to see Alastair being pulled out [of a drawer] like you see on television.' In fact when her husband went to the hospital, Alastair was lying in a bed looking as if he was asleep. Now she regrets not having been to the hospital because:

> that was really [my] chance to say goodbye which I have never done . . . When he was in the chapel of rest I didn't want to go because I thought they would have put make-up on him and combed his hair wrong and dressed him in something funny and I didn't want to see him in a coffin

. . . I'm glad I didn't go then. I only regret not going to the hospital. I think if somebody had explained to me that it would be all right, persuaded me to go, I'd have been better off because I haven't seen him dead, and I think that's important. I think I would have been further along if I had actually seen him dead.

The fact that their child's hair was combed the wrong way was something several parents mentioned; it obviously mattered to them. Of course there is no reason why undertakers should know how the person wore their hair when they were alive, but there may be ways of overcoming this problem. Relatives could perhaps be asked for a recent photo. Or they could be invited to come and help to arrange the person's hair themselves.

This sort of measure is not always practicable, of course. Sometimes the body has been so badly mutilated, that there are virtually no recognisable remains. Faced with this, survivors may find it hard to accept that the person is actually dead. When Brian's wife committed suicide he was only able to identify Judy by her wedding ring and watch; though he is glad to have been spared the ordeal of seeing her remains, he has found it hard to accept her death, and in his dreams, Judy is often still alive.

In Judy's case there was a funeral, there was a coffin . . . [but] I didn't know where Judy was; I mean, maybe she was there . . . Sometimes I wonder whether there's a part of me that hasn't accepted that she's not here any more because, although there was a funeral, I can't actually say that I felt she was involved . . . I found the service very remote.

Raphael suggests that where there are no recognisable remains, the bereaved 'may still need to say goodbye and may need to talk through his or her feelings about what remains of the person' (1985: 36). But some survivors may need to do more than this. When Jennifer's brother died on a railway line, his body was very badly mutilated. As a result, not only were the family told it would be best not to see Tim's remains, but they were also advised not to look at the photographs used as evidence at his inquest. At the time of his death, Jennifer felt strongly that she needed to know that what had been found was indeed Tim's body, and that feeling persisted. But it was only months later that she discovered that she could see Tim's file at the coroner's office. So nearly a year after the death she went to the office and spent time looking at those photographs. She did not find this easy, but it gave her a sense of acceptance and she has no regrets about what she did. Not everyone would choose Jennifer's way of confronting the death, but survivors who are left with no recognisable body to see may have to find other ways of saying goodbye.

The time immediately after a death is rarely easy for the bereaved, and survivors of suicide face additional stresses, not least the legal investigations which have to be set in train. These, combined with the sometimes violent nature of suicide death, can leave the survivors in a particularly vulnerable state. Sensitive attitudes and behaviour on the part of the police, the coroner's officer, and others who may be involved can, however, help to minimise the survivor's distress.

Chapter 5

Looking back

He was talking about suicide all that week and had actually threatened suicide . . . that was the most terrible thing of all and I just couldn't cope with it, I just couldn't handle it at all . . . I can remember saying, 'But you couldn't love me if you're saying you're going to leave me' . . . and to me it wasn't a reality, you see, that's the awful thing, to me he was just talking, I never really believed it, that's the terrible thing. (Lois)

You think, well, how could you be there and . . . it happen despite you being there? On the other hand, you're not almighty, and can't control everybody and everything. (Marie)

At times, people will take their own lives seemingly unexpectedly. Survivors may have been aware that the person had problems, but the death still comes as a complete surprise, as was the case with Caroline's family. To Robert and Pat, their daughter was 'a twenty-year-old who thought she should have a boyfriend and thought she should be thinner'; the weekend before she died, Caroline had said she felt unwell and had spent time in bed, but, as Robert explained, it never entered their heads that 'she was in trouble that way'.

For other survivors, despite the fact that the suicide is unexpected, when it happens it is as though all along they had been half expecting something like that. When Jane heard the news from America that her brother, Christopher, had died she remembers thinking that it had probably been a stroke or something similar: 'I was bracing myself to hear "coronary thrombosis" or "stroke" . . . I was summoning all my strength to hear something coming from a direction I expected it to come from.' But what she heard was that Christopher had taken his own life with a gun:

and it had never entered my head. He had never mentioned anything of this sort, never mentioned suicide. It was never a thought I had entertained in relation to Christopher, ever, and simultaneously I thought, yes, yes, I can see that.

Living with a suicidal person

Parkes has suggested that 'the greater the area occupied by A in the life space of B, the greater the disruption that will result from A's departure' (1998: 119). The strength of reaction to a death may be related less to love and more to the intensity of involvement between the two people (Marris 1978). At the point when many young adults are leaving the family home and parents are anticipating a well-earned breather, Mark and Francesca found themselves embarking on what turned out to be ten years of frequently intense involvement and caring for their daughter. They coped with the suicide attempts and the other crises; like many family carers they became the backstop when the official services failed, and it was to them and to the family home that Patricia always returned.

The completed suicide may be the culmination of years of difficulty, often marked by previous attempts, threats of suicide, and repeated crises. People who deliberately self-harm have a risk of suicide some 100 times greater than the general population (Hawton and Fagg 1988); and between a fifth and a quarter of people who die by suicide have been seen in hospital for deliberate self-harm episodes in the year before the death (Hawton 1998).

Frank and Ursula spent five years trying to care for their daughter before Josie finally died as the result of an overdose. Labelled 'schizophrenic' by the psychiatric services, Josie's adult life had been punctuated by crises: admission to hospital would be followed by discharge and the inevitable re-admission; there were other times when her parents had no idea where she was living; on one occasion they found she was serving a prison sentence, twice she attempted suicide. Ursula often felt torn: mental health professionals told her she should not let Josie return to the family home; her instinct was to want to look after her daughter. At the time of her death Josie was living in a bedsitter nearby, but frequently returning home in the daytime when Ursula would look after her.

Sometimes the suicidal person's difficulties can threaten to disrupt totally the lives of those around them. Andrew was a GP in a busy general practice when his wife's problems began. Although Gwen had suffered from intermittent depression for some years, her brother's suicide three years before her own death seems to have upset an already fragile balance. Andrew can remember those last years clearly:

the vicious circle of the depression and the booze and the attempts at killing herself . . . in and out of psychiatric clinics, repeated attempts at suicide, codeine tablets, barbiturates . . . putting her overcoat over her dressing-gown and going down to the off-licence to buy her whisky in the morning.

Despite all his efforts and despite the fact he was a doctor, Andrew admits that in the end he was powerless to help her.

Living with the knowledge that someone has attempted suicide and may do so again adds to the stress of what is often already a fraught situation. Isabel's husband took two overdoses during fifteen years of severe depressions, which led to unemployment and periods of in-patient psychiatric treatment. After the second attempt, Eric's doctor told Isabel that if her husband made no further attempts in the next four years then everything would be all right. His prediction was somewhat over-optimistic. Seven years later, Eric finally killed himself with another overdose.

Facing threats of suicide

In four out of five suicide deaths, the person will have given clear verbal or behavioural clues that they are intending to take their own lives (Shneidman 1993: 41). They may have told someone outside the family such as their general practitioner, but are equally likely to have told a relative.

Bridget was seventeen and in the middle of taking her A-level exams when her older sister Catherine killed herself; their mother had died some years before, their father (who was also to die by suicide later that year) was unable to cope, and it was left to Bridget to try to talk her sister out of the suicide threats:

> I eventually worked out that I couldn't stop her by persuasion; I couldn't talk her out of it because it wasn't a logical thing . . . I'd try and talk her out of it but in the end she'd just say 'I've just got to do it and I will' and so I didn't feel I could stop her like that at all – I tried.

Sometimes survivors find themselves on the receiving end of what is tantamount to emotional blackmail. Melanie found herself in that situation with her husband. Things at home had become impossible, so she and her baby daughter had moved out and were staying with her parents. Ian wanted her back and began threatening that he would kill himself if she didn't return; on one occasion he sent her a farewell note and when she informed the police, they discovered that it was a false alarm. When it became clear that she was not coming back, though, he did kill himself.

As a response to threats of this kind, some survivors become drawn into bargaining with the suicidal person. Miriam's son, Ben, had made it plain for some years that he had no wish to go on living; he often told her how he envied the dead. The year before his death, he announced that he had made up his mind to die. Faced with this threat, Miriam can remember saying to him: '"Well, let's have an agreement: not this year", and he said "OK". I was beside myself with anxiety and I said to him, "If you do this, you will finish me off" and he said "Well you come too".' Late into the night, Miriam was forced to sit and listen as Ben explained how he had to tell her of his plans to die because he didn't want it to happen out of the blue:

> the feeling that it gave me was that it was rather as if somebody in the family had announced their intention of committing murder, and the fact that the person he was going to murder was himself didn't take away the fact that it would have felt like betraying him.

Miriam found that any attempts on her part to intervene and try to get help only made her relationship with her son worse. When she wrote to Ben's college telling them that he was suicidal, he saw it as an act of betrayal. Miriam found herself trapped, living on a knife edge: 'It was like carrying something that was going to be spilled if you weren't very very careful.' She knew what was likely to happen, but felt powerless to prevent it.

Susan lived with the feeling that she was carrying round a precarious secret during her husband's three crisis periods. She coped alone, as Richard refused to go and talk to anybody or have any treatment; his problems had to be hidden from everybody except her. The strain on her was, at times, considerable; Richard would be pacing up and down all night, after which, Susan recalls, 'he would pick himself up and go off to work', leaving her feeling absolutely shattered and wondering how much longer she could go on coping without support. The final and worst crisis lasted about nine months and Susan began telling Richard that she did not think she could carry on supporting him alone; he would have to get outside help. Now she is left wondering whether that was what made him decide he would rather take his own life.

Not everyone will threaten suicide as explicitly as Ben or Catherine. Suicide may be hinted at, with the person saying they feel hopeless, or life has no meaning and that they have had enough. Shame and guilt may inhibit more open communication (Hill 1995). It can seem as if the person is using coded language, so the message may not be understood. After Heather and her son had been watching a programme on teenage suicide one evening Alastair remarked, 'Now I know how to do it':

> and I didn't take a blind bit of notice because it didn't mean anything to me, it just seemed to be a flippant remark that he threw at me . . . and now I think he probably thought that he'd almost told me and 'why didn't Mum help me when I told her what I was going to do?' But I didn't pick it up . . . It was only when he was missing, then it crossed my mind . . . and I thought, that's it, he's gone to do it.

Previous attempts to find help

Estimates vary but between a quarter and a third of people who die by suicide will have received some specialist psychiatric care in the year before their death (Foster et al. 1997; Department of Health 1999), and it is thought that 90% of all suicides have a diagnosed mental disorder, including two-thirds with a depressive illness (Smith 1995). Six out of ten will have been in contact with their GP in the month before their death (Vassilas and Morgan 1993).

Some survivors, realising that things were seriously wrong and that the other person needed more help than they could give, turned to professionals of one kind or another for assistance; but sometimes they were disappointed. When Josie was suffering from what the doctors decided was 'a drug-induced psychosis', a diagnosis which they subsequently changed to schizophrenia, Ursula recalls going to psychiatrists for help: 'I very naïvely thought "Ah, the experts will know what to do. They will deal with everything", and it came as a great blow to learn . . . that they really did not know much more than me.'

Some people had displayed problems which did not fit into any psychiatric classification, and mental health services often seemed to be as much at a loss as relatives when it came to explaining what was wrong and deciding what treatment should be given. When Carol's son was seen by psychiatrists, nobody could decide what was causing his difficulties. They thought he might have a schizophrenic illness or a personality disorder. He was given large quantities of medication and offered a day-centre place but no one ever seemed sure what was wrong. Lois had similar problems when Simon was referred to the local mental health services. There was mention of 'a psychotic episode' but the only advice she remembers being given over the years was 'be firm but kind'.

Faced with mental health services which may be unable to meet the needs of the suicidal person, relatives inevitably become the backstops – the ones who end up providing the care and support. Over a period of ten years, Mark and Francesca (see p. 54) tried to get help for their daughter from a range of services and professionals including psychiatrists, social workers, psychotherapists, day centres, and hostels; but as Mark recalls: 'there came the slow realisation that the so-called medical authorities . . . [and] the social workers, had nothing to offer, no understanding, no genuine caring for the individual . . . The worst thing [was] that Patricia was on her own.' This realisation that no one could really help was, Mark believes, one of the reasons which in the end led Patricia to take her own life.

Mental health services in Britain have often been described as the 'poor relation' of the NHS, a description Jean recognised when she tried to get help for her daughter. Even though she managed to get Anna admitted to the psychiatric unit of a large London teaching hospital, she soon realised that that was not going to be sufficient to help her daughter. 'I was doing the best I thought I could do for her', she says, 'but it wasn't good enough.' It didn't begin to address the problem. Even with the resources of a large teaching hospital, for example, Anna only saw her consultant for ten minutes each week.

The strain of knowing that a close relative is suicidal can be intolerable. In a recent newspaper article, a mother described her feelings after fifteen years of her daughter's repeated attempts at taking her own life:

> I wished it could be over. Ended, for ever . . . I can't take the continued uncertainty . . . I have to try and save myself, to cocoon myself against the day when the voice on the telephone will say 'I'm sorry' . . . The awful thing is, I long to hear that phrase. I wish it could be over and I could mourn for the daughter I used to love.
>
> (James 1988)

Faced with this situation, survivors may decide that if someone else in the family is not coping, then, whatever the stresses, they must be the ones that cope; they must remain on an even keel – or at least give the appearance of doing so – if the suicidal person is going to remain alive. Miriam felt that whatever was happening to Ben, and whatever her own distress she at least had to give the appearance of coping:

> I actually thought, if he's going to be saved, then I have to control myself because it's not fair to beat him over the head and [to] have a mother that's distressed is something else that makes him feel that life is not worth living.

Lois found her life becoming dominated by constant worrying about her son, and she remembers begging Simon, 'just give me one day without my having to worry about you because I do so desperately need it'. The strain of caring for someone who is distressed and suicidal day after day, and sometimes for years, is bound to take its toll. In some cases, relatives may also be having to provide basic physical care; there were times when Ursula had to do everything for her daughter, when Josie could not even make herself a cup of tea or wash her hair. She recalls how Josie just drained her utterly, physically and emotionally.

Survivors may even become suicidal themselves. Both Christine and her husband had been under considerable stress. Graham had been having problems with his college lecturer's job, in addition to which their son had developed leukaemia and was extremely ill; as Christine admits: 'I'd been thinking in terms [of suicide] the previous year anyway, because things were so dreadful . . . it could have been either of us quite honestly.' She managed to cope, despite her own suicidal feelings. When Irene's husband, Bill, hanged himself though, Irene was already in hospital being treated with electro-convulsive therapy (ECT) for severe depression; as she admits: 'it was me that wanted to die . . . not Bill'.

Survivors who are feeling under stress may find themselves trying to balance their own needs with those of the other person. Janice lived with this dilemma for many years. During childhood she was somewhat protected from her mother's problems, not really aware that her mother was being treated for depression. But she can remember the university vacation when she decided she could not face going home, she just could not cope with her mother. When her mother attempted suicide some years later, Janice again began to feel that she was going under herself: 'I knew that I couldn't go and live with her and make it all right – for my own sanity – and I knew really that writing letters and ringing weren't enough . . . I just felt myself going down and down.' Faced with this dilemma, survivors can feel that their own survival is under threat. Like Janice they may be forced to make difficult choices.

Other stresses in the family

For some families, threats of suicide may be only one cause of stress in their lives. Like Christine, who was also coping with her son's leukaemia (see above), Paul's family had also been struggling with the impact of cancer. The day that Paul shot himself, his mother was staying with relatives, recovering from a course of radiotherapy. Looking back, though, Maureen still feels that despite her own needs at that time, she somehow failed her son by not being there when he needed her. 'Once you're a parent', she says, 'you're a parent for life and that is it . . . I should have been there. My son needed me and I wasn't.'

For families like those of Paul and Graham, the suicide occurred at a time when they were already facing other life-threatening situations. For John, however, his wife's death came at a time when he was already trying to come to terms with other major losses. Two years before, Averil's son by a previous marriage had murdered his grandfather, for which he had received a life sentence. For John and Averil, it was, effectively, a double bereavement. When Averil's body was washed ashore, John found himself utterly alone.

Power in relationships

When a person decides that life is not worth living, they are saying, in effect, 'I have this right. I am responsible for my own actions.' But others are not likely to see it that way, and the result can be the emergence of a power struggle, but one in which there are no ultimate winners.

We have created a power relationship between ourselves and that person. We have made him or her dependent on us. We have also given that person the power to threaten us – to threaten suicide, so that we dare not end the relationship and relinquish our power over that person for fear of failing. The result is that the two of us are locked into the classic power relationship of jailer and warder. Both are equally prisoners . . . power and love are not compatible. Fighting replaces feeling.

(Lake 1984: 125)

The jailer's job is to guard the prisoners, and survivors may find themselves continually watching over the suicidal person. When Betty's other children told her about Jonathan's two previous attempts she found herself watching him constantly. More than three years after Jonathan's death, Betty is still angry; despite her vigilance, it feels to her as though he slipped through her fingers. She thought she could have saved him: 'I know I could have done it. It's too late. I'm very angry.'

Trying to stop someone committing suicide can be highly disruptive for all those concerned. When Judy became suicidal, Brian found he was caught up in a sort of cat-and-mouse game, trying to watch his wife constantly and finding this meant he could not even go to work. When this strategy became impossible he tried getting friends and neighbours round to keep an eye on her. Eventually she was admitted to a psychiatric clinic. Despite all these efforts, Judy still managed to attempt suicide several times, and Brian finally had to come to terms with his own powerlessness in the situation:

I think by the time [she died] I'd sort of realised that if she was going to make that many attempts when we'd had good professional help, she was just determined . . . I obviously find it hard to accept that there was nothing I could have done which could have stopped her.

Bridget's sister had developed paranoid thoughts, so that Bridget's attempts to watch over Catherine became virtually impossible: 'Basically we were torn between wanting to make sure that she didn't damage herself and also not wanting to reinforce her delusions of being watched.'

Survivors may try to prevent the suicide happening by taking steps to ensure that the person is forcibly protected from harming themselves. For some survivors, though, the prospect of seeing a relative detained in a psychiatric hospital against their will is unacceptable. Frank realised that long-term compulsory hospitalisation would have been his daughter's future life, had she remained alive: 'She would obviously have been detained somewhere indefinitely', he says, 'and there was no way that Josie would have wanted that, certainly.'

Despite her misgivings, Jean had originally agreed to her daughter being compulsorily detained in hospital, but found the experience unbearable:

She was on a section [of the Mental Health Act], we did get her sectioned because it was the only way to make her continue treatment, but when they did lock her up after she made the first [suicide] attempt . . . she was only there for three days and I said 'I simply can't stand it'; she was standing there like a little bird, it was terrible, and I thought, she's going to get much more ill like that, she must have more freedom.

Faced with someone who is determined to end their life, survivors will sometimes have come to terms with their own inability to control events even before the suicide happens. Before his daughter's death, Mark had realised he was in a no-win situation: 'One felt powerless, one felt up against a force, a death wish if you like to mythologise such power; it's the life instinct inversed, such power that nothing you could do would stop it.'

For other survivors, though, it is only after the suicide that they can begin to come to terms with their own sense of powerlessness. As Ursula discovered, this can be a painful and confusing struggle wavering between feeling they should have been able to save the person and thinking that perhaps that would have been the wrong thing to do anyway.

I'm a bit confused . . . I feel I could have convinced Josie that life was worth living . . . actually that's belittling her because it makes out that she would have been an idiot, because it wouldn't have been true and she wasn't unintelligent. I do sometimes feel I should have tried to convince her that things weren't as they were, but she would see through me, she would have known that I was lying.

In the end, she decided that Josie did have the right to take her own life:

if you deny someone that right, you're taking away something that is a vital part of them. You're imposing tremendous power if you deny that right. But I wanted to impose that power . . . so it was a terrible conflict . . . a complete contradiction.

For survivors, acknowledging their own lack of omnipotence also means recognising the other person's autonomy; as Francesca admitted: 'I have to give Patricia some responsibility for her own life, I can't take that all on myself.' Handing over the responsibility for running one's life can be very demeaning, as Jennifer realised after her brother's death: 'Why should he hand over that power to me? Why should he? He wouldn't want to feel that small.'

Denying the possibility of suicide

Even when survivors are faced with threats of suicide, they may react with denial. The possibility of suicide is blotted out, repressed from consciousness. Following the suicide of his girlfriend's aunt, the journalist William Leith wrote: 'Where suicide is concerned, thinking of the act as a definite concrete possibility becomes a kind of blasphemy' (1993). Survivors may need to protect themselves, as a character in Susanna Mitchell's novel, *The Token*, found.

> She closed her eyes to face the old self-deception. It was clear to her now, subconsciously she had always known that Julia's suicide had been no sudden brainstorm. All the signals had been there if she had been prepared to read them . . . She had considered Julia better because she wanted her better. She had assumed her pathetic façade of recovery to be real because it suited her to do so; she had refused to admit that her friend was still tormented and bewildered, edging towards the point where self-destruction seemed the only answer.
>
> (1985: 57)

Even when the survivor knows what is likely to happen, they may find they are ignoring their instincts, as Colin found:

> I regret I didn't follow what had been my instinct at the time [which] was to go round and talk to her . . . I knew what her situation was and what moved her to do things, but I don't suppose I was really conscious of . . . what was going to happen.

Writing of his friendship with the poet Sylvia Plath, Alvarez describes this sort of mental gymnastics survivors may perform: 'In common with her other friends of that period I chose to believe in this cheerfulness . . . or rather *I believed in it and did not believe* . . . but what could one do?' (1974: 42).

The question 'But what could one do?' illustrates the unbearable sense of helplessness which survivors can feel when they know someone is likely to commit suicide, a reaction which Litman has aptly described as the 'immobilisation response' (1970: 441). Survivors may feel unable even to raise the subject with the other person. Janice had been told by her sister that their mother had several times talked of feeling 'near to suicide', and she knew that her mother had phoned the Samaritans, but she found herself quite unable to discuss any of this with her mother. 'It was', she admits, 'just much too threatening.'

When Pam and Harry received a telephone call from the hospital where their daughter nursed, telling them to come immediately as Frances was seriously ill and unconscious, both in their different ways realised that suicide was a possibility. It was as if once it had actually happened, the conscious mind could admit what had hitherto been repressed: 'My mind turned immediately that she'd done something to herself – I suppose it must have been at the back of my mind' (John); 'I had my own suspicions that this might happen [but] you just think oh no, I must be going mad, I must be imagining it, but the suspicion was there all right' (Pam). Marie, whose husband committed suicide, acknowledges now that 'all the warning signs were there', but she ignored them, despite her professional training and experience as a psychiatric social worker. Yet like some other survivors, she knew that, in spite of a superficial normality, something was very wrong: 'something awful was happening', she recalls, 'and I couldn't do anything about it'. But then, she realised afterwards, neither could he: 'We'd say "How did he keep that to himself?" But at the same time it's so awful, how do you tell anyone?'

Occasionally, the survivor's fears about possible suicide seem to force themselves abruptly into consciousness. Several people mentioned sudden and inexplicable feelings of acute distress before the suicide, as though in some way they knew what was about to happen. Eileen remembers the day she was having dinner with the man she was later to marry. It was Valentine's Day, and as she says, it should have been a perfect evening; she had no idea that one of her twin daughters was about to commit suicide:

> We sat and had dinner and we reached the cheese stage and I just burst into tears, and I said 'I feel so unhappy and I've no reason to feel unhappy' and I couldn't stop weeping . . . and then next morning, of course I had the news that Donna had died and it must have been about the time that she killed herself that I had started to cry.

Point of no return

How the bereaved person copes with the loss will depend partly on their relationship with the deceased immediately prior to the death (Bowlby 1985; Clark and Goldney 2000). Kast suggests that guilt feelings will be 'substantially less if the communication between those remaining behind and the dead had been good, if there had been a genuine leave-taking, and if problems could still be discussed with one another' (1988: 56).

Survivors of suicide, far from being close to the other person, may have had the opposite experience. They may have found themselves living with someone who grew more and more distant from them, a situation described (from the suicidal person's perspective) by Alvarez, writing about the time leading up to his attempted suicide. He describes 'the closed world of suicide' and how his life was being lived for him 'by forces I could not control' (1974: 293). The suicide victim, he writes, experiences an 'imperviousness to everything outside the closed world of self-destruction' (1974: 144).

In the last weeks of her husband's life, Marie felt that same sense of distance developing between them:

I just could not get through to him; he looked so lost . . . as though he was drawing away; and the last evening I saw him sitting in the chair and [it] was just as though he wasn't there – and that was frightening.

Marie had realised something was very wrong with Oliver but in Nancy's case she only saw with hindsight how Clare had shut herself off so completely that no one in the family realised how desperate she must have been. Now, with hindsight, she feels that 'when a person knows that they're going to do that, they shut off completely. They cover up, and they make up their minds they're not going to consult anybody.'

Trying to understand what her daughter had been going through before she died, Phyllis felt that 'it must have been like being in a tunnel'. This echoes what Shneidman has described as 'constriction':

A synonym for 'constriction' would be a 'tunneling' . . . or 'narrowing' of the range of options usually available to the individual's consciousness . . . one's ordinary thoughts and loves and feelings and responsibilities are simply not available to consciousness . . . In this tunneled vision, the focus is on the unbearable emotion and on the way to escape from it – for that is, psychologically, what suicide is.

(1993: 40, 127)

This sense of a black and white world, of the victim living in an 'either/or' situation, was mentioned by numerous survivors. It seems to be something which victims may carry around for much of their lives – a striving for perfection which says 'only the best will do, and if that's not possible then nothing else will do'. It is an 'all or nothing' world.

Looking back to the time leading up to the suicide, it felt to some survivors as though death had become a magnet for the suicidal person. For Isabel this was borne out by an article which Eric had written after his first suicide attempt; entitled: 'Half in love with easeful death', while it did not explicitly mention his own recent attempt, he talked of how:

the boat he is embarked on has room for one passenger only and with no pilot to steer him he must take the wheel himself . . . self-destruction is seeking him out, drawing him to it like a magnet, and he lacks the strength of the vertigo sufferer to draw back . . . the time for weeping is past.

In some cases, though, the survivor's perspective on the matter will be different. Susan questioned whether the suicidal person's choice of death really is inevitable or whether, at some earlier point, the person could have made an alternative choice. 'You do have some control at the beginning', she says, 'before you slip totally into depression', but, she admits, echoing the title of Eric's article 'there is a point where they almost as it were fall in love with death.'

Bereaved people will often return in their minds again and again to the events leading up to the death 'as if, by so doing, they could undo or alter the events that had occurred' (Parkes 1998: 75). For the survivors of suicide this may become part of a continuing, sometimes unending, search for understanding why the suicide occurred, a search which is explored in the next chapter.

Chapter 6

Why did it happen? The search for understanding

> It's a riddle that goes round and round and round in your mind and drives you absolutely crazy for years and years and suddenly you think – I'm tormenting myself. I shall just never know the exact and precise reason. (Pam)

The search for meaning

When someone dies, it is not uncommon for the bereaved to question why the person died, to try and reach some understanding of the meaning of the event. According to Parkes, the process of grieving includes the attempt to make sense of the loss, to fit it into one's assumptions about the world or, if necessary, modify those assumptions (1998: 78). Finding meaning can play a critical role in adjustment following a bereavement, involving both making sense of the event but also finding benefit in the experience (Davis et al. 1998).

With suicide, the search for an explanation may be particularly important. As Suzy, a survivor of her father's suicide, commented:

> I'm sure if someone commits suicide, it's not at all like they died of a heart attack or a stroke . . . it isn't straightforward; there's an awful lot of things to be sorted out, about why they did it, what was wrong.

In today's largely secular Western societies, while there are probably relatively few people who would see a death as 'God's will', we still tend to cling to a belief that says death is beyond the control of human beings. That explanation may be less plausible for survivors of suicide who are faced with trying to understand a self-inflicted and possibly self-chosen death. Stengel (1973) has suggested that people intending to take their own lives have less need to make sense of death than those who will be bereaved as a result.

The survivor may be left with many different questions. When Alan died, Carol remembers asking herself:

Why did it have to happen? Why do I have to go through this? Why did I have to lose my son who was such a good quiet boy? Why does [her other son] have to be an only child now?

The questions can seem endless. Why do people commit suicide? Why did *my* relative commit suicide? Did they really mean to do it? Why didn't they tell me how they were feeling? What sort of person were they? Did I really know them? Why did this happen to me? Where did I go wrong? Why did this happen to *my* family? Why am I having to suffer so much? Am I the only one who feels this way? The survivor is faced with trying to understand the meaning of suicide in general terms, but also to understand why this person apparently chose to die (Calhoun et al. 1982).

Needing to search for reasons is commonplace amongst survivors, but by no means universal. If the suicide came to be seen as inevitable as the deceased's mental health deteriorated, family members may have accepted that mental illness was the cause of death (Clark and Goldney 2000: 472).

Neither Ann nor the rest of her family ever felt the need to question why Giles committed suicide:

because it seemed to us to be totally logical, exactly characteristic of him, that if he suddenly felt that he had had enough, he would [commit suicide]. I never consciously thought before it happened that he would, but when it happened, it seemed not unexpected.

The nature of the search

For some survivors the search can be unending; they find it hard to stop asking themselves why. Eighteen months after her son's death, Heather still worries that she has not found the answers:

I'll never know. I've accepted I'll never know, but it does seem important that I don't know. I *should* know. Why don't I know? I'd like to know why. I don't know why I want to know. It doesn't change anything.

Particularly in the early stages of the bereavement, searching can become an obsession which dominates the survivor's life. Nine months after her son's death Maureen asks herself why, 'every day of the week, all the time'. Cain's description of the 'driven endless repetitions and reconstructions of different versions of the events preceding the suicide and a groping quest for the "meaning" of the suicide' (1972: 14) conveys something of the obsessional nature of the search. The answers to this quest, he adds, will often be painful:

For too many this floundering search to construct a meaning, an interpretation of suicide, of *the* suicide, provides too few answers not coloured with guilt, with perceived responsibility, with despair beyond redefinition or reparation.

(1972: 14)

There are probably few people who, having survived the suicide of someone close to them, have not, at some point, felt guilty in the way Cain describes, and who have not felt themselves to be, in some measure at least, responsible for the death.

If guilt becomes unbearable, the survivor may search for a reason which will remove their self-blame. In Hauser's words, this 'relentless pursuit of the why . . . represents the hope of finding that which will assuage the guilt' (1987: 64).

Some survivors embark on a lengthy search for evidence of an illness or syndrome that affected the victim which will provide them with the definitive answer as to why the suicide occurred. Searching for an answer has not stopped Carol feeling guilty about her son's death but she is determined to try and find out why young people take their own lives. Recently she has been collating and analysing information from questionnaires sent to other parent survivors, in which she asked them about the personality, behaviour, and circumstances of the victims. Her hope is that some common factors will emerge which could aid research into youth suicide prevention.

Since her son's death, Miriam too has been busy searching for the answer to why he committed suicide. Although she had already realised there was something wrong with Ben as a small child, she believes she may now be closer to identifying the reason for Ben's death. She has been reading all the literature on the particular syndrome from which she now believes he was suffering and has corresponded with relevant experts. Looking back, though, she wonders whether, in the early stages, this led her to more or less deny Ben's death:

The immediate aftermath of his death was a making sense of his life . . . and it was almost as if I sort of deferred the recognition that he'd gone for good because I'd made what seemed like a miraculous discovery of something which had been perplexing me since he'd been born . . . it was as if I felt that when I had mastered the subject I could then apply it and perhaps set myself the task of making his life tolerable; and in this way, you know, this sort of magical sense of things fitting together, I've kind of postponed in a way the recognition that there were going to be no second chances.

Like Miriam, other survivors may search the literature, hoping to find an explanation of the suicide, reading anything they can lay their hands on, in the hope that this will help them make sense of the event. For Carole, the search began after Jon had attempted suicide:

> I went into the newsagent's . . . staring out from the front of *New Musical Express* newspaper were the words 'Youth suicide'. For the first time the words had a sort of meaning for me. How many times in the future was I to actively seek out that word in the indexes of many books. The answer to the riddle of my son's death was to be found in one of them, I felt sure . . . The need to read about suicide became my priority. I scoured libraries and bookshops, hoping to find the key to Jon's death.

Searching for information in books may also help to lessen their sense of isolation. A survivor may feel as though they are the only person who has ever been through this experience. Jennifer remembers how, in the weeks following her brother's suicide, she would come home from the library day after day with a pile of books:

> I read anything on death, dying, and suicide. I was almost obsessional about it. I so wanted to read about other people who had lost someone by suicide, what their feelings were, to reassure myself that I was not losing my mind.

Survivors may have few opportunities for meeting with each other and comparing their experiences and feelings, but those who are able to do so often find it a very helpful experience (see Chapters 15 and 16). Talking even to close friends about the suicide is often difficult and, when the survivor does find someone prepared to listen to them, they may still feel that the other person cannot really understand what they are going through (see Chapter 11).

You cannot ask the victim why

Alvarez suggests that 'the real motives which impel a man to take his own life . . . belong to the internal world, devious, contradictory, labyrinthine, and mostly out of sight' (1974: 13). At the same time, the person who dies by suicide is making a dramatic public statement. After the event, survivors are left with the task of trying to interpret what was behind that statement. Like Suzy, they may have reached certain conclusions but even so, she admits:

> I've offered one explanation . . . my father didn't want to go through his depression again . . . but that's not a total explanation . . . you will never be able to talk to them about what happened, you will never be

able to ask them why they did it, you will never be able to discuss it with them . . . it's the complete finality of it and I think that is the most difficult thing.

The survivor cannot ask the person who died for an explanation. Instead they may try and explore the state of mind of the deceased (Clark and Goldney 2000: 472). They may, Staudacher suggests, 'try and mirror what [the] loved one was doing or feeling' (1988: 178). David could recount in some detail the events of the day Paul died, but after telling his story, the picture remained incomplete. He was still unable to get inside Paul's mind. What was Paul thinking and feeling that day, he wondered? How could he have been calmly watching a video only two hours before he shot himself? What *had* happened to him in that last half-hour when he was alone in the house? Did he have a complete brainstorm? What *was* going on?

For some survivors it was helpful to find out more about the actual circumstances surrounding the death; it enabled them to piece at least some of the story together, even if the picture was incomplete. Jane's brother was living abroad when he took his own life; when his wife returned to England, Jane remembers how they talked at length: 'and I just couldn't get enough of hearing about the circumstances . . . and the more she talked the more plain it became. And I will never know completely – but I feel I do know.'

What sort of person was the victim?

Some of the survivors I met hoped that this book would offer a definitive explanation of why people commit suicide. In fact there already is a substantial and growing literature on suicide causation; as Alvarez somewhat cynically comments: 'As a research subject, suicide has, as they say, come big' (1974: 100). But whereas researchers will be taking an objective look at the suicidal person, the survivor's quest is of a more personal kind.

When someone commits suicide, survivors can be left feeling unsure as to whether they ever really knew the person. Perhaps they had always thought they understood them well enough; now they may feel less sure. They may wonder whether there were things about the person and their life of which they were unaware; sometimes that will turn out to have been the case. More often, though, it will seem as though the person was acting completely out of character, leading survivors to conclude that when the suicide occurred 'they were not themselves'. Sometimes, though, survivors will cast doubts on whether the death really was self-inflicted. In Pauline's case, although the verdict on her son's death was suicide, the rest of her family are all convinced, she says, that Michael would never have taken his own life, and Pauline herself seemed unsure.

The phrase 'while the balance of mind was disturbed' no longer has any legal significance but some coroners still append it to a verdict of suicide.

For some survivors, its use can make acceptance of the suicide easier because they see it as an accurate assessment of the situation. The implication that the person committed suicide while their mind was not 'balanced' may strengthen the survivor's belief that the person was acting out of character at the time (Barraclough and Shepherd 1976).

Whatever conclusions survivors reach about what triggered the actual suicide, they may also need to try and understand the rest of the survivor's life and how that may have contributed to the death. In conversation with survivors, two words used to describe the victim seemed to crop up frequently – 'perfectionism' and 'loss'. Neither can provide the complete answer, nor can they be regarded as proven causes of suicide, but because they were mentioned so often, they may have some relevance as possible contributory factors. The previous chapter mentioned how the victim may be the kind of person who constantly strives for perfection, a point echoed by many survivors when trying to describe the victim's personality:

> Susie was impossible about the idea of failure . . . [she had] a sort of refined perfectionism about things . . . she was an ultimate perfectionist. (Peter)

> Lesley was a perfectionist and I think perhaps that was part of the problem, you know. She always liked things just so. (Joan)

> From the start Patricia was a perfectionist. She had to have A's in everything. (Mark)

But there are pitfalls for the perfectionist:

> Many suicidal people have very high expectations for themselves which makes perfectionism even more mandatory than it might be for the average person. The suicidal individual often makes unrealistic demands on himself or herself. The person often wants more than actually exists or is possible to obtain.
>
> (Staudacher 1988: 178)

> Perfectionism may also be a dangerous trait . . . Achieving standards becomes integral to their self-esteem and fear of failure is a threatening prospect.
>
> (Hill 1995: 61)

People often set themselves goals; they may aim to be a better worker, or a more successful student, or a more considerate spouse, but these are usually seen as ideals, as desirable rather than imminently achievable goals. With suicide victims, though, a different set of rules seems to operate; it is almost as though they are setting themselves up for failure, for what Keir describes as 'the frustration of desires' (1986: 57).

> She had this sort of desire to do something that everybody else knew she wouldn't be able to do. It was as though she lived in this strange dream world of desperately wanting to be something she could never be and all she ever did was face herself with failure. (Pat)

> Frances was a perfectionist who could never reach the perfection that she tried to achieve. (Pam)

Significant losses of various kinds were a feature of some victims' lives, leading the survivors to question whether the impact of these losses had contributed in some way to the suicide. Individuals can react very differently to the same kind of loss, and research into the impact of losses sustained in childhood has frequently produced contradictory results (Bowlby 1985). Nevertheless, many of the survivors felt that losses which the victims had faced as children or young adults had possibly contributed to their deaths. Of the seventeen young people who had taken their own lives, seven had lost a parent through death or divorce, and a further two had experienced the death of a close friend shortly before the suicide occurred. As Caroline remarked, not long before her death: 'Everyone I love dies.' Other types of loss may contribute to the victim's decision to commit suicide. Wendy's father, for example, took his own life when terminal cancer meant he no longer enjoyed good health or a pain-free existence. Anticipation of loss may also affect some people; after her husband's suicide, Marie wondered whether Oliver had taken his life because he was possibly losing his sight.

Suicide notes

Almost half the survivors interviewed had been left a note or letter by the deceased, a substantially higher proportion than Stengel's (1973) estimate of 15%, Shneidman's (1982) estimate of 15–30% or Conley's (1987) 25%.

Shneidman, who has undertaken many studies of suicide notes, concludes that 'they are not the royal road to an easy understanding of suicidal phenomenon', despite the fact that they 'would seem to offer a special window . . . into the thinking and feeling of the act itself' (1993: 93). Studies of notes may have not produced significant new insights and information about suicide, but they can affect the survivor's reactions to the death.

Whatever researchers may have concluded, for some survivors, the note will assume great importance in their attempts to understand the suicide. Irene has read and re-read Bill's note, hoping that it will yield fresh evidence: 'I've studied it so many times, so many hours, looking for a clue –

even [reading] between the names, just anything', but, she admits, 'I can't find any peace in it.'

Notes do not always provide the hoped-for answers. Pat and Robert felt that, if anything, Caroline's letter to them made her death even more of a mystery. Although Robert read it constantly for the first two weeks, they have since thrown it away. Perhaps notes do not provide all the answers because, they are no more than 'cryptic maps of ill-advised journeys' (Shneidman 1993: 102). Staudacher warns survivors against assuming that the note will give them the definitive answer:

> It is important to put the note in perspective. That is, it is one item which reflects your loved one's thinking along a whole continuum of thought. The note is not necessarily representational of the same mind which conceived the suicide and carried it out. The note only represents your loved one's state of mind when the note was written. It is a mistake to try to extract the essence of the tragedy from this one piece of communication, however lucid it proves to be.
>
> (1988: 179)

Nevertheless, even if notes do not yield any answers, they are messages to those left behind. Attempts have been made to analyse suicide notes and categorise those messages. Osterweis and colleagues (1984) suggest that there are two types of notes: those which are overtly hostile to which survivors may react defensively, and those which aim to relieve the survivor of any responsibility for the event but may leave survivors feeling remorseful. Staudacher (1988) and Keir (1986) suggest that notes may also include statements about: the victim's low self-esteem and sense of failure; the person's inability to continue living; and messages of farewell.

In one study, quoted by Keir (1986), over half the notes were found to include statements to the effect that the victim felt unable to go on; life was perceived as intolerable. Survivors are often left with these messages about the victim's sense of utter hopelessness. Frances's note is typical: 'Much as I love the world', she wrote, 'I can no longer live with myself.' Suicide becomes the only solution to the person's problems; as Caroline wrote: 'I'm a total failure. I keep thinking things are going to get better, but it just gets worse.'

Messages telling the survivors not to blame themselves for what has happened are a common feature of suicide notes (Osterweis et al. 1984). Jon wrote that 'too much had gone too wrong' but he wanted his parents to know they were not to blame for this. Whatever the survivor's own feelings of guilt or responsibility, it can help when the person who died at least is saying 'I don't blame you'. Brian found this to be the case when his wife left letters which he described as being 'very kind'.

Graham and Christine were in the middle of an argument when Christine told her husband to leave the house. Graham drove off, and that was the last time Christine saw him alive. They had both been under considerable stress for some time (see p. 58), but when Christine realised what had happened, she blamed herself because she had told him to go. In his note, though, Graham made it plain that she was not to feel responsible for his death, a message she has been able to accept. It confirmed what she had begun to realise anyway: it had not been a spur-of-the-moment decision; Graham had almost certainly been thinking of committing suicide for some time.

However, not all suicide notes are intended to make the survivors feel better; some are clearly intended to hurt those left behind by blaming them in some way for the suicide (Staudacher 1988). Jan, who was thirteen and away at boarding-school when her father shot himself, remembers reading his farewell message a few days later: 'He'd left a very long letter to the three of us girls . . . saying that we'd let him down, that we were bad, awful daughters, that we'd all gone away and left him and a lot of very blaming stuff.' In the twenty-five years since his death, Jan has struggled to accept that despite what he wrote, the responsibility for her father's death does not lie with her – it belongs to him.

Melanie's husband left two farewell letters, and although she actually never read them, she was told by her father that one was full of anger towards her, and the other was only slightly less hostile. Although she now regrets that her father destroyed the letters, if she had read them at the time of Ian's death, she knows they would only have reinforced the guilt she felt anyway; as she admits, she felt that by leaving him and asking for a legal separation, she 'as good as killed him'. Nearly four years later, though, she can see things in a somewhat different light:

> Now I can see that it was his responsibility and he had a lot more options than killing himself. I don't believe Ian was that depressed. I think he made a decision and it was all anger to get at me . . . I found a tape in the house . . . and it was addressed to [their daughter], saying how he hoped one day she would forgive me for what I'd done, and he didn't want this to blight her life.

If the survivor suspects, or has been told, that the note expresses angry feelings, deciding whether to read it can be difficult. When Nick's mother died she left behind detailed notes about how she felt, but at the time of her suicide he didn't read them; he only knew that they apparently said some 'nasty things'. Five years later he is still undecided as to whether he will read them at some future point.

When a suicide happens unexpectedly, and the survivor has not even seen the body, the death can seem very unreal; but having a note which makes it clear that the victim intended to die can help survivors accept the reality of the death. Clare's suicide took everyone by surprise. Nancy and her husband were abroad when she died, and they never saw her body afterwards. It must all have seemed very unreal. It could not have been easy to read that Clare felt she had made a complete mess of her life, but Nancy is glad they had a note, otherwise she feels she would never have been absolutely certain that it was suicide; she would always have wondered whether someone had murdered Clare by pushing her on to the railway line.

Since suicide victims rarely give other people the chance to say goodbye, the note may be important because it represents their only farewell. Although Maureen does not believe that Paul's note gives any answers as to why he committed suicide, she feels that if he had died without leaving the note, it would have made things even worse. This is borne out by the behaviour of some survivors who described how they desperately searched the house, unable to believe that the person could have died without leaving any sort of farewell communication. Susan never doubted that her husband's death was suicide, but she still feels hurt that Richard left no note for her or their son, even though he did leave a note (not addressed to anyone in particular) saying, among other things, that 'Susan has been the support of my life'.

Suicide notes are the final communication from the deceased to those left behind but have to be handed over to the coroner's officer, who may also take personal belongings such as diaries or tapes as part of the evidence needing to be gathered for the inquest. Survivors have no legal rights of ownership to notes and while they may be handed back after the inquest, this does not always happen. Practice varies between coroners' courts. Survivors may find that notes or other effects have been 'lost' or can only be reclaimed with difficulty (Biddle 1998).

When the police discovered her husband Eric's body, they informed Isabel that a note addressed to her and the three children had also been found. According to the policeman who gave her this news, the note said something to the effect that he just could not go on any longer; but, the policeman added, he could not remember what the rest of the note said. She never had the chance to read the note herself because the police subsequently told her they had lost it. As a result, she feels she has been deprived of Eric's last message to her and fifteen years later still feels frustrated and angry at times because she can only speculate as to what the rest of the note said and whether the note really was lost.

For Pat and Robert, although they had found and read Caroline's note before it had to be handed over, when the letter was returned they were told, quite wrongly, that this was not the usual procedure.

Doubts about the person's intentions

Of the fifty survivors I talked with, most had no doubts that the victim had intended to commit suicide, even in those instances where the coroner had passed a verdict of accidental death or where there had been an open verdict (see pp. 86–87). Since they had volunteered to talk about their experiences as survivors of suicide this was not entirely unexpected. But there were still occasional instances where survivors seemed less sure. After Julie was found dead, the verdict was accidental death, and Phyllis referred to her daughter's death as an 'accidental suicide':

> I thought that she contemplated suicide; in fact I mean really it wasn't . . . well, she did take her own life, but it was an accidental suicide . . . in the back of my mind I can see the reason, but in another way I know for certain that it wasn't deliberate because she didn't leave a note . . . I don't think [people who commit suicide] know what they're doing.

Even for someone like Suzy, who talks about her father's death as suicide, there can still be doubts about what happened at the end; she still wonders sometimes whether he really intended to take his own life on the night he died:

> Someone once said to me that after he'd been sick on the landing he might have felt that perhaps . . . he wasn't going to die after all and I have found that awfully hard to cope with, that he might perhaps have died when he didn't really mean to after all; and that gave me an awful shock . . . I've got absolutely no way of proving that.

Survivors, as she says, have no conclusive proofs of the person's intentions. They can only make guesses. Do people really intend to take their own lives? Are they perhaps hoping to be rescued in time? Do they see it as a gamble with death? Or, as Phyllis suggested, is it the case that people committing suicide simply do not know what they are doing?

Wisdom with hindsight

For many survivors, going back over the events leading up to the suicide is often about the 'if-onlys' – 'if only I knew then what I now know':

> What suicide does is to curiously give you sight, but it is hindsight. (Mark)

> It's very easy I think to look back retrospectively and understand things that you don't actually understand at the time. (Peter)

> It was completely out of the blue, but since [then] we've had so many clues. I mean, hindsight has told us we had a lot of warning but [suicide] never came into our thoughts. (Nancy)

The suicidal person may provide unspoken clues about their intentions but many survivors were unaware of the meaning of these veiled communications and only understand their significance after the event. This is the wisdom survivors achieve with hindsight; survivors can become experts on suicide when it is too late.

A common warning sign is when someone who has been very depressed or very disturbed appears to be in a calmer and more positive frame of mind. Sudden upswings in mood can be deceptive. Miriam's son had given plenty of explicit warnings of his intention to commit suicide (see pp. 55–56), but when, shortly before his death, he seemed very composed, she thought that things were looking up. Only now does she realise that he was, as she says, 'laying false trails'.

Some suicidal people destroy or give away favourite personal possessions shortly before their death. After Alan died, Carol discovered he had destroyed all his certificates, together with his college notes, and all the photographs he had taken. That was not the only clue: early in December he told his mother not to buy him any Christmas presents – he died ten days before Christmas. Liz, who was living abroad at the time of her brother's suicide, found out subsequently that there had been at least two classic warning signs: not only had Tony stopped wearing his jewellery, but shortly before he disappeared, everyone had noticed how much more cheerful he seemed to be.

Living without all the answers

However many clues they may find, and however much of the story they piece together, ultimately survivors will invariably have to live with something which they can only understand in part. One stressful event may be the catalyst, the factor which tips the balance, but will not be the sole reason why someone commits suicide.

According to some survivors, the victims had often been faced with a whole series of problems and setbacks; it seemed as though they had reached a point when 'enough was enough': bereavements, the ending of relationships, exam failures, physical ill-health, and redundancy or problems at work were common events in their lives, but despite this, many survivors, like John, were still left without the full story:

> It would be much easier to be able to say to myself that this is exactly what happened. But even if somebody told me that, I couldn't accept it, because I know from my own experience that life is far too complicated. There are no simple answers.

For others like Christine it is a matter of finding answers that they can live with: 'I still think about it', she admits, 'but I don't really ask why. I mean

I'm fairly satisfied that I know why he did it. I may not be right, but it seems right to me.'

This need to search for clues, to try and understand what led the person to commit suicide, is one of the most difficult legacies which the survivor will inherit. In the end they may, like John, decide there is no single answer, or like Christine, they may find answers they can live with. Whichever path they go down, survivors need to be able to reach a point where the search for answers to 'why' can be given up.

Chapter 7

The inquest

I just wanted to be part of it. I didn't want it to be something done by strangers . . . the last thing that would happen to Patricia, where, in a sense, there was some sort of decision to be made. There were certain possibilities, certain choices to be made, and I suppose I just wanted to have something to do with it. I just wanted to say my bit. (Francesca)

Introduction

In England and Wales, all unnatural deaths are subject to legal investigation, including suspected suicides, and enquiries usually begin immediately after the body has been discovered. The police will take statements from relevant people such as members of the dead person's immediate family, the person or persons who discovered the body, and any other witnesses; additional evidence will include farewell notes or letters, and the pathologist's post-mortem report. The coroner's officer (see below), who acts as the coroner's agent, is responsible for ensuring that the necessary evidence is available to the coroner before the main inquest takes place.

Coroners can be either medically or legally qualified (though, in practice, the majority of coroners currently hold a legal qualification, and a minority are both medically and legally qualified). Local authorities are responsible for the appointment of coroners and for meeting the cost of running the courts; the coroner's officers who staff the courts are former members of the police force, although a government sponsored committee of inquiry has proposed that they could be replaced by specially trained civilians (HMSO 1971).

In accordance with the Coroners Rules (HMSO 1984), the coroner's brief is to ascertain the identity of the deceased and how, when and where they died. The inquest will usually be opened formally by the coroner within a day or two of the death, and this is normally a brief hearing; formal identification of the person is made, after which the body can be released for burial or cremation. The inquest is then adjourned. In the ensuing weeks, the gathering of evidence will continue, and the full inquest will take place at a later date when statements are read out in court, witnesses may be cross-examined, and the coroner's verdict will be given.

Does the inquest represent a medical or a legal investigation? Barraclough and Shepherd, who researched the inquest system in the 1970s, have described it as 'a formal court of inquiry, conducted in public' (1976: 110), the word 'court' implying that this is a judicial exercise. Although the inquest is *not* a trial in the legal sense, they suggest that the inquest is, effectively, 'a survival of a medieval trial for self-murder which results in a verdict' (1978: 795).

Biddle, who has recently carried out research into the inquest system in relation to the experiences of families bereaved by suicide, suggests that the courtroom setting and many of the procedures are reminiscent of a court of law:

> The inquest opens with the instruction 'please stand in court', issued by the coroner's officer who plays the role of court usher. It is at this moment that the coroner enters. The coroner's officer must then take an oath as must each witness . . .
>
> (Biddle 1998: 32)

The whole process still has a strongly legal flavour, with the paraphernalia of statements, evidence, summonsing and cross-examination of witnesses, verdicts, and, in certain cases, the presence of a jury. It is hardly surprising that to some survivors the inquest feels like a trial where both they and the person who died are under judgment.

For survivors of suicide, the inquest brings further public exposure. Not only are very personal aspects of the victim's life likely to be investigated and discussed in court, but their own actions, and the nature of their relationship with the dead person, can also be called to account. Maureen remembers how shocked she felt at her son's inquest when she had to answer questions such as 'did you row?' For Frank, the very worst part of the whole experience was this contact with 'officialdom', at the very time when he was struggling with his worst feelings of grief.

For suicide survivors, their personal tragedy becomes a matter of public interest (Biddle 1998). The circumstances surrounding the suicide are open to scrutiny by public officials such as the police and coroner's officer, and members of the public as well as the press (see below) are also permitted to attend the inquest.

Waiting for the inquest

It is not uncommon for the full inquest to be held up to two months after the death has occurred. The coroner's officer will usually need several weeks to obtain all the relevant evidence and ensure that relevant witnesses are able to attend on the same day. Sometimes, though, survivors may have to wait even longer. Several people had waited at least three months, and Frank and Ursula, who had originally been told they could expect to wait about two months, actually waited six months for Josie's inquest. Ursula knew that though the inquest would be an important event, it would also be a stressful occasion, and she found the long wait very distressing: 'You felt that you were in limbo. You knew this had got to happen and you'd got to steel yourself to deal with it.' Survivors may feel that their grieving is suspended until the inquest is over, although Biddle (1998) also found that in some cases where there were delays, 'far from putting their grieving on hold, the inquest caused it to re-emerge and moved them backwards' (1998: 112).

Anticipation of the inquest can leave survivors feeling extremely apprehensive, particularly if they have been called as witnesses; postponement only adds to the stress, particularly when the survivor is only told about the delay at short notice. In Christine's case, the date of her husband's inquest was changed several times, and each time, having steeled herself to go to court, she was only telephoned with news of the cancellation the evening before.

These postponements could be due to the fact that evidence such as a psychiatric report was still awaited or there were problems with assembling the witnesses on a particular date. Whatever the reason, survivors were not always kept in the picture and this could create additional pressures in an already stressful situation. Delays can occur with the preliminary inquest too, as Heather found, when they had to wait a week for the inquest into her son's death to be opened:

> He died in the early hours of Wednesday and it must have been all over the weekend that we didn't know what was happening. We rang the police and they didn't know. We rang the coroner and he didn't know. Nobody seemed to know what was going on . . . It was an extra pressure on us because I kept worrying about what else they might have found [during the post-mortem]. In fact they found nothing. He hadn't even been drinking.

Because both the police and the coroner's officer are involved, families are sometimes unclear who is responsible for liaising with them. Clearer systems of communication are needed so that relatives are kept properly informed about what is happening.

The survivor's reactions to the inquest

For the vast majority of survivors, this is likely to be their first experience of attending a coroner's court and maybe the first time they have been inside a court building. They may not know how the inquest will be conducted, what sort of evidence they are likely to hear or see, or what part, if any, they will be expected to play. At the same time, they may not feel they can ask about these matters. Biddle found that

> Numerous people [had] experienced the anxieties and distress caused by being kept in a state of ignorance in the time leading up to the inquest, ill-prepared for what happened on the day, and unaware of their rights regarding leaving the court room.
>
> (1998: 88)

Liz was unaware of what might be said about the post-mortem on her brother and choked when she heard detailed evidence about the state of his body (which had only been discovered seven weeks after his death). Carol, too, had no idea whether or not she and her son had to remain in court:

> I was terrified . . . very hyped up about it . . . terrified about whether or not they would be showing [her son] photographs which I didn't want him to see . . . I wish somebody had told me that you didn't have to see the photographs at the inquest and things like that.

On the other hand, when one of Eileen's daughters died on a railway line, it was suggested that she might prefer to remain outside the courtroom while evidence about Sheila's body was being read out.

Brian has hearing difficulties and that, together with the fact that the full inquest and the preliminary hearing were in different places (the former also being a jury inquest), could have added further stress to an already difficult experience. Meeting with the coroner's officer and looking round the courts made the experience much less difficult. It would be relatively straightforward for relatives to be routinely offered written and/or verbal information before the inquest. This could include a prior visit to the courtroom or a floor plan of the court, together with a full explanation of what was likely to happen on the day (Biddle 1998).

Sometimes the inquest can be less daunting than the survivor had expected, as Nancy discovered when she attended her daughter's inquest: 'I got the idea that it was going to be something terrible, and in some ways it was just like being in an office . . . It wasn't so terrible as I'd been led to imagine.' That was Nancy's experience but coroner's courts vary considerably in the way they conduct their business:

> The recurring and outstanding discovery that I made was the total lack of rules and structure applying across the entire system. However, it was also clear that individual coroners do not follow their own rules in

the absence of general guidelines. On the contrary, many courts seemed to rely solely upon discretion and improvisation.

(Biddle 1998: 27)

Individual coroners have considerable discretion in deciding matters such as whether or not they use a witness-box, whether witnesses sit or stand, but also on more significant issues such as how much of the post-mortem report or other evidence is read out in court. However, although inquest proceedings are generally conducted in a less rigid manner, the inquest is a public inquiry with the degree of formality that that implies. As Biddle points out: 'the coroner's duty is to serve the Crown and not bereaved families' (1998). Some people may find this somewhat formal approach less upsetting but, in other cases, survivors can feel that the inquest is too impersonal and that it has little or no relevance to their personal tragedy. To Lois, her son's inquest seemed pointless; she felt that it had little to do with Simon, and she only attended because she had been summonsed to appear as a witness:

> The inquest was horrendous . . . to have it all read out . . . the deadpan way they read these things . . . you know it's your son they're talking about; they're talking about a body [but] it isn't just a body, it's a person . . . I think for me the inquest was the worst ordeal of the whole lot.

Survivors are often very vulnerable when they attend the inquest. Kindness and a compassionate manner are appreciated, and survivors who felt the coroner did not treat them in this way remembered the experience (Barraclough and Shepherd 1976). Fifteen years after her husband's death, Susan still had vivid memories of the coroner's behaviour at Richard's inquest:

> Each time the coroner just gabbled and I was asked to identify the handwriting of this note he'd left in his pocket . . . and his age and who he was, and so on. But that's all, and the whole thing was over in about three minutes. I couldn't decide whether he was doing that because he was totally uninterested or because he was trying to spare me. I can actually remember standing and wondering why the coroner was behaving in such an offhand manner.

Some of the survivors interviewed by Biddle (1998) also had somewhat negative experiences of the coroner's behaviour but there was a common expectation that the coroner would show show them understanding and respect, would acknowledge their presence in court and would address them directly.

The evidence

Survivors may see the inquest as an opportunity to listen to evidence which can help them piece together more of the story. Jennifer went to her brother's inquest knowing little about Tim's death. Her only sources of information had been local newspaper and radio reports and she hoped that the evidence would tell her more about the actual circumstances of Tim's death. Obtaining accurate information can be an important means of making the whole event feel more real (Hauser 1987), and if survivors have not seen the body, this can be particularly important. Brian's wife died on a railway line and he was not able to view her body, but hearing about the last few moments of her life from the train driver meant being able 'to complete the bit I didn't know'.

As Francesca said at the beginning of this chapter, the inquest was about her daughter and she very much wanted to be part of the proceedings. Like Francesca, Janice felt that when such very personal matters were at stake, they should not be dealt with solely by strangers. In her case, she also wanted to find out more about the circumstances of the death which had happened at some distance from where she lived (see p. 43):

> I felt it was really important that either I was there or my sister . . . because they would be discussing my mother, and discussing what they'd found in her stomach and I felt that it would be wrong . . . not to be there. I wanted to see the policeman [who found the body] and hear his story.

For some survivors, the inquest is an opportunity publicly to state their version of events, to tell the story as *they* see it, but they may not always get the chance to do so, as John discovered. His wife's inquest was scheduled as the last of four cases that day, and although it was already past the court's normal time of adjournment, the coroner said he would proceed. John was eventually called as a witness, but his attempts to talk about Averil's problems, to explain about how she had gone downhill after her son's life sentence for murder, were all forestalled. The coroner did not seem to think that any of it was relevant, and appeared to want to complete the inquest as quickly as possible. As a result, John felt the whole thing was very incomplete.

> I wondered why the devil we'd gone there. And I felt offended, bruised inside . . . All he was concerned about was did she use the word 'suicide' . . . and I was waiting to get up and tell him about Averil, about what had happened and about how she felt . . . even to tell him I'd failed. I was ready to say all this and when my turn came – no . . . and I came out feeling that the inquest wasn't over.

John wanted to tell the coroner how he felt partly responsible for Averil's death but for other survivors, feeling they were on trial or, however unintentionally, being blamed in some way, was extremely upsetting. Jean was on holiday when her daughter committed suicide. It was a much-needed break, but she still found it hard when the coroner asked when she had last seen Anna: 'And I had to say two weeks, and I felt dreadful. I thought, what kind of a mother am I?'

Heather was waiting outside the courtroom where her son's inquest was being held when the coroner decided he wanted to question her about a remark Alastair had made (see p. 56) and which was mentioned in her husband's evidence. It was a remark which, at the time, she had not understood as a suicide threat and she had no idea that he was even feeling suicidal. Although she explained this, the coroner responded by saying that he found this 'a little strange'. As Biddle suggests, when the deceased person's relationships with others come under scrutiny, 'this creates a potential for blame . . . though in an implicit and inconclusive way' (1998: 27).

For some survivors, the inquest may be seen as an opportunity to set the record straight. They may hope that those they feel contributed to the suicide will be publicly identified, perhaps even reprimanded, even though inquests are not held to apportion blame. After her sister's suicide, Bridget felt that although Catherine's psychiatrist could not be held directly responsible for what happened, he had, at the very least, been negligent in not arranging to re-admit her to hospital when it was obvious that she was in a highly vulnerable state. The situation had been somewhat complicated by the fact that staff at the hospital in question were taking industrial action at the time. When it came to the inquest, though, only the industrial action was mentioned and nothing was said about the psychiatrist's role. As a result, it was left to Bridget and one of her brothers to pursue the matter directly with the health authority.

In some instances, survivors felt that unreasonable levels of stress at the person's place of work had contributed to the suicide, and they hoped that this would emerge during the course of the inquest. Before her husband's suicide, Christine had warned Graham's employers that problems at work (which, she felt, were not of his making) were placing him under severe stress. Apparently no one had thought it necessary to act on her warning and she had no opportunity to raise the matter at the inquest. Graham's former employers, having been wrongly informed by the police that Christine was planning to take legal action against them, appeared in court with their solicitors. As in Bridget's case, Christine was left to pursue the matter herself and eventually Graham's employers held an internal inquiry. Christine felt sufficiently strongly about the issue to want to pursue it herself, but it was an additional strain at an already difficult time.

Survivors may arrive at the inquest with their own version of events, only to hear another version from others giving evidence. It can be upsetting for the bereaved when others 'get the story wrong', while creating an 'official version' of the event (Biddle 1998). Ursula agreed with the verdict of suicide at her daughter's inquest but was annoyed by the pathologist's report which implied that Josie had been injecting herself with drugs; she believes they could equally well have been marks from injections Josie had been given while in hospital, and the pathologist offered no evidence to substantiate his claim. In other instances, survivors were angry because their relative had been given a diagnostic label such as 'schizophrenic' or 'manic depressive' which they considered inaccurate.

As mentioned above, survivors sometimes found evidence distressing but remained in court, unsure whether they could leave. In fact, coroners do not have to make public all the evidence collected. King (1997) suggests that they are usually concerned to minimise the survivors' trauma and will only admit strictly relevant information, but given the lack of uniformity in procedures identified by Biddle (1998), it seems likely that practices will vary as to what evidence is read out in court.

The verdict

In the case of unnatural deaths, there are several possible verdicts but a verdict of suicide can only be reached if the evidence proves 'that the fatal act was both *self-inflicted* and that the *intention* was to die as a result of the act' (King 1997; italics in original). As a result open verdicts are returned on a large number of self-inflicted deaths, which can cause confusion, distress and anger among relatives (Cline 1996; King 1997; Biddle 1998).

The verdict can be seen to represent the official, public pronouncement on the death, and to survivors, what the coroner – often seen as an authority figure – decides may assume great importance, precisely because it is seen to be an official, authoritative statement. At the same time, having what the survivor believes to be the correct verdict is also very important. Ursula, for example, was relieved when the verdict on Josie's death was suicide because, as she said, 'any other verdict wouldn't have been right'.

Others are content to accept a non-suicide verdict. Joan is still unsure whether her sister really intended to take her own life, so she can accept the verdict of accidental death: 'I don't think you'll ever know. I mean, she never ever suggested it at all . . . she'd never said about taking her own life.'

It is often assumed that coroners will try and avoid bringing in a verdict of suicide in order to protect the family (Keir 1986; Staudacher 1988). But this assumption may be false says Audrey Walsh, herself a survivor:

> Coroners think they are being sensitive to relatives by bringing in an open verdict, but they are doing everyone a disservice. Parents know how their child died, and have to face up to what happened. By

avoiding the word 'suicide' coroners are merely increasing the stigma and disguising the size of the problem.

(Quoted in Lyall 1987)

However painful the idea of suicide may be, the truth can be preferable for some families, even though the legal constraints mentioned above mean this is not always possible. Liz found herself unable to accept the open verdict on her brother's death. As she says: 'I think all the family and friends believed he'd done it himself'. She wrote to the coroner asking him to re-open the inquest; but he expressed surprise that 'you even want to . . . bring out the fact that your brother perhaps did commit suicide'.

Christine was also convinced that her husband had taken his own life, and felt that by 'choosing' suicide, Graham was also wanting to make a public statement. So when the coroner passed an open verdict, she asked if he would change it to one of suicide which he refused to do, on the grounds that there was insufficient proof of intent. Despite the verdict, she remains convinced that Graham's suicide was a conscious and intentional act.

John describes the open verdict on his wife as 'an albatross around my neck', but with no firm evidence that Averil intended to take her own life, that was the only possible verdict. At the time he found that hard because he felt that it laid him open to suspicion. Four years later the verdict remains problematic; he finds it hard to mourn her death properly; he has found it virtually impossible to visit her grave, and feels the verdict has left him with a sense of incompleteness. Unlike a verdict of suicide, an open verdict can leave the survivors unsure as to what sort of death it is they are really mourning.

The role of the press

The discussion of suicide and the media in Chapter 1 raised the issue of the media's contact with survivors, which can cause distress and anger (Barraclough and Shepherd 1976, 1977; Dunne-Maxim 1987; Biddle 1998)

While very few members of the public exercise their right to attend inquests, the press are 'an unwelcome but common presence at suicide inquests' (Biddle 1998: 100). Reporting of suicides in local newspapers is common practice. In fact the story is often covered twice: a brief mention immediately after the suicide, and a longer report after the full inquest. In a small number of cases, there will also be national media coverage.

Opinions have been divided as to whether the media should have the right to attend inquests. A government committee recommended that there should be no restrictions on reporting of suicide (HMSO 1971), a view with which others have disagreed, arguing that the presence of the press and subsequent reporting often caused unnecessary distress to survivors (Barraclough and Shepherd 1976).

For some survivors, knowing that details of the suicide are there in black and white for everybody in the local community to read is felt to be a major invasion of privacy. When Heather's son committed suicide, his death was reported not only in the local press but in several national dailies as well, all of which she found very distressing. She felt Alastair's death was something 'very, very private indeed', and the intrusion on her privacy was made worse by finding that reporters from two national tabloid dailies were not only on her own doorstep, but had been approaching her neighbours as well.

Where the suicide is not talked about openly within the family, survivors can find it painful to see the death freely discussed in the press. When Suzy's father committed suicide, she felt that because she believed in press freedom, she had to accept the reports in the local newspapers. Her mother, on the other hand, had been devastated to read the headline 'Principal Died From Taking Aspirin'. As Suzy said: 'Things weren't discussed in the family, so you certainly don't have it in the newspaper . . . [because] the whole of [the city] would see that he actually killed himself.'

Survivors often find it hard to tell other people about the suicide (see Chapter 11), but they may still prefer to have the choice rather than discovering that not only do other people already know, but that they have a version of events gleaned from newspaper reports. As Francesca said after her daughter's suicide: 'I didn't want anyone to know if I had not told them . . . I wanted to be responsible for telling people. I didn't want it to be a general statement.'

What appears to survivors to be inaccurate reporting of suicide deaths is not uncommon and can be a particular cause of distress (Barraclough and Shepherd 1976, 1977; Dunne-Maxim 1987); even seemingly minor inaccuracies can be upsetting. Pam and Harry remember how, on the day of the inquest, the front page headlines of their local newspaper referred to their daughter as 'Nurse Susan', when although that was her first name, everyone had always called her Frances. Heather was particularly cross when the local newspaper got its facts wrong about where her son's body had been discovered. In contrast, though, reports that are factually accurate and non-sensational can make it easier for survivors to cope with the involvement of the press; Ursula had been terrified about reading the newspaper report because she thought they would probably 'twist a few words and totally misrepresent something' so she was glad when what she read was an accurate description of the inquest proceedings.

Reporting on suicides can vary between a brief factual paragraph on an inside page to front page banner headlines, but inquests on younger people and suicides where the death was violent are reported more often, are given more column inches, and have more eye-catching headlines than other suicides (Shepherd and Barraclough 1978). When Bridget's sister committed suicide her death fulfilled both of those criteria; the headline in the local paper was 'Blast girl once took overdose' with a report which Bridget described as being 'completely useless'. Bridget (herself a journalist) argues that the paper could have written a much more constructive story about some of the issues surrounding her sister's death (see p. 85). Instead, as she recalls, 'they just chose this sort of horrible, sensationalised [reporting]'. What this approach also does, as Peter pointed out, is simplify and trivialise an issue which is far from simple. Several survivors mentioned how they felt that a more considered and informed approach might have helped to educate the public about suicide and suicide prevention, a point also made by Dunne-Maxim (1987).

Robert was convinced that his daughter's suicide was triggered by a newspaper picture published the day of Caroline's death, which showed someone jumping to their death. However, his contacts with the press were quite positive. A reporter from their local paper appeared on the doorstep shortly after Caroline's death and the family decided that they would talk to him and would give him a photograph of their daughter. Caroline's former nursing colleagues were also interviewed, and the result was a story which not only discussed her death, but talked about how Caroline had been a hard-working nurse and how fond of her the patients had been. As a result, Robert and Pat feel that they were able to cope with the attentions of the press, despite the banner headlines and newspaper placards. Stories which include positive comments about the person who died can not only help survivors (Dunne-Maxim 1987), but can also educate readers about suicide victims. As Carol pointed out, if there was more positive coverage maybe 'suicide would not be looked upon as a thing done by baddies'.

Several survivors mentioned that while the publicity was not particularly welcome, it was inevitable because the press attended inquests, and so was something they had to accept. As Marie said: 'It has to be reported, something has to be written up, and I think it's difficult, to put it mildly, to see it there in black and white, but you know that it's happened.' Pam and Harry found the banner headlines about their daughter's suicide not only unexpected but rather hurtful; but at the same time they felt that complaining would not have been particularly useful. As Harry said: 'It wouldn't have brought her back; it wouldn't have done any good.'

Press reporting may be inevitable – suicide tends to be considered newsworthy – but insensitive approaches to families and inaccurate or sensational coverage could be avoided if the media were to adopt a more sensitive approach.

Chapter 8

Funerals

> I was very worried about the suicide aspect of it, and thinking what if there is a God in heaven? What on earth is happening to Alastair now? (Heather)

> I just wanted to be surrounded by people. I felt very strongly about that. All the flowers and all the people . . . it was a beautiful funeral . . . I thought it was as good as it could be. (Francesca)

People who die by suicide are no longer denied a proper funeral service and burial, but deep-seated, age-old and primitive beliefs about suicide are not easily shaken off. Regardless of whether they hold any formal religious beliefs, survivors may still be worried that their relative has been condemned to some kind of eternal punishment (Clark and Goldney 2000).

Pam and Harry wanted to bury their daughter's ashes in her grandmother's grave, but thought that because Frances had committed suicide, perhaps this would not be permitted (though fortunately their fears were unfounded). Heather, who described herself as a non-believer, was still worried about whether her son was being made to suffer for taking his own life, until she was reassured by her local vicar:

> [He] was really good, he said all the right things . . . He put my mind completely at rest, and said that God wasn't vicious like that, and Alastair would be looked after, and he'd be all right; [and] although I didn't believe, I thought, well just in case it's true, I can rest in that.

Rather than asking for definitive theological pronouncements, survivors may be looking for reassurance that the person who died is not suffering. When the bereaved have witnessed someone's mental suffering for a long time, it may be particularly important to know that the person's emotional pain is over and they are 'at peace'.

Members of the clergy are likely to be in contact with families soon after the death to make the funeral arrangements. What they say and the way they are seen to react to the situation, will be important to survivors. Individual members of the clergy will have their own attitudes and feelings about suicide. But although trained to minister to the bereaved, not all clergy are able to cope with suicide, as Jane and her family found when the local curate – obviously unaware of how Christopher had died – came round to discuss the funeral service:

> He did his stuff and then eventually he said . . . 'How long was your husband ill?' and [Jane's sister-in-law] said, because she'd said it so many times before it just came out – 'Oh, he wasn't ill, he wasn't ill at all, no. He committed suicide, he shot himself', and the teacup began to rattle . . . and the curate was out of the house in five minutes. I've never seen anyone move so fast.

Eileen was headmistress of a Church of England primary school so knew the vicar well, yet despite the fact that she was twice bereaved by suicide, on neither occasion did he say anything at all to her about the deaths.

If clergy relate to families in a sensitive and non-judgemental manner, this can be an important source of support, particularly in the days immediately following the suicide. Heather and her family found their local vicar extremely supportive; she remembers how 'he sort of took over and steered us through; he was wonderful'. He acknowledged and respected the different beliefs of individual family members, encouraged them to plan a service which would be a celebration of Alastair's eighteen years, and suggested that they might like to include some of their son's own music in the service.

The funeral service, if done well, can contribute to a healthy resolution of grieving. It can help make real the fact of the loss, give people the opportunity to express thoughts and feelings about the deceased, reflect the life of the person who died, and draw together a social network of support for the bereaved family (Worden 1991). Survivors of suicide may find the prospect of a public funeral difficult. Guilt and shame may lead them to feel undeserving of the supportive presence of a wider circle of friends and relatives. They may worry about how other people will react towards them and what they really thought about the deceased (Van Dongen 1993). On the other hand

> If a public funeral is not held, [there may be] regrets about not giving adequate tribute to the deceased . . . and the opportunity is denied for other significant mourners such as school friends or work colleagues to commence their grieving. If the funeral is private or if there is no funeral at all, the bereaved may also deprive themselves of the usual demonstrations of support.
>
> (Clark and Goldney 2000: 478)

In fact, very few of the survivors I met had reacted in this way, and for many the funeral had been a very positive, even if painful experience which had left them with good memories:

> It was really good. We had some very popular hymns that everyone sang very loudly . . . lots of friends, lots of people. (Marie)

> It was a good memorial service . . . Her friends read poetry that she had loved . . . It was important to us at the time and to her friends. (Pam)

The funeral is usually the last act which the bereaved can perform for the dead person, and for people bereaved by suicide, the chance to do something for the other person may mitigate the survivor's sense that whatever they tried to do when the person was alive was not enough or was not accepted.

The funeral can also be the chance to plan a proper farewell where no other goodbyes have been said. In the weeks following her husband's death, Christine found everyone was urging her to 'get the funeral over with' but she knew that this was not what she wanted to do. Because it was the summer holidays and people were away, she wanted time to contact as many of Graham's friends as possible to enable them to be at the service; and she wanted time to plan a funeral that would be meaningful to her; so she and her son wrote the service together, chose suitable poetry to read, and were able to include some of Graham's favourite music. They also found a clergyman more than willing to help them with these arrangements.

Christine also had a particularly helpful undertaker who did not mind when she rang him at two o'clock in the morning to discuss details of the funeral. In an increasingly secular society, funeral directors may have as much if not more contact with newly bereaved survivors than members of the clergy. The issue of viewing the body (see Chapter 4) can be a particularly sensitive issue when the death was suicide and undertakers need to be fully informed about the circumstances of the death. Otherwise survivors may have to face the sort of question which Susan was asked: 'I'm very sorry my dear . . . and what did he die of?'

Suicide can seem very meaningless to the survivors, and being able to plan ceremonies and rituals which inject some meaning into the event may be even more important than with other deaths (Lukas and Seiden 1987). Suicide is also a violent, often ugly act and a funeral which is made beautiful – whether by flowers, music, the support of friends, words that are spoken, or all of these – can help to counteract the survivor's more disturbing memories. Jean has some very positive memories of her daughter's funeral:

> I certainly like things [to be] beautiful and Anna would have wanted a beautiful ceremony and I'm sure a lot of people would tell you that it

was extremely beautiful . . . it's a good memory. I was absolutely shattered with the people who came . . . so many people when someone dies young . . . and the flowers were fantastic. The house was filled with flowers, the crematorium was filled with flowers which Anna would have loved, and we planned a very beautiful ceremony . . . only half an hour but we made it as beautiful as we possibly could . . . So it was good, yes . . . and her school friends sang beautifully . . . It was just amazing . . . I think about it a lot.

Idealising the deceased is common, particularly in the early stages of bereavement, and funeral addresses often refer to the person's more positive qualities while perhaps refraining from mentioning less endearing characteristics. But what will be said at the funeral of someone who has committed suicide? Will the manner of death even be mentioned? Reference is sometimes made to the suicide during the funeral service, and when there is no attempt to mete out criticism or blame for the death, this straightforward acknowledgement of the manner of death can be helpful to the mourners. At Patricia's funeral, both her life and her death were mentioned; the person who conducted the funeral spoke of the mental pain she had suffered, but also of how her life had been complete in itself; her right to choose suicide was acknowledged, and those present were asked to respect that choice. Other survivors remembered being urged not to blame themselves for what had happened, and while this may not have totally relieved them of their guilt, statements of this kind at the funeral and in the context of a public ritual, could help to place their guilt in a more realistic perspective.

To many people, suicide can seem a negative and destructive act, and it can easily be forgotten that the suicide was only one final act in a person's whole life. Honouring the person's life may be as important as marking their death. As one survivor explained:

it became more and more important to me that we plan a memorial service for my mother . . . I wanted to honour my mother in a formal public setting. I had become her defender and advocate since her death and . . . I did not want her suicide veiled.

(Alexander 1987)

People who commit suicide often do so believing that they are of no value either to themselves or to others, but the fact that other people choose to come and pay their respects to the dead person can be a positive experience for the bereaved. For Janice, the fact that her mother's friends came to the funeral was an affirmation that, despite her mother's often difficult behaviour, there were people who had cared about her: 'a lot of them had probably been at the raw end of her accusations maybe a few times, so I felt they obviously appreciated the other side of my mother as well, so that was good'. The presence of the victim's friends can be a support to the family, as Pam found when many of Frances's friends came to the funeral 'as a tribute to [her] and to help us on our way'.

For some survivors, inviting non-family members to view the body at the undertakers can also be helpful. After their son took his own life, David and Maureen were amazed at how many young people came to see Paul's body and to leave gifts and letters in his coffin. Although a suicide may have the greatest impact on surviving family members, other people will be affected too (see Chapter 2), so it may be important for them to be able to attend the funeral and perhaps to visit the undertakers.

Not surprisingly, funerals are often very emotionally charged events, but the social gathering afterwards can be a release of tension and a chance for people to share, talk, and reminisce about the dead person. It can also be another good memory for the immediate survivors; Heather recalled the gathering held after her son's funeral: 'We had a nice party here because the youngsters came; we had drink, plenty to eat, there was plenty of laughter. It made a real party afterwards. It was a lovely day.' Though painful at times, many parents appreciated having their son's or daughter's young friends around them at this time.

Occasionally survivors are left with less positive memories of the funeral. The funeral may become a focus for feelings of ill-will. Where specific family members are being blamed for the death (see p. 104), the funeral can become fraught, as Nick found when his mother committed suicide:

> My father reported that her side of the family had been threatening him, and so I attended [the funeral] and [took] the biggest, strongest friend with me . . . sort of as a bodyguard . . . I didn't look up in the church, I just sort of went into the funeral and was aware of her side of the family . . . but I didn't look at them.

Melanie was blamed for her husband's suicide by her mother-in-law who refused to attend her son's funeral. Sometimes, though, relatives may not be given the opportunity to attend, as Carol found when her son died; her sister's children, aged between seventeen and twenty-three, were not told of their cousin's death initially and had no choice about whether to attend Alan's funeral, which Carol found hurtful.

The funeral is an important marker in the process of grieving; it confronts the bereaved with the reality of their loss and the finality of death. But it can also be a point where, if sensitively handled, healing can begin to take place. Studies of suicide survivors have paid little attention to the role of the funeral but Van Dongen found that the most helpful experiences 'appeared to be those in which the clergy provided an appropriate service, many people attended and the survivors were able to cry and express their grief' (1993: 132–3).

Chapter 9

Facing suicide as a family

> I was ignorant of suicide. I didn't think it could happen to me, an
> ordinary, decent, well set-up, middle-class family with everything going
> my way . . . I would never have believed it could happen to my family.
> (Carol)

The death of one its members will have an impact on family life and
relationships and the balance within the family. The effects of loss on the
family system will depend on the role the deceased played within the family
and whether the death leaves a gap which someone else must now fill. The
emotional integration of the family will affect the degree to which its
members can help one another cope. And whether families value or hinder
communication, particularly when it comes to expressing emotions
(Worden 1991).

The earlier literature on suicide bereavement often presented a rather
negative picture of the impact of self-inflicted death on the family, as in
Cain's dramatic portrayal of the family bereaved by suicide:

> Psychological processes . . . are often shaped by and amidst family
> interactions contorted by individuals too deeply preoccupied with their
> own grief to be helpful to each other, brimming with needs to blame
> and externalise, contending with newly erupted affects and problem
> behaviour in themselves and each other, abruptly forced into restruc-
> turing delicately intertwined family roles and skills . . . buffeted as well
> by major practical problems which weigh towards further dissolution
> of the already harshly rent family structure.
>
> (1972: 15)

Subsequent research presents a more optimistic picture in relation to some
families. A study of parental bereavement after suicide and accident (Seguin
et al. 1995a) found that while suicide had a negative impact on some
families this was not necessarily true for all families. Some parents in the
suicide group felt that the event had brought the family closer together,

calm had returned to their lives and they no longer had to worry all the time. Similar findings were reported by Van Dongen (1993): the majority of survivors in her study felt that family relationships were as close or closer than before the suicide. Other families, however, are likely to cope less well (see Chapter 2, pp. 24–25) because of pre-existing vulnerability (Seguin et al. 1995a; Clark and Goldney 2000).

This chapter is about how some families coped with the impact of suicide, their altered perceptions of themselves as a family; the difficulties some individuals experienced in their attempts to talk to one another; how some family members struggled to support each other in the face of their own grief; the difficulties in allowing individual family members to grieve in their own way; how some families could rewrite history and thus deny the fact of suicide; the temptation to blame one another for what happened; and the fear that suicide 'runs in the family', and that other relatives will now take their own lives.

The chapter focuses on the family as a single unit or system but though most survivors are part of a family, they are also individuals who will have had a particular relationship with the dead person. The relationship will have been different for each survivor; it may have been warm and intimate, or distant and hostile; it may have been an intimate but hostile encounter. So for each survivor the loss will mean something different. Survivors also have family relationships; they may have lost a brother or sister, son or daughter, mother or father, husband or wife. Not all siblings, for example, will feel the same; nevertheless, certain reactions are more likely to occur with some groups than with others (McIntosh 1987b). The following chapter looks at particular issues facing four such groups of survivors: parents, spouses, siblings and children.

How the family sees itself

Suicide, it has been suggested, 'seems to challenge the family's entire belief system, including their own sense of themselves as a unit' (Nelson and Frantz 1996: 132).

Suicide happens in all sorts of families but survivors often see themselves as having a shared identity with others similarly bereaved. This was also what could make them feel so different from other families. Sometimes they thought they must be bad, even wicked, families. Families may even feel there is a 'tainting of the family tree' and that the suicide was caused by evil in the family (Clark and Goldney 2000: 474).

After her son's suicide, it seemed to Heather as if 'we must be an absolutely horrendous family to have had a child who could be so unhappy'. So when survivors encounter negative reactions from friends and neighbours (see Chapter 11), this may only serve to reinforce and confirm their own sense of shame.

Suicide leaves some survivors feeling as though they have undergone an amputation, and that a part of them is missing. 'There's a hole in our family' is how Pat described it. Spouses sometimes compared the suicide to loss of a limb (Chapter 10). Like any death, suicide leaves a gap in the family, and the effect may be far-reaching. Within the group which constitutes the family, individuals will usually have particular roles and functions (Worden 1991; Parkes 1998). For example, the dead person may have been the main or even sole breadwinner in the family; they may also have played less obvious roles – as the family member who did most of the worrying, or the one who made all the major decisions; on the other hand, they may have been the person who was always seen as 'difficult' by the rest of the family, the one who relied heavily on others, and was unable to cope with everyday life. When that person is no longer around, it is as though one of the actors in the drama of family life is missing; to get round this, other family members may take over the dead person's roles. The survivor who has always been independent may suddenly become the person who relies on others.

Some changes can be quite positive. While Irene's husband was alive, she had been the dependent, non-coping partner in their marriage. When Irene was going through periodic bouts of depression it was always Bill who took care of things, who kept things going at home. Indeed, this was what seemed to be happening at the time of Bill's death; Irene was in a psychiatric hospital being given ECT in an attempt to relieve her depression. Although she still needed further help, four years after Bill's death, and after many struggles, Irene is aware of how much she has changed. She has discovered she is more capable than she ever dreamt was possible, and she feels in control of her own life for the first time; she has recently attended a counselling course and has started up a local support network for other survivors.

Communication in the family

Communication within the family can be difficult after any loss, but in comparison with families bereaved by a natural or accidental death, families bereaved by suicide are more likely not to want to discuss the death (McIntosh and Kelly 1992: 88). This is significant because research suggests that families able to communicate directly amongst themselves are more likely to support one another and will adapt better to the loss (Nelson and Frantz 1996: 132).

The survivor may have to break the news to other family members. Jennifer was told by the police that Tim had been killed on the railway line, but although she soon realised that it was probably suicide, her mother had not guessed the truth, and Jennifer felt she would have to tell her, but: 'I was frightened of saying, and I was worried [about] what to say because I wanted her to realise for herself or I wanted the police to have told her so that I wouldn't have to tell her.'

Allowing or encouraging other family members to talk about the suicide can be difficult or impossible. When their son died, Carol was away from home, and it was her ex-husband who discovered that Alan had hanged himself. Although she knows that the memory of what he saw that morning stayed with him, and that perhaps he needs to talk about it, she has so far been unable to let him do so. They will talk about other things to do with Alan, but not that.

Family survivors may talk intensely with one another in the weeks immediately following the death, discussing the person's behaviour in the time leading up to their suicide and questioning why the death occurred (Van Dongen 1993). However, for some survivors submerged in their own grief, the idea of having to support someone else can seem to be an impossible demand. After Ben's suicide, both Miriam and her daughter, Ruth, felt they were a blight on each other, although fortunately this only lasted a few weeks:

> My daughter . . . would hear me saying to friends on the phone, 'I shall just have to go and see Ruth as often as I can', and her heart would sink with that and . . . in the first few weeks we were simply a torment to each other . . . I went to see her a couple of times and she found me absolutely unbearable . . . She would say, 'You're so weak', because she, in fact, couldn't bring herself to tell her contemporaries how he died . . . She said he'd been killed in a car crash . . . What was completely unfamiliar and unexpected for me was that my passionate desire to see Ruth survive and my desperate need to see her didn't mean that I wasn't compounding her pain.

On the other hand, 'if family members are able to act openly and share feelings, they feel much closer and safer with each other' (Nelson and Frantz 1996: 143). Pam and Harry acknowledge that they were fortunate in being able to talk together and share their feelings about their daughter's suicide – although this was not always so in the early days, when Harry was going off to work every day, and Pam was at home on her own.

Sometimes a survivor will decide that they can only cope by cutting off all communication, and refusing to discuss the suicide with anyone else. Feeling lonely and desperate after her husband's suicide, Irene rang one of her sons only to be told: 'Don't phone me, I can't handle it.' An attempt to talk with her brother produced a similar response: 'Irene, I don't know what to say to you, I can't handle it. I can't even come and see you; just leave it.' If survivors cannot handle their own feelings, the thought of facing other people's pain may be too threatening. As Marie said: 'I think there's only a certain amount you can put on your family really.' This may be the point when survivors will look for help outside the family (see Chapter 12).

Survivors may need encouragement from others to mention the dead person; family members may sometimes have to give each other permission to talk. When her daughter committed suicide, Jean found that her son would not talk to her at all about Anna; after several months, though, when Jean decided to broach the subject with him, Richard's response was 'it's for you to make the first move'. As a result, although Jean will not force the issue, now they can at least talk about Anna sometimes.

Where family members refuse point-blank to discuss the suicide, family relationships can be severed completely. When John's wife died, he had virtually no immediate family to whom he could turn. He did, however, look to his mother for support:

> After the funeral I went to my mother's house and she said: 'Now you mustn't bring your grief here or it will kill me' . . . Well, my reaction was that of sheer, utter bitterness and anger, sheer unadulterated anger, and my answer was, 'Well, if you won't let me bring it here in these circumstances, I'll never come here again', and out I walked. I didn't go near them for two and a half years, and that's what I call my two years of wilderness. It was totally a wilderness.

In some families, though, the opposite will happen; the loss of one person in the family will draw remaining members closer together (Van Dongen 1993). Since Judy's death, Brian and his two sons have become much closer; although Chris and Rob were both in their twenties when their mother died and were no longer living at home, Brian feels that as a family they have learned to share much more with each other, and they have been able to talk together about her death. Family relationships often change and regroup themselves after a death, and for Dick it was the realisation after his sister's death that 'there were only the two of us left' which he feels has resulted in a much closer relationship with his brother.

Even when immediate family members are able to talk to one another, survivors can find it painful when more distant relatives no longer mention the person who died. After her daughter's death, Phyllis felt very hurt when everyone outside the immediate family simply stopped mentioning Julie: as she says, when they did this, 'It felt as though she was never there'.

Talking with children

The following chapter (pp. 115–120) describes the experiences of some adults, one of whose parents had died by suicide during their childhood. But how do adults cope with talking to children? As we have seen, discussing the suicide with other adults can be hard enough, but what do adults tell children? When Richard died, Susan found having to break the news to their twelve-year-old son one of the hardest things she had to face at that time. As she says, 'How do you break the news to someone who has never known of his father's depressions . . . who only knew of him as a jolly dad who played rugger with him? . . . That was terrible.'

Research findings and individual case studies suggest that children bereaved by suicide are often not told how a parent died (Shepherd and Barraclough 1976; Bowlby 1985; McIntosh 1987b), even though concealing the truth can cause problems subsequently. In the absence of an honest explanation, children may reach their own inaccurate and harmful conclusions: 'He must have died because I did something naughty that day'; 'She can't really have loved me, otherwise why would she have gone away?' 'Perhaps I should have done something to stop this happening'.

With an actual or suspected suicide death, media reporting, the involvement of police and overheard conversations can make it more likely that a child will find out by accident or will hear a version of the death which conflicts with what they have been told by an adult. (Winston's Wish 2001) As a result, children may find it hard to trust adults.

Some children will be too young to understand the meaning of death, let alone suicide. Hannah was only about two when her father committed suicide; Melanie has since told her daughter that he died in a car accident (in fact, he died in his car by carbon monoxide poisoning), but even though Hannah seems to have accepted her mother's version of events, Melanie is not altogether happy about this. Four years later, Hannah has not asked any more questions about her father's death, but Melanie hopes that one day she will be able to tell her what really happened.

Nick's baby daughter was born some years after her grandmother's suicide, but Nick has already been thinking about what he should tell her. Although he worries about 'getting it right', he feels very strongly that she should eventually be told the truth: 'I feel it would do her an injustice . . . for that to be a secret. I feel secrets like that are very bad . . . they can dog people's lives.' Suicide can easily lead to the creation of family myths and harmful secrets (see below).

Children need consistent information and explanations from adults but this can be difficult when family members disagree about what children should be told. If parents have decided not to tell their children about a relative's suicide, this can be difficult for other family members. When her husband took his own life, Irene's grandsons, who were seven, eight and nine, were told the next day that their grandad was dead but not how he had died. Four years later they are still unaware that he died by suicide although Martin, who was particularly close to Bill, sometimes asked Irene about his grandfather's death. She believes that 'someone's going to have to tell these boys', but acknowledges that this is their parents' responsibility.

Children's understanding of death depends largely on the developmental stage they have reached (Raphael 1985), but even fairly young children seem capable of some understanding of suicide, if they are told in clear, simple terms along these lines:

> It can help even very young children to have a simple story that they can use to re-tell, and slowly make sense of what has happened. Use words they understand. Always ask them what they think about what you have said to make sure that they have actually understood. Try to avoid secrets and unnecessary details.
>
> (Winston's Wish 2001: 7)

When Suzy's father committed suicide, she and her husband decided that they would tell the whole story to their two older daughters, then aged six and nine: 'We both explained that . . . he got depressed, that he felt it was too much for him to cope with being like that, it was sad, and that he had killed himself taking aspirins.' Although Suzy is unsure what they made of this, she thinks they probably did understand.

Even though older adolescents' understanding of death is likely to be more or less the same as adults (Raphael 1985), talking about the suicide may not be any easier, as Lois has discovered after her oldest son look his own life. Simon had two brothers, both of whom were in their late teens when he died. Lois finds it hard that they don't talk about Simon with her; she feels that if no one mentions him, then 'there will have been no point in him being alive'. Partly to try and counter this, she has been compiling a booklet of some of his poems and other writings to share with family and friends, but his brothers have not wanted to take part in this.

Lois wondered whether her sons' unwillingness to help her compile the booklet was due to an inability to engage with something connected to Simon, rather than a lack of interest. She could well be right. Bereaved adolescents may react to a sibling's death with apparent lack of emotion because they are afraid that they could be overwhelmed by grief to the point of not being able to function (Nelson and Frantz 1996).

Same family, different reactions

Grieving is complex and individuals will often react in different ways to the same death and within the family arena, survivors may find themselves 'caught between divergent, if not conflicting patterns or pace of grief' (Cain 1972: 15). When individual family members react very differently to the same event, this can cause problems, as Caroline's family discovered. Pat went through a phase when she resented both her surviving daughter, Nicola, and her husband, Robert, 'because they weren't grieving the same way as I was . . . I thought they weren't grieving, you see. I thought "Look at them, they've got over it".' When Nicola did not visit Caroline's grave as often as her mother, Pat found it hard to come to terms with that too:

> I didn't like to say anything . . . I knew she hadn't forgotten [Caroline] . . . It just appeared that Robert and Nicola were able to adjust better than I was, and get on with their lives quicker and better than I was, and I resented it.

As a family, Pat, Robert and Nicola found there were other differences, apart from the timescales of their grieving. In the early days at least, Robert felt driven to discover why Caroline had taken her own life, something which the other two have never felt they needed to do. Nicola believes her sister's suicide was a 'spur of the moment thing', and she prefers not to think about what actually happened on that day. Their initial physical reactions were very different too: while Pat was rushing around being constantly active, all Robert wanted to do was curl up and sleep. It was only when Pat had the chance to talk to other survivors that she was able to accept that she and Nicola and Robert were all different, and 'their way of grieving wasn't mine, and they had to be left to get on with it in their way'. Now, talking together as a family, they can recognise and accept these differences.

Where one person feels that others in the family are not grieving properly, this can be an additional strain: 'If one member cries more or less than another, this is noticed and conclusions drawn about the nature of their relationship with the dead member' (Parkes 1998: 175–6).

Someone who displays their grief more openly may conclude that other people do not really care as much as they do about the person who died. At one stage after their daughter's suicide, Frank began to feel that he and Ursula were not as close as they might have been because they were grieving differently. Ursula felt that Frank didn't care as much as she did. 'I don't feel that now', she admits, 'and when I thought of it logically I didn't . . . I realised that different people deal with things differently and at different speeds.'

Individual reactions to the death and styles of coping will be partly determined by the survivor's relationship to the dead person, as Peter realised after his sister's suicide:

> I think each of us in the family views all the events differently. I mean for each of us it's a different investment, and a different relationship, and inevitably each of us will account for everything in a different way . . . [will] understand things differently.

After Susie's death, Peter went back to New Zealand to spend time with his family, and although he found he could talk about her with some members of the family, this was not always the case, and was something he had to learn to accept:

> One has to accept people's reactions and my father can't talk about it, and you simply have to understand that. He was the person who found her; he was devastated, and he never fully understood what was happening in Susie's life . . . and I can't ever put myself in his shoes . . . He's eighty-four . . . and I simply can't imagine what it's like at that point in life to find your youngest daughter [dead].

Differences in coping strategies, such as those experienced by Frank and Ursula (see above), may be linked to a number of factors, but research on bereavement in general (i.e. not specific to suicide) suggests that gender plays a part. The literature supports

> the view that men may cope with bereavement by seeking distraction, turning to activities to take their minds off their grief and avoiding memories, while women will cope by expressing their emotions, confronting the loss, talking to others about it and dwelling on their grief.
>
> (Stroebe 1994)

Blame within the family

Anger is a common reaction to loss and may be directed at the dead person, at other people, or at oneself (Bowlby 1985). It can be turned inwards, causing feelings of guilt and self-reproach, or directed towards other people who will be blamed in some way for the loss. When someone commits suicide, blame will often be directed towards self and others simultaneously. How could he have done this to me? How could I have been so stupid not to have stopped him? Why didn't that doctor who was treating him realise he was suicidal? Potential targets for blame are numerous:

> On the one hand, the dead person can be blamed for having deliberately deserted the bereaved; on the other, one or other of the relatives can be held responsible for having provoked this action. Very often blame is laid on close kin, especially the surviving spouse. Others to be implicated are parents, particularly in the case of suicide by a child or adolescent; sometimes also a child is blamed by one parent for the suicide of the other. Those who mete out such blame are likely to include both relatives and neighbours; and not infrequently the surviving spouse blames him or herself, perhaps for not having done enough to prevent the suicide or even having encouraged it.
>
> (Bowlby 1985: 184)

Compared with people bereaved from natural or accidental deaths, suicide survivors blame family members for the death more often (McIntosh and Kelly 1992: 89). At a time when survivors are looking for comfort in their grief, the eruption of these feelings can be particularly distressing and painful. When Alastair died, Heather remembers how she and her husband started accusing each other:

> which was horrendous. I was expecting that to happen . . . I'm not sure who started it, but I was very aware that we shouldn't do that and yet we just did. We just ended up shouting 'It's *your* fault!' 'It's *your* fault!'

Parents may blame each other for the death of a child, but they may also be accused of causing the death by surviving brothers and sisters. Betty can still remember how, after her son's suicide, one of Jonathan's sisters when she was feeling particularly distressed, angrily accused her mother of killing him.

Spouses are sometimes considered to be responsible for the well-being of their partner, so that when something goes wrong, then the surviving spouse will often be a target for blame (Bowlby 1985; Clark and Goldney 2000). When Melanie's husband took his own life, members of his family made it plain that they thought she was to blame. In the four years since Ian died, his mother has never spoken to her, because she holds Melanie responsible for what happened to her son.

Accusations of this kind can result in family relationships being permanently severed. When Nick's mother committed suicide, both he and his father were blamed by his mother's family (and, as if that were not enough, by some of his father's family too). Looking back, Nick thinks that his mother's relatives probably blamed them as a means of avoiding their own sense of guilt, but the hostile telephone calls and the way his father was generally hounded has left both of them with unpleasant memories. As a result of all this, Nick is now completely cut off from one half of his family and does not expect he will ever see them again.

Blame can drive a wedge between survivors even at times like funerals when people are generally expected to be mutually supportive. What is often a highly emotional experience can become even more fraught when feelings of blame are in the air. When Liz's brother died, she felt that though Tony and his wife had separated, his wife was at least partly to blame for his death. Despite the separation, his wife came to the funeral with her parents, and although Liz never spoke to them and made sure they did not sit together at the crematorium, she remembers how 'it was kind of them and us . . . it was horrible'.

Sometimes the only way survivors can cope with feelings of blame or guilt, whether directed at themselves or at others, is to remain silent:

family members don't want to expose the guilt and blame they feel; the blame they feel towards other family members, the guilt they feel about themselves . . . The silence is an attempt to keep the cap on terrible accusations . . . towards others and towards oneself.

(Lukas and Seiden 1987: 111–12)

Not talking about the suicide can be a way of not having to face the truth of what happened. The result may be the creation of family secrets.

Secrets in the family

'You must not tell anyone', my mother said, 'what I am about to tell you. In China your father had a sister who killed herself. She jumped into the family well. We say that your father has all brothers because it is as if she had never been born.'

(Kingston 1981: 11)

Of course by no means all families react in quite such an extreme fashion, but many people have inherited family secrets about suicide. When I asked survivors whether this was the first suicide in the family or whether, in the past, other family members had committed suicide, they were often unsure. They *thought* perhaps there had been an uncle, a great-grandparent, or some other relative. As children they had perhaps overheard the whispered conversations of adults, but it was something never really talked about in the family.

But this 'ritual of secrecy' (Nelson and Frantz 1996) does not just belong to the past. It is four years since Dick's sister committed suicide, and he still regrets the fact that Sally's death was not talked about more in the family:

We did talk about her to some extent, but I don't think the whole thing was all that talked about. I think that might have helped. My mum tended to deal with things by carrying on regardless almost, and trying not to acknowledge it too much . . . but I used to think sometimes it was a shame; it was almost as though Sally had been wiped off the map practically.

Of course it is possible to prevent the development of family secrets. Survivors like Nick and Melanie with very young children had already made up their minds that at some point their children would be told the truth. Their children, at least, would not become the bearers of family secrets.

Living with the aftermath of suicide can be painful, and rewriting the story can be one way of removing the source of pain; according to Pincus and Dare, 'secrets in the family are often an attempt to avoid guilt and the pain of loss' (1978: 134). If the death was 'an unfortunate accident' or 'due to natural causes', no one is to blame, no one need feel guilty, no one has been rejected.

When Wendy's father committed suicide with an overdose, the fact that he took his own life was not mentioned except by those members of the family who had been in the house at the time. But even they did not mention suicide again once the funeral was over. After a few days Wendy's stepmother started saying that perhaps it had been an accident; 'she had all sorts of explanations', Wendy recalls, except suicide.

Secrets created at the time of the death can subsequently be unravelled, but it is not always straightforward, as Isabel discovered. When she visited her family, who live abroad, shortly after her husband's death, Isabel told them Eric had died of a heart attack. Her family are Roman Catholic, and she felt that if she told them the truth they would see it as a sin. At that time, she wanted to protect her three children from finding out the truth. When, at some later stage, she told her family that Eric had taken an overdose, her assumption that they would consider his suicide a sin was correct, and her brother's response – 'we forgive him' – left Isabel feeling very angry.

Does suicide run in families?

A radio phone-in caller to a programme on suicide described how his brother and sister had both taken their own lives and now he felt people were thinking: 'Two down, one to go'. Perhaps he was actually voicing his own fears.

Bereavement of any kind brings an increased risk of suicide (Parkes 1998; Clark and Goldney 2000), particularly in the very early stages after the death. It may be seen as a way of being reunited with the person who died, or associated with severe depression. However, when the death was suicide, additional factors are present, not least that the deceased has shown a means of escape from intolerable pain or seemingly insoluble problems.

Within the family there may also be fears that 'suicide runs in the family' and that they or other relatives will take their own lives. This can bring added complications. Nick believes this is one of the reasons why survivors avoid mentioning suicide because if they do, 'people think, oh gosh, it's in you, sort of thing'.

Jan was thirteen when her father, who had an alcohol problem, shot himself. Later on she found herself wondering whether suicide and alcohol-ism run in families:

> One of the things that horrified me when I read about suicide and about alcoholism was about how it runs in families – and that felt very alive for me because I could see that that was a very real option for me

. . . I was certainly afraid that I might become an alcoholic, and afraid that I would find myself, when I was low, thinking, oh well, I'll show them, I'll commit suicide.

After a lengthy period of therapy, Jan reached the point where she felt that neither alcoholism nor suicide was a real option for her and she remains reasonably certain about that. At the same time, though, she is aware that it remains in the background – and will surface from time to time.

People like Jan may have to confront fears about their own potential for suicide or other self-destructive behaviours, but other survivors will worry more about whether children or grandchildren will be affected. Ann went for genetic counselling when she was planning to get married. Because of her brother's suicide and her sister's chronic mental illness, she worried about whether it would be safe to have children (though she now has 'four perfectly normal children and ten perfectly normal grandchildren').

Survivors sometimes have to face the real possibility of history repeating itself. Martin's mother had taken her own life when he was an adolescent, and when his teenage daughter was going through a phase of self-destructive, quasi-anorexic behaviour, he realised he was reacting in exactly the same way as he had when his mother was alive. The young boy who had felt he should be looking after his mother reappeared as the grown man who felt he had to persuade his daughter to eat; as he says: 'again I found myself being a caretaker, and making all sorts of arrangements'.

Friends and acquaintances may wonder whether the family has an inherited tendency to mental illness or insanity (see Chapter 11), but this may also concern survivors themselves. It may worry them more than the possibility of suicide. Seven years after Bridget's father and sister committed suicide, it is not so much the possibility of suicide that worries her, but what she describes as 'madness'.

There's a whole history of it in my father's family and though I figure that if I was going to go mad I would have done it by now . . . if I have children, then that's going to be something I have to think about and so that side worries me.

When someone takes their own life, 'the previously unthinkable becomes thinkable'. It can feel very frightening, it can lead to overwatchfulness between family members and can inhibit family members from communicating freely with one another. These fears may sometimes be unrealistic but it has been suggested that educating survivors about the possible causes of suicide can not only help to alleviate guilt but may reduce fears about subsequent suicides in the family (Clark and Goldney 1995).

Chapter 10

The impact of suicide on individual family members

The family network plays a central part in some people's lives, while in others, family members may have little regular contact with one another. Whichever is the case, though, our place in the family contributes to our sense of identity. We are a son or daughter, perhaps also someone's brother or sister; as adults, we may have established our own family, creating new identities – husband or wife, and father or mother. Whatever our place in the family, when one of its members dies, it will affect us. With one exception, the people whose stories are told here included parents, siblings, children and spouses of people who had died by suicide. It is the particular issues facing these groups which are the subject of this chapter.

Parents

> I think there's self-doubt in what you've done . . . your role as a father or as a mother . . . the thought that you'd done something wrong or didn't play your part right in the bringing up of your daughter. It's that that chisels away at you. (Robert)

> And I am pregnant
> With your death
> I carry you again
> – a dead weight –
> No birth to come.
> J.C. (1987)

Prior to the twentieth century, the death of a child was a frequent event and most parents could expect to lose up to half their children in infancy or early childhood. These losses were expected and perhaps accepted more readily than is now the case. Deaths of children are now much rarer, so parents are generally less prepared for these unanticipated losses (Parkes 1998).

Only 19 children aged 14 and under died by suicide in England and Wales in 1998 (Samaritans 2000), but the recent increase in the suicide rate among young adults in recent years means more parents are bereaved by the suicide of one of their children. While it would be undesirable to create hierarchies of loss by suggesting that the death of a child is necessarily the 'worst' bereavement, many would agree with Gorer's conclusion that this particular loss, especially when it involves a fully grown child, may be 'the most distressing and long-lasting of all griefs' (1965). The fact that the child may have reached adulthood does not usually make it any easier. For many people, parenting involves a continuing commitment and responsibility for their children's well-being into adulthood. For some parents whose only child dies by suicide, there is an abrupt and complete cessation of their parental identity and role.

For many parents, children provide a sense of continuity; they themselves will grow old and die, but their children will live on, and perhaps have children of their own. When a child dies, regardless of whether there are other children, this line, this sense of continuity, will be severed. That was how Francesca felt after her only daughter committed suicide: 'You see when a daughter dies – when a daughter chooses to die – you've lost the mother–daughter–grandchild . . . it's gone.'

Children are often seen as representing their parents' future, but when a child dies, parents 'are victimised by loss of the dreams and hopes invested in that child' (Nelson and Frantz 1996: 132). Parents who did not go to university, or who may have spent their life in a rather mundane job, may look to their children to achieve their own unfulfilled ambitions. When Frances died, although she left behind a brother, her death seemed like the end of Pam's hopes for the future:

> You don't expect to lose your children, do you? You expect that you will die and leave them behind . . . we just didn't imagine . . . I mean we'd always looked to the future, and our future and the children's future all wound together, and suddenly there wasn't much of a future . . . We always thought she'd do pretty grand things . . . go abroad and nurse and do great things.

Parents do not expect their children to die before them, that is not the natural order of things, a point echoed by Mark whose daughter, it seemed to him, 'went too soon . . . went out of order'.

When a child seemingly chooses to die, for whatever reasons, parents are left with an overwhelming sense of rejection and Gibb suggests that the bereaved parent may feel that their dead child is 'inflicting punishment for [the parent's] wrongs or deficiencies' (1998: 124) – a severe rebuke which can impede mourning.

As Pat said after Caroline's death: 'It's the ultimate rejection of you as a mum if your child cannot face life and cannot face you. There can't be any greater rejection than to obliterate yourself and detach yourself totally from that person.' Invariably this leads parents to question why? What was there about me as a parent that led my child to do this? Where did I go wrong?

In the days and weeks following the suicide of a child, many survivors will place their parenting under a microscope, often going back over many years, searching for clues as to where things might have gone wrong, and wondering if they can pinpoint a particular incident which could have caused the death. Carole was preoccupied with this for some time after her only son died. She recalled how, nearly twenty years before his death, Jon had been separated from her when his sister was born. According to Carole, he returned home traumatised by the separation: 'I had unwittingly and unthinkingly hurt him deeply . . . I have suffered deep distress and anguish over this since Jon's death. This has caused me more pain and guilt than any other episode in our life together.'

Parent survivors commonly feel that their parenting is in question:

> Parents have the responsibility for the growth and protection of their children. When a child commits suicide, therefore, the competency and credibility of the individuals as parents are called into question . . . How could the parents have been so insensitive, so unaware of their child's mental state? . . . For some of these parents the self-doubt resulted in a 'parental identity crisis'.
>
> (McIntosh 1987b: 74)

In their study of suicide bereaved parents, Seguin and colleagues report that: 'Almost all the parents have the impression that they have failed in some way, thus putting their parental competency into question' (1995a: 495). After her son's suicide, Anne Downey wrote: 'I'm sure every mother, under the circumstances, digs and digs and finds so many areas where she went wrong. We aim at perfection, which is impossible' (1987: 71). When a child dies by suicide, even 'good enough' parenting can feel like failure.

As with other survivors, though, retracing the past only brings wisdom with hindsight (see Chapter 6). Mark's daughter was twenty-nine when she died and much of her adult life had been punctuated by breakdowns and crises, including suicide attempts, but he has found it hard to come to terms with the fact that, as her parents, they failed to notice anything seriously wrong during her childhood; for Mark, that was 'the most shattering discovery of all'. There is a kind of double burden: not only have they apparently failed as parents, but they did not even realise that they were failing. As Heather said, after her son died: 'We failed him . . . without realising that we had.'

This sense of failure can affect the way parents feel about their relationship with surviving children. If parents believe they have failed one child with such devastating results, 'they may no longer feel they are competent providers for the rest of the family' (Seguin et al. 1995a: 495). They may fear that their other children will take their own lives or will be harmed in some way. After her son died, Maureen remembers how she started following her two teenage daughters round the house, always needing to know where they were, and frightened to let them go out on their own. This excessive concern about other family members is not unusual (Wrobleski 1984–5).

At the same time, though, parents may feel, however irrationally, that because fate has dealt them one blow, this should confer immunity from any further tragedies. Since her daughter's death nine years ago, Nancy has struggled with anxieties about her two sons:

> I have a sort of angry feeling inside me which is quite illogical . . . that it ought to have been one of the rules of life that if you've lost one of your children, that should be insurance against losing any others.

Parents may find they are caught up in a sense of despair, almost convinced that further family tragedy is now inevitable. Lois has two surviving sons, the youngest of whom is still at school:

> I can't watch over him all the time, and I'm not basically a possessive person . . . but it's hard . . . you know it could happen again . . . that's the sort of pessimism that comes over you; you think, oh that'll be the next thing I've got to cope with – a car crash.

Parents' own feelings of guilt, and their sense of failure, may be compounded by the belief that other people must see them in the same light. As Lois said: 'You know that suicide is bad in the sense that there's still this social stigma of failure, and you feel you've failed as a parent, or mother, or whatever.' Feelings of shame can lead parents to isolate themselves more frequently than other bereaved parents, making it harder for family and friends to offer support (Seguin et al. 1995a).

With the death of a child, both parents are confronted with a major loss, making it more difficult for one to support the other. The person they might otherwise rely on is faced with their own grieving. Sharing their feelings may be difficult or even impossible. One parent may be trying to protect the other from their pain; one may be silently blaming the other person for the death; in some cases, one of the couple may be refusing to accept that the death was self-inflicted.

Although none of the mothers I interviewed suggested that their losses were worse than those of their husbands or partners, women may be more vulnerable than men following the death of a child (Parkes 1998). Writing about women, death and dying, Cline (1996: 249) considers that there are specific issues for female suicide survivors, related to women's identities including that of 'primary parent'. Women's chronic grief may be intensified by their difficulties in expressing rejection and anger (Cline 1996), which may in turn lead to increased vulnerability to depression. There is certainly some evidence that although suicide bereaved fathers and mothers have an increased risk of depression, this was greater in the case of mothers who over time showed an increased risk of recurrence of depression (Brent et al. 1996a).

Siblings

> We've had the time for grieving, and although I don't want to forget her . . . I think I want to go on now. (Nicola)

Despite being faced with the loss of a brother or sister and the added strain of grieving parents, siblings can become the 'forgotten victims': 'The removal of a sibling from the family constellation often results in additional temporary loss of love, due to the grief-stricken parents' withdrawal' (Nelson and Frantz 1996).

For adolescent survivors, there are the added challenges of negotiating the transition to adulthood. The dearth of research into the experiences of sibling survivors was noted by Henley (1984), McIntosh (1987b) and Valente and Saunders (1993), although some studies have since been published (Brent et al. 1996a; Nelson and Frantz 1996).

Sacksen has also noted the paucity of material on sibling survivors. In addition, she found a lack of support services for this group, despite the fact that participants in her study said that they would like to meet others in a similar situation, wanted someone to listen to them and would have welcomed the opportunity to talk to a trained professional (Sacksen 1999).

Although it is over fifty years since Ann's student brother committed suicide, she can still recall the events of that time. On the day Giles died, though she very much wanted to accompany her parents to the university, she was told they would manage without her. Similarly she did not attend Giles's inquest, and when it came to the funeral her parents again said they would be going alone. Although she now realises they were probably trying to protect rather than deliberately exclude her, she had no chance to say goodbye to her brother. She was an 'absent mourner'.

The relationship between siblings sometimes becomes more distant after they leave home but adult survivors can be devastated by the loss of a sibling with whom they had a particularly close relationship as did Jennifer and Tim. For Jennifer, her memories of childhood were that 'it was never just me . . . always me and Tim'. Close to each other in age, as small children they played together constantly; as young adults, they purchased their first car jointly; and they always went together to the local disco. Tim had always been a permanent fixture in her life: 'I can't think of any time growing up when he wasn't there.' Tim's death has left its mark on her childhood memories, because her own childhood and Tim's were inseparable. Now she is an only 'child'.

For survivors from larger families, the suicide can mean losing the favourite brother or sister, the one with whom the survivor had had a special relationship. Although Peter was the eldest of four, it was Susie, the youngest of his three sisters, who had always been closest to him. Even after Peter had left his family's home in New Zealand, and come to live in England, Susie remained his favourite sister.

> I was always entirely besotted with Susie, right from the beginning . . . I mean one shouldn't perhaps, but one inevitably does have favourite siblings and we had lots in common . . . there was an indulgent relationship too because she was much younger and I was the eldest.

Siblings will sometimes take on the role of caretakers and assume responsibilities which prior to the suicide were their parents' (Gaffney et al. 1992). The adolescent survivor may take on the role of parent-substitute, where the actual parents are, for the time being, unable to fulfil that role. Research findings suggest that younger sibling survivors may have more difficulties, possibly because they are more involved in family life than older siblings who spend little time at home (Brent et al. 1996a). However, even older children can sometimes find the parent–child roles are reversed.

When Francesca's daughter committed suicide, she remembers how her son, then in his late twenties, and suddenly an only child, 'somehow stepped out of being a son and became a parent'. Pam and Harry's experience was similar; they felt as if their twenty-year-old son had literally grown up overnight. The more usual roles of parents and child as carer and cared for are reversed. This may be more likely to happen where the surviving sibling is now the only child, and as a result may feel they have the sole responsibility for their parents.

But what about the siblings' own needs? As Jean's son complained after his sister died: 'It was my only sister, and I'm all on my own, and no one makes a fuss of me!' Eileen's sole surviving daughter, Marjorie, experienced similar reactions; after Marjorie's twin sisters had committed suicide, it seemed that her own needs were being ignored; everyone kept asking how her mother was coping, but nobody thought to ask how she was feeling. It can be difficult for young adults to know who they can turn to for support. They may feel they need to protect already grieving parents from further distress, and as a result, parents may conclude that the suicide has not really affected them that deeply. Talking to friends of their own age can also be difficult; peers may be unsure how to respond and the survivor feels embarrassed or ashamed about the suicide. Meeting new people can be difficult if the sibling survivor is unsure how to respond when asked about brothers and sisters (Gaffney et al. 1992).

Where parents appear to be totally wrapped up in grieving for the dead child, surviving siblings may start to feel unloved and neglected, as happened to Jon's surviving sister. When her mother started crying at Christmas, Gilly's response was: 'I'm here and you've got me, so don't spoil the day.' As Carole realised afterwards: 'I could feel in a way jealousy, you know . . . She felt I was thinking about him and I wasn't thinking about her.' Siblings can feel excluded by parental grief.

Survivors like Nicola may feel guilty about being the one who survived and wonder if somehow they contributed to the suicide:

> I hate myself sometimes because . . . she obviously did think 'Nicola does this', and 'Nicola's that', and put herself down and [she] always said 'Oh, I wish I was thin like you, and I wish I had blonde hair like you', and I sometimes think that if there hadn't been such a difference between us or she hadn't looked at me and thought I was everything she wanted to be . . . She never saw any faults, although there are lots, she never saw any, and sometimes I find that hard.

An integral part of growing up is the young person's increasing independence from their family of origin, but if a sibling takes their own life during this time, it may be difficult for the surviving siblings to exert their wish for greater autonomy. They may feel they need to be at home supporting one or both parents when otherwise they would be spending more time outside with peers.

Young adult survivors may be torn between feeling that they should be around supporting their parents, but at the same time wanting to get on with their own lives. After her son's suicide, Carole saw that this might be a problem for her daughter who had just left home for university, as she has realised: 'I don't want to be a burden to her . . . she might feel she's got to come home every so often, and she's got to ring me up, and she's got to see how I am.'

Eighteen months after her sister's suicide, Nicola felt the time had come for her to look to the future:

> I think that is the difference between Mum and Dad and me. They're always looking back on what was . . . and I want to [say] it's happened, and we've had the time for grieving, and although I don't want to forget her and not talk about her and forget things that happened, I think I want to go on now . . . I feel that now's the time to, hopefully,

when I get married and move into a house; it's going to make a big change for me, a new start.

The fact that young people may have a different perspective on death does not mean that they are immune from grief, but on the threshold of adulthood they need to be able to look to the future as well as mourn the past; it is a normal and healthy reaction at that stage of life. As Carole's daughter told her: 'I've cried for him for a year; I'm going to get on with my life now.'

Parental suicide in childhood

Her death has been buried for so long and there has been a conspiracy, almost to the extent of wiping her away, as though she never existed, and that really makes me very angry. And so now, if anything, there's a sense of wanting to get back a sense of her, and a value for her. So I don't feel stigma; there's a sense of wanting to honour her. (Kevin)

Bowlby has suggested that 'relative to deaths due to other causes, the death of a child's parents by suicide is not altogether uncommon', and the proportion of parental deaths due to suicide 'for children born to parents in their twenties . . . may be as high as one father in fifteen and one mother in seventeen who die' (1985: 381). It has been estimated that in Britain, each year as many as 2,000 children under sixteen may become survivors of parental suicide (Shepherd and Barraclough 1976).

Studies of child survivors of suicide are rare, although a recent study compared the emotional and behavioural responses of children (aged 5–17) bereaved by parental suicide with those of children whose parent had died from other causes. The researchers found that although both groups displayed common emotional reactions, the suicide bereaved group were more likely to show anxiety, anger and shame and they had more behavioural difficulties over the first two years (Cerel et al. 1999). As Black (1998) has pointed out, children who have gone through a sudden and particularly traumatic bereavement, are more likely to need some kind of specialised help.

The survivors whose experiences are described below all lost a parent through suicide during their childhood, the youngest being four and the oldest eighteen at the time. Despite the fact that in some instances the suicide had occurred over twenty years previously, their memories of the event were often still very vivid.

Given the difficulties many adults have in talking with each other about suicide, it is hardly surprising that children are often told little or nothing about how their parent died; even when they are told something, the information they receive may not even be an accurate version of events. Non-existent or distorted communication is common in this situation; as

Cain and Fast discovered when studying a group of child survivors of parental suicide, many of them had received 'the message . . . that they *should not tell* and they *should not know*' (1972a: 103, italics in original). Shepherd and Barraclough's findings (1976) were not dissimilar; in a group of thirty-six child survivors, only half were given any sort of explanation about the suicide; of the remaining eighteen, some of whom would have been too young to have understood about suicide at the time of the death, twelve still knew nothing about the manner of death between five and seven years later. A more recent report on adolescent survivors suggests that some young people may still struggle to ascertain the facts about a suicide in the family (Gaffney et al. 1992).

Kevin's story is worth recounting in some detail at this point because much of what happened to him around the time of his mother's death is typical of the experiences of child survivors. When he was ten, Kevin came downstairs one morning to find his mother lying on the kitchen floor with her head resting in the gas oven. He decided that she had probably fallen over and banged her head; he certainly had no idea that she was dead, let alone that she had taken her own life. He remembers lifting her head from the oven, after which he was sent upstairs to his bedroom; he can recall next looking out of the window and seeing the bright red blanket as the ambulance men carried her away. All that day, relatives came and went from the house, but Kevin and the other children were told nothing until that evening when their father told them their mother was dead; there was no proper explanation, though, of what had happened, and suicide was not mentioned. Feeling numbed and shocked, Kevin was sent off without his siblings to stay with relatives. No one suggested that he might want to attend the funeral, and he only realised that his mother had gone for ever when, on returning home, he looked in her wardrobe and saw that all her clothes had disappeared. About two months later, playing at a friend's house, he overheard something which suggested that his mother had committed suicide, but within the family, the manner of her death remained a secret. Within a year of losing his mother, he had left home to go to boarding school.

Seeing or hearing things but not having them properly explained; being sent away from home, or being looked after by distant relatives or by neighbours; not having the chance to attend the funeral; finding out about the suicide by overhearing adult conversations; going away to school (or moving home); all these are common experiences of child survivors.

Although some parents who take their own lives will ensure that their children are not around at the time of the suicide, this is not always the case; Kevin's experience is not that unusual. In their study of families (see above), Shepherd and Barraclough (1976) found that almost half the children had been in the vicinity of the suicide, and even this they consider to be an underestimate since the information was not obtained directly from the children.

Denise was four when she saw her father hanging from the staircase, but despite having had to live with that memory, at least she had that information: 'I just think if I hadn't found him, that I wouldn't have been able to fit it into my understanding . . . I don't think it would have been explained adequately.' Indeed, for the next twelve years no one did explain to her what had happened and Denise kept quiet, sensing that the subject was taboo in the family. As she reached her teens, she would spend hours alone in her room, crying, and trying to make sense of what she had seen as a small child. It was only finally when she was sixteen that she and her mother were able to talk to one another about what had happened.

Despite these difficulties, in some ways Denise was fortunate because even if the suicide was not discussed, at least it was not denied; Cain and Fast (1972a) came across families where the child who had witnessed the suicide was either given a version of events which clearly contradicted what had been seen, or they were told that they must have dreamt the whole thing. This can seriously affect the child's entire sense of reality (Dunne-Maxim et al. 1987); if a child sees her mother has cut her wrists and is told that death was the result of a drowning accident, what and who is she to believe? What is real and what is make-believe?

In Martin's case, there were secrets in the family long before his mother's suicide (which happened when he was in his early teens). Looking back to his childhood, he *thinks* his mother was probably having a series of mental breakdowns; he can remember fetching her from hospital on at least one occasion. He *thinks* she may have been addicted to morphine; he can remember coming across phials and syringes around the house. But he is not too sure about any of this, because no one told him what was going on. He is not even sure exactly what month and year it was that his mother died. What he can remember is that one day his mother disappeared, their home was suddenly full of police who practically seemed to live in the house, the story was in the national newspapers, and then she was found dead. With the lack of communication from adults about what was happening to his mother, it is hardly surprising that, as he admits: 'I was the one person who hadn't twigged.' After her death that secrecy was maintained:

> It was sort of in a sense not spoken of, and it was never really discussed afterwards in the family at all . . . I can never remember having a conversation with my father about it, ever . . . that was the way the family coped.

Now, almost forty years later, he feels that he will probably never be able to piece together the story of his mother's death. He still has dreams in which he is searching for her, and when he finds her, it is always as though she never really died. Perhaps for Martin she never has died.

One of the few things which Martin does recall clearly from that time is hearing his father crying in the night. Realising that the last time he saw his mother alive she had been cross with him about something, he decided that he must have been in some way responsible for her death:

> I did feel that I was to blame and that I'd angered her and upset her in some way . . . I really felt that I'd done something . . . I think I've spent a lot of my life trying to resolve and make reparation for it . . . I remember my last memory of her being angry, very angry, and I now can't remember what it was about and what I had done.

Child survivors may attempt to avoid feelings of helplessness and abandonment by deciding that they must have been responsible for the suicide. This may help them feel more in control but can also lead the child survivor feeling that they are capable of doing immense harm. As Jan recalls, following the death of her mother and three years later the suicide of her father: 'I spent years trying to be such a good girl so that I couldn't do any more damage.'

Even when children are aware of things going wrong at home before the suicide, because they are not adults they are likely to feel helpless to alter the situation. As Jan found, children tend to have very little power. Although she disliked the publicity surrounding her father's suicide, at least she felt that the secret, which she had been powerless to deal with, was out in the open:

> I hated the [publicity] at the time, I felt it exposed, and at that time I just saw it as a negative thing, that it had exposed what had been a kind of secret all that time [but] I suppose at some level there was relief that it wasn't a secret any more. Prior to the suicide his drinking never led to any sort of intervention and I can remember every time he got picked up [for drinking and driving] thinking now they'll do something about it – but it never happened.

Until her father died, it must have seemed to Jan that even adults were powerless to change things. One of the ways in which the child survivor may try to deal with what has happened is to become the family carer. Kevin talked of how he felt responsible for ensuring that everything was all right; he became, as he says, 'the carer, the coper, someone that the others might look to'. Dunne-Maxim and her colleagues suggest that these children (in common with some sibling survivors, see above) may 'seek to "parent" their parents in an apparent effort to bring some order to their disturbed lives and homes' (1987: 238). Assuming the parental role may also be a way of identifying with the dead parent:

The identification may take the form of noting the many similarities between oneself and the deceased parent, taking on the dead parent's role within the family, or displaying the same behaviour or symptoms as the parent who committed suicide.

(McIntosh 1987b: 78–9)

Hilary was eighteen, and had just left home to attend secretarial college when her mother committed suicide. She returned home the same day, and, despite being the youngest of three children, she made all the funeral arrangements. She never went back to college, but took over her mother's role and kept house for her father until her marriage some years later. Thirty-five years after her mother's death, Hilary has discovered that 'this is where the scars lie'; her sister, who lives abroad, has recently announced that she does not plan to return home when their elderly father dies. Although Hilary is in many ways a natural carer and coper, she is surprised how bitterly she resents her sister's attitude. Once again, she is going to have to deal with a family funeral on her own; once again she is going to be the one who copes.

Identification with the dead parent can take more subtle forms. Martin's mother was a doctor, and he spent much of his early adult life unsuccessfully attempting to become medically qualified – despite being advised against this by other people. It was, he subsequently realised, 'a blanket attempt to try and be her almost' – and an attempt perhaps to repossess that which he had lost?

At its most tragic, identification with the dead parent can result in the child survivor also taking their own life (McIntosh 1987b). Others may not actually die by suicide but may grow up feeling that suicide is their fate. Worden suggests that 'many [survivors] seem to carry with them a sense of fate or doom' (1991: 95). As he suggests, this preoccupation is not unusual but some will cope with this by volunteering for Samaritans or other suicide prevention schemes.

For Denise, being a survivor has meant facing the question 'Will I do it too?' As she grew up, it became increasingly important for her to feel sure that even if she resembled her father in some ways, unlike him she was not going to take her own life:

I do remember in my teens my mum used to say, 'oh, you're very highly strung', and that I was just like my father and . . . it was terrible . . . There was always this fear that if something happened, I might end up taking my own life . . . I might not be strong enough [not to]. There was a fear, yes.

On reaching adulthood, child survivors may feel they need to make some sense of the suicide. Some, like Kevin and Jan, go into therapy, wanting to understand better how the suicide has shaped their lives. Like adult survivors, they may also embark on a search for the person who died. What sort of person were they and why did they do this?

What they find can be quite conflicting and confusing, as Jan found after her father's death. The man she had grown up with was someone who had a serious drinking problem, whose idea of a joke was to fire his gun and pretend he had shot himself, and who left a note blaming his daughters for his suicide. But to other people in their local community in South Africa, he was a courageous and highly respected lawyer, a man to whom many people had cause to be grateful, and who had even been known to save people from capital punishment. Piecing this sort of picture together can be difficult.

For Kevin, the silence which surrounded his mother's suicide has left him even more determined not to let her disappear into oblivion. With the help of a therapist, he has been trying to get back in touch with some of the 'good parenting' which he believes he had from her as a little boy. On a more practical level, he has acquired a copy of her birth certificate and newspaper reports of her inquest. He has also made contact with family members who knew her, and has been to talk to them about his mother.

For any child, the loss of a parent will be a devastating experience. The feeling of having been hurt and abandoned may be translated into feeling 'I won't trust anyone again because then I can be sure of not being hurt or rejected again'. To some extent this has been Denise's experience; although she has made some close relationships with men, she is always afraid they will leave her, and aware that her father's suicide makes it hard for her to sustain trust in important relationships, particularly where men are involved.

Anyone who has been bereaved by suicide will carry that experience of survivorship with them for the rest of their life, unwelcome though that may sometimes be. Denise knows that she cannot shed her past: 'I suppose I do feel that I should not be living in terms of it any more, [but] I still feel it's very much part of me.' She is right, but perhaps what matters ultimately is how far people can confront and integrate that experience into the rest of their lives. Some survivors like Jan and Kevin have chosen to confront their childhood experiences very directly by entering therapy. For Kevin, the decision to seek help came when he realised that he did not have to remain frozen as the ten-year-old whose mother committed suicide – indeed, that he could not do so: 'I [could] either continue to live a lie, or actually confront the past.'

Spouses

> I felt as though I had been forcibly divorced. I mean, that's the only way I can put it, that I had no say in the matter . . . I wasn't ready to give up on him and he gave up on himself. (Susan)

The survivors of suicide perhaps have more in common with the innocent parties of divorce or separation, because there's this feeling of rejection, of inadequacy. (Brian)

The death of a spouse or partner is potentially one of the most stressful life events. Depending on the age and circumstances of the couple, it can mean raising children alone, financial difficulties, loneliness and social isolation. Suicide bereavement has added dimensions.

Suicide regularly represented an implicit statement that the suicide's spouse could not or did not help him towards happiness or at least out of despair . . . the entire history of the marital relationship often seemed put on trial as to 'responsibility' for the suicide.
(Cain and Fast 1972b: 150)

If marriage or partnership is a contract freely entered into by both parties, the person who takes their own life breaks the contract unilaterally. The sense of rejection can be particularly acute for suicide survivors, as Marie discovered after Oliver's death: 'I mean, you go through the "why" business anyway, but why should someone choose to kill themselves rather than live with me?'

Surviving spouses may also feel in some way responsible for the death, as Susan discovered. Because Richard had been good at covering up his feelings outside their home, some of their friends found his suicide quite inexplicable. As a result, she felt people were somehow implicating her in his death. They wanted to know what her role had been, and although she believes that their marriage was happy, she feels that other people placed a question mark over the relationship.

For some spouses or partners, the suicide occurs after a lengthy period of difficulty and stress, but this is not necessarily experienced as unmitigated relief by the survivor. Isabel's husband, Eric, had fifteen years of treatment for mental health problems before he finally took his life; his difficulties had considerably disrupted family life; but despite that, Isabel found that no longer to be one of a pair was one of the most painful aspects of her bereavement: 'just being cut in half, and feeling so alone really, even though he had been so ill . . . Just the isolation, because it's not the same [being] with the children.' At the same time, after coping with recurring crises including Eric's previous suicide attempts:

It was a form of relief really, when he died, to be honest . . . You know I had had to live with this business of the suicide for a long time, so for a while it was like a relief, a sense of peace in a way.

In some cases the needs of a suicidal spouse or partner may have had to be balanced with the needs of young children. Isabel remembers how on one occasion she decided to try and look after Eric herself, rather than have him re-admitted to the local psychiatric hospital, but his aggressive outbursts and heavy drinking disturbed the children, and she found herself caught between competing demands: 'It was hard going for all of us . . . He was suffering but we were all suffering as well.'

For Melanie, trying to cope with her husband and a small baby meant facing painful choices. Things had started to go wrong soon after Hannah was born and became worse as Ian became increasingly demanding. She began to feel that if the three of them stayed together she would be looking after two babies. It felt as though Ian was forcing her to choose between him and Hannah. After his death, Melanie found that, for a time, caring for Hannah 'became no more than going through the motions', and she resented the fact that Ian had left her to be a single parent. Any widowed parent may find single parenting hard work, but the suicide survivor may also feel aggrieved that the other person deliberately forced them into that role.

Susan remembers how she felt about being left to cope with the aftermath of Richard's suicide. In the next four years, Susan's father, an aunt and a sister all died. As well as her son, she had a widowed mother to look after. Despite the strain, Susan carried on coping – 'I was the coper and I had to keep going' – but subsequently developed a painful physical illness which, she now realises, was probably a delayed reaction to these losses and to not having enough space for her own grieving. Having to cope with other people, whether they are dependent children or elderly parents – or, as in Susan's case, both – can mean having to put your own grief on hold.

The rejection inherent in spousal suicide can make it hard for survivors to consider starting another relationship. Four years after her husband's suicide, Irene still feels unable to consider the idea: 'I don't think I would ever trust again . . . I would never marry again, no. I wouldn't dare.' Irene is not prepared to risk a possible further rejection. In Isabel's case, although friends have urged her to remarry, she feels unwilling to risk the possibility of another fifteen years of the sort of difficulties she experienced in her first marriage.

As Susan found, the survivor may be left wondering whether there is something about their personality that attracts suicidal people. Before she married Richard, Susan had had two other serious relationships; one of these men subsequently committed suicide, and the other she described as 'impossibly neurotic'. Although in some ways she would like to marry again, she reluctantly admits that 'on reflection I have realised that I have an apparently calm personality which seems to attract neurotic men'.

Despite some survivors' reluctance to commit themselves to a new marriage or partnership, by no means all surviving spouses will remain widowed (Shepherd and Barraclough 1976), and remarriage can turn out to be a very positive experience. While he was married to Gwen, Andrew always felt that their marriage was not all he felt it could be. After what he describes as 'the sixteen most wonderful years of his second marriage', he knows that he was right: 'Now', he says, 'I know how marriage should be.'

Chapter 11

Facing the world

Some people can't handle it. I mean, if you say somebody killed themselves, it's a real conversation stopper. (Melanie)

Society somehow expects us to sweep our feelings of horror and guilt and grief away. (Jennifer)

She was so much there. The one thing of any importance to me was my own daughter . . . I wasn't going to talk trivialities. (Nancy)

Bereavement and social support

Bereavement research suggests that the support of family and friends is critical in the period following a bereavement. It can help the mourner in their grieving and reduce the impact of sudden loss. Amongst the suddenly bereaved, 'social support from family and close friends plays a major and consistent role in alleviating separation anxiety, feelings of rejection and depression' (Reed 1998).

Apart from the family members, the bereaved person's support network may include friends (of varying degrees of closeness), acquaintances, neighbours and colleagues in the workplace. Support may also be offered by others such as GPs. In the days immediately following the death, the bereaved will often withdraw from their wider social network, remaining at home with immediate family, perhaps seeing just one or two close friends. But at some point, often after the funeral has taken place, they will gradually re-emerge, go back to work, and resume social and leisure activities.

Sometimes the bereaved person will find other people reacting to the loss in ways which are not particularly helpful: friends may be embarrassed, they may not know what to say; they may want to help but say the wrong thing; or, if really unable to cope with the situation, they may avoid the bereaved person. In general, though, as a society we would probably like to think we are becoming a little more comfortable with death and bereavement. But can the same be said about society's response to suicide deaths?

And how do the survivors themselves feel about facing other people? That is the focus of this chapter.

Like anyone who has experienced a major loss, survivors of suicide need the support and informal assistance of others. When Shepherd and Barraclough (1979) asked a group of survivors what sort of help they had needed, just over four-fifths mentioned comfort and support, together with practical help – but a third of that group felt that these needs had not been met. This may well have been the case, but other researchers have questioned whether 'survivors actually *are* given less support, or whether they *feel* a lack of support' (Wagner and Calhoun 1991–92: 62; italics in original). Does the shame felt by many suicide survivors mean that they socially isolate themselves?

Shame and stigma may also affect the degree to which survivors of suicide feel able to avail themselves of the support of others. As Doka (1999) suggests, lack of social support may create what he has termed 'disenfranchised grief':

> The circumstances of the death [can] create such shame and embarrass-ment that even those in recognised roles (such as spouse, child or parent) may be reluctant to avail themselves of social support . . . Death . . . from suicide or other self-destructive causes (e.g. drink-driving, drug overdose, etc.) . . . may all be illustrations of disenfranch-ising deaths. Each of these circumstances may carry a stigma that inhibits survivors from seeking or receiving social support.
>
> (1999: 38)

Norms of suicide death and bereavement

Significant events such as births, marriages and deaths are usually marked by specific rituals. We have baptisms, christening parties, wedding ceremonies and funerals, and there are generally accepted ways of reacting and behaving on these occasions: we are expected to congratulate the newly married couple or the new baby's parents, we offer sympathy to the widow whose husband died from a heart attack; and hold military funerals for members of the armed services. Where the person had a long illness, people may say how glad they are that the suffering has ended.

Unlike some of the more primitive societies which have developed certain prescribed behaviours for mourning a suicide death: 'Western societies have generally failed to develop such guidelines, leaving a highly ambiguous situation for survivors and their social networks in the event of a suicide death' (Hauser 1987: 67) – a view echoed by Rudestam who concludes that 'the rules (norms) regarding suicide bereavement may be less clear and more restrictive than the rules for other types of death' (1992: 43).

Studies of the social rules and behaviours governing suicide were undertaken by questioning members of the community and undergraduate students respectively (Calhoun et al. 1986). They concluded that in the case of suicide, other people can find it hard to talk either about the cause of death, or about any positive aspects of the death.

As Nick discovered, when trying to talk with friends after his mother's death, there are no conventional phrases for commenting on suicide: 'People sort of had grave expressions and nodded . . . and there was nothing they could say.'

Other studies point to this lack of clear 'rules' or expectations when it comes to talking with suicide survivors. Nearly all the participants in Van Dongen's study 'perceived friends and relatives (outside the immediate family) as also uncertain and uncomfortable when interacting with them' (1993: 133). Similar findings emerged from an earlier study where again, the overwhelming majority of survivors referred to being aware of other people feeling uncomfortable (Wagner and Calhoun 1991–2).

Given the potential discomfort of many people in the survivor's social network, it is hardly surprising that survivors sometimes feel it would have been easier if the person had died from some other cause. Carol feels that people would have reacted very differently if her son had died in an accident; instead: 'it's almost as if you're not allowed to have gone through suicide, or to be a survivor of suicide or the death hasn't happened that way – it's happened some other way'. As Dick commented after his sister's suicide, 'if it had been a painful cancer or something they might have said "at least she's not in pain" or something like that'. Although he felt able to talk about Sally's death with certain people (particularly female friends), he soon realised that the fact that she had taken her own life made some of his friends very uncomfortable.

In one of Bel Mooney's novels, the highly respected village doctor disappears. When his body is found in nearby countryside, everyone assumes he has had a heart attack, but when the real cause of death emerges, his son finds attitudes have changed:

> it all sounds as if everybody thought it was perfectly okay for Dad to be dead. Nice normal heart attack . . . no problem. But *now*, when we all know it wasn't normal – that he *decided* to die, we all avoid each others' eyes as if something rude had been said.
>
> (1985: 116, italics in original)

Breaking the news to other people

The aftermath of suicide can draw everyone into a conspiracy of silence. Survivors sometimes have as much difficulty in talking about the suicide as do those around them. Rudestam (1987) found that roughly half the respondents in his study did not want to discuss the suicide with friends and acquaintances, and nearly a third admitted that they sometimes lied to other people about the cause of death.

Survivors may sometimes resort to ambiguities; Brian found it difficult to talk openly about his wife's suicide; as he said, 'I think all parties involved in suicide try to hide it to some extent, don't they? I mean, I used the expression "Judy was killed". I don't say that she took her own life.'

Survivors can find it particularly hard to face other people in the early days. As Pam recalled: 'at the time you're so vulnerable that everything hurts, everything. You're bruised so easily.' Having to tell other people can feel like rubbing salt into a wound, as Peter discovered. Although he has never felt any particular sense of stigma about his sister's suicide, telling other people about Susie meant it was impossible to deny what had happened: 'Every time I had to say that Susie had died, I had to admit it to myself.'

Jane felt that she needed to tell other people as part of coming to terms with Christopher's death; she also did not want people to hear the news at second hand; so, when she returned to work after her brother's death and found that a colleague had already told people about the suicide, she reacted extremely angrily:

> I felt violated, and also it made me realise that telling people is part of the process of coming to terms with what you're telling them . . . I felt the ground had been pulled away from under me, and I resented it bitterly.

Some survivors find it is easier to tell people in the early days, when they are still in a state of shock and everything seems somewhat unreal anyway. For the writer Peter Handke, talking about his mother's suicide could seem almost dangerously easy: 'I would not be extorting personal sympathy from my listener or reader', he wrote, 'I would merely be telling him a rather fantastic story' (1976: 6). That sense of the suicide becoming a sort of fantasy – something completely unreal – was echoed by Ursula. After her daughter's suicide, she asked her sister to telephone people and tell them about Josie's death because, as she explained, 'I knew that . . . if I had to keep explaining to everybody, and going over it, it would have lost its meaning. It would sort of become banal by repetition.'

Peter Handke's sense of wanting to keep it to himself in order to maintain a sense of reality left him feeling ambivalent about whether he even wanted attention from other people:

> The worst thing right now would be sympathy, expressed in a word or even a glance. I would turn away or cut the sympathiser short because I need the feeling that what I am going through is incomprehensible and

incommunicable; only then does the horror seem meaningful and real. If anyone talks to me about it, the boredom comes back and everything is unreal again. Nevertheless, for no reason at all I sometimes tell people about my mother's suicide but if they dare to mention it to me I am furious.

(1976: 4)

Marris suggests that these conflicting emotions are a common reaction to bereavement. 'The behaviour of the bereaved', he says, 'is characteristically ambivalent: they may be lonely but shun company . . . they complain if people avoid them, embarrassed how to express their sympathy, yet rebuff that sympathy irritably when it is offered' (1978: 28).

Anne Downey experienced that sense of confusion and ambivalence after her son's suicide. Should she say something, or not? Are people really sorry for her, or just curious? Does she want their sympathy anyway? Are they judging Stephen in some way?

I wish the lady in the bank would not be so pleasant. She knows about you taking your life. I blurted it out one day to her friend who must have told her . . . Now she looks at me with that face, and I become confused, almost apologetic. I am afraid of suddenly saying 'Yes, I'm the lady whose son killed himself. Please do not treat me differently because you make me feel guilty and he would not like that. He never meant to hurt me. It was just something he did without thinking. If he had been killed in a car crash you would not look at me like that'.

(1987: 41)

But even an open and truthful approach does not necessarily elicit a sympathetic response. Other people can find the unexpected news of the suicide deeply shocking. When Betty's son died from an overdose, she rang the woman she used to work for and told her the news:

I said, 'A dreadful tragedy has happened, I've lost my son', and she was terribly upset, and then, when she found out it was suicide, never a word; she'd gone. It's incredible. How did he die, you know, what did it matter? I'm never going to say he died any other way because it's not true.

Having to deal with people who are not coping with hearing the news can be an added and unwelcome burden for survivors, but avoiding this situation by not talking about the victim was not always what they needed either; survivors mentioned how there were times when they would go around almost compulsively talking about the suicide – occasionally telling complete strangers. After her son's death, Heather really wanted to talk about what had happened, but she found that just mentioning Alastair's name, let alone his death, made everyone freeze. Even finding an acceptable way to talk about the death can be difficult, as Nancy discovered after her daughter died: 'I learned quite early on not to say "my daughter committed suicide" because that embarrasses people. Then I toned it down a bit to "she took her own life"; but now I say "she died".'

Faced with other people's reluctance to talk about the suicide, some survivors will decide that the only way to deal with the situation is to broach the subject themselves. Being able to talk about her daughter mattered a great deal to Phyllis, and she found that other people were quite willing to talk about Julie provided she mentioned it first. As she says: 'then they know it's all right'. Not that survivors necessarily find it easy to be the instigators. After his sister's suicide, Dick realised that other people were tending to wait for him to mention Sally, and although he recognises now that they were probably only trying to be tactful, he sometimes found it hard having to make the first move.

Other people's reactions

Survivors can find it hard to make any sense of the death themselves and if asked by other people, they may find it difficult to explain why the suicide occurred. Sometimes, however, other people will offer their own explanations, presumably believing that this will be helpful. In fact, it can have the opposite effect. After her son's death, there were well-meaning people who assured Maureen that Paul had obviously committed suicide because he wanted to, implying that this was some freely made decision, rather than – as she sees it – an act of desperation:

> Don't they realise what torment that boy was going through? Would they have wanted that for their son? Would they have wanted that mental torture or heartache that he must have been feeling for weeks and weeks? . . . They're the remarks I find very unkind, and very hurtful, although they're not meant to be unkind; they weren't said maliciously.

Confronted with the survivor's unhappiness, other people may feel that by offering some sort of explanation they will lessen their distress. When another person is clearly distressed, it is tempting to want to 'make things better', but, as Lukas and Seiden suggest, 'You need to know that as a helper you do not have to fix things up for people . . . Survivors need help in working out their answers. Ultimately, it is their answers that are the only ones that are not irrelevant' (1987: 146–7).

The exhortation to 'never speak ill of the dead' is generally accepted (in public, at least), but may be ignored when a person has taken their own life. Other people may feel free to pass judgement on the person who died, despite the pain this can cause; as Janice discovered, even when the comment is made by a comparative stranger, it can still be hurtful:

> [She] wasn't actually someone that I do know very closely; there were a lot of people there, and we were all sort of like-minded people getting on well, so I felt quite easy saying to her 'Yes, my mother's just died and she took an overdose and it's been difficult' and she said something like 'wicked woman' – that she thought it was really wrong – and I felt very upset by that because I didn't think it was wrong.

Seeing the survivor's distress, friends may feel it will help to tell them how selfish or wicked the victim must have been to cause them this much suffering. But regardless of the survivor's own feelings about the death, having to listen to criticisms of this kind from other people can be extremely hurtful. Jean was pleased when friends told her how much they had loved and valued Anna; but there were others who criticised her daughter, including one person who told her, 'Anna was such an awful child to you and an awful nuisance; years and years from now, you'll think it's the best thing that ever happened.' Losing her only daughter has never felt like that to Jean, and she certainly never wanted to be told that Anna was an 'awful child'.

I came across survivors who had been on the receiving end of all kinds of negative remarks about their relative, such as 'Why did she do this to you?', 'What a waste of a life', and 'We forgive him'. Survivors found such comments unhelpful, partly because there was often an implied judgement about the victim's worth, and as Suzy said: 'I think you need exactly the same as other [bereaved] people get . . . a valuing of the person.'

Avoidance

Although survivors may understandably feel hurt when people in their social network appear to avoid them, they may also accept that other people simply do not know how to react to them (Van Dongen 1993). As Jean discovered, part of coming to terms with the loss can mean having to acknowledge that other people will not always be able to cope with the suicide:

> I've lost a number of friends whom I've had to let go. It's no use being angry with these friends that they cannot share my grief . . . unless someone has experienced our sort of pain how can they possibly share? Once upon a time we were lucky not to know what it was like either.

Even if people listen and are sympathetic, they may still avoid mentioning the death (Rudestam 1987). After her brother's suicide, Liz found that although other people knew the circumstances of Tony's death, no one would actually use the word 'suicide' when talking to her. If friends cannot cope with the idea of someone taking their own life, they may even want to try and convince the survivor that the death was not really suicide, as happened to Isabel, some of whose friends told her they were sure Eric had not really taken his own life. It can be hard enough for survivors to face the fact that it was suicide, but when other people try and persuade them that the truth was otherwise, survivors may end up unsure what sort of loss it is they are really grieving.

For some survivors, one of the most difficult aspects of their bereavement is finding that other people will not even mention the person, let alone talk about their death. As Pam discovered after Frances died: 'You're allowed to mention your son who's living, you're allowed to mention *his* childhood, but you're not allowed to mention your daughter's childhood.'

Even when survivors have initially been able to talk about the suicide, after a time other people may presume that the survivor will have recovered, and that the best thing is not to mention the person any more. Like people bereaved by other deaths, suicide survivors may feel under pressure to recover and return to normal (Wagner and Calhoun 1991–2). A year after her daughter's death, Pat finds this very painful:

> I find now that other people don't mention Caroline, and that hurts me . . . Her name never comes into the conversation unless we bring it into the conversation . . . Someone might be talking about dieting and I would probably say 'Oh Caroline tried this or tried that', and there's this silence and the subject is changed . . . I get angry . . . I don't express my anger but I want to say, 'She was here, she was a person, she lived with us and with you for twenty years, and she laughed and she cried, and she did all the things that we do' . . . Whether they think it's because it would hurt us, but it hurts far more for people not to talk about her . . . I don't honestly think it's because they've forgotten her. They probably don't feel the need to keep her alive as much as I do.

This behaviour may also be other people's way of avoiding their own painful or disturbing feelings evoked by death:

> the expectation is that the bereaved will be brave . . . and not embarrass others with his grief. For unlike the pleasant feelings stirred up by lovers, the loss of a loved one reactivates everybody's most painful nightmares, the most primary infantile fears and panic, the anguish of abandonment and the terror of being left alone, having lost love.
>
> (Pincus 1974: 42)

When the death was self-inflicted, other people may react even more strongly. As Rudestam concludes, 'It is very difficult for members of a support network not to be emotionally threatened by a friend or relative's bereavement in connection with a suicidal death' (1992: 43). Writing of the aftermath of her son's suicide, Diana Davenport had this to say to the people she felt were avoiding her: 'Many still are the stalwarts to whom death is a conversational avenue not to be trodden . . . Oh can't they realise that I want to speak of him, want their soft and stumbling words?' (1989: 129)

Faced with their own unease, friends may try to divert the survivor with a 'let's take your mind off it' approach. After his sister's suicide, Peter found some people were trying to jolly him along in an attempt to stop him thinking about Susie. But as he said: 'I didn't want to be taken out of myself. I didn't want not to be thinking about Susie, I didn't want not to be thinking about what was happening at home.'

Talking about the deceased

Some survivors will be reluctant to mention the suicide to everyone, selecting who they will or will not tell, perhaps deciding not to mention the fact that it was suicide except to close friends or to people with whom they would have some sort of continuing relationship. Susan's approach to responding to questions about Richard's death is typical: 'If I think they're going to remain an acquaintance, I just say he had heart trouble.'

Talking to other people immediately after the death has its own problems, but how do survivors deal with this if the issue arises at some later point? Do they even mention the person who died? Parents whose children had committed suicide often found themselves faced with this dilemma when people asked how many children they had. Brothers and sisters may also be asked about their siblings.

Parents who decide to mention the child that died can find that their honesty is not always well received. After Alan's suicide, Carol decided that if people asked her about the children, she would tell them she had two sons and that one had died. But, she says, if the fact that Alan committed suicide emerges, 'they shut off immediately; they don't ask any more questions . . . it's almost as if you've said something [that] upset them'. Just the mention of suicide can shock people; as Lois commented: 'It is hard to say I've got three children, my eldest son committed suicide, hope you have a nice day . . . It would have been easier to say my son died of cancer or anything . . . anything would have been easier.'

As survivors like Carol and Lois have discovered, coping with other people's reactions can be difficult; at the same time, though, parents sometimes feel very strongly that they do not want to deny the existence of the son or daughter who has died – or, as in Eileen's case, the two daughters she had; since Donna and Sheila died, she has found a way of talking about them which gives other people an opening:

> I usually say, 'I've now got one'. If they pick up the 'now' that's fine; if they don't, that's okay. Because I cannot, l will not, deny the fact . . . I won't say 'I have one', because that denies the fact that I had Sheila and Donna, and I did have them, and they were a big part of my life.

Others like Frank will decide they are not going to tell people, and his way of coping has been to say he has two – rather than three – children. His wife, on the other hand, feels she really wants to tell people about Josie 'because it's so much a part of me'. There are no straightforward solutions, no rights or wrongs. Individuals will work out what they feel is best for them. For many survivors, though, the situation creates a dilemma; to keep silent can feel like denying that the person ever existed; on the other hand, they know that if they mention the suicide, other people may well retreat into embarrassed silence.

Shame and stigma

Any bereaved person can feel set apart from other people. After his wife died of cancer, C.S. Lewis wrote: 'I'm aware of being an embarrassment to everyone I meet . . . perhaps the bereaved ought to be isolated in special settlements like lepers' (1966: 11). This sense of being set apart from other people may be further accentuated when the death was a suicide, as Maureen recounts:

> people on the outside [need] to try and understand how we are feeling, what we are going through . . . because [we] can't cope with people on the outside . . . So it's important for them to know that it's far from normal for . . . the people who are left . . . I feel like some sort of sect; we are different. Yes, that's how we feel, different, totally different, not normal any more. We never will be normal.

Several survivors I met referred to other people as 'outsiders', yet it often seemed that it was they who felt they were the outsiders, the ones who had become 'a sort of sect' in Maureen's words. They have the 'spoiled identity' and belief that they are not 'normal' described by Goffman in his book on stigma (1968).

After her husband committed suicide, Irene imagined how, if she were to tell people what had happened, 'they were going to stand in the market square and shout to everyone, "this is the lady, this is the one"'. Survivors may feel that the person who died 'has made a public declaration that he prefers death to them' (Smith 1978: 62). Survivors like Irene may feel branded by the rest of the world, as though the stigma attached to the suicide victim becomes attached to the whole family, or as Harry said, 'You're a bit of a funny family if something like this happens, you know.'

Survivors may feel that they are the only family to whom this has happened, even though suicide has directly touched the lives of more than one in five people in the UK (Samaritans 1996). Carol discovered that both sets of neighbours had had suicides in their families; yet she has still found it hard to accept that someone in her family could commit suicide. Before Alan's death, she realises, she would have viewed such a family in a negative light. 'I don't think I should be ashamed of the manner that Alan died', she says, 'I shouldn't feel that people look at my family as I would have done previously.'

The reasons why survivors may feel stigmatised and set apart from others are complex and can be difficult to disentangle. What does seem reasonably clear, however, is that the survivor's feelings and behaviours will contribute to the ways in which they and members of their social network will interact. Other people may be uncomfortable with the idea of self-inflicted death but that is not the whole story.

In a comparative study of bereavement after suicide and accident, Seguin and her colleagues found that shame appeared to be 'unique and central to the experience of suicide bereavement' (1995a: 495) and was such a key part of survivors' grieving that 'it may in some circumstances interfere with the way survivors of suicide interact with other people, and the manner in which social support is offered to them' (1995a: 495). If shameful feelings predominate, survivors may isolate themselves more than other bereaved people do, making it difficult for family and friends to provide support. Survivors, in turn, will then not perceive their family and friends as supportive and their sense of isolation will become even greater (Seguin et al. 1995a). This idea of a 'feedback loop' – or vicious circle – may sound depressing but it may also provide useful clues to the kinds of interventions which could improve support for survivors of suicide.

What helped the survivors

Despite these difficulties, survivors can still find people with whom they can grieve openly and who can offer them emotional support. Several of the survivors I met mentioned how much they had been helped by someone (usually a close friend) who had been prepared to sit and listen, had allowed them to talk at length about what had happened, and had not been upset or overwhelmed by their distress. For Susan, this was one of the things which had helped her most: 'it was a relief to talk to her at length . . . she didn't get upset like family members would, and she helped me a great deal just by listening'. The value of 'just listening' is frequently undervalued.

It can be reassuring when those nearest to the bereaved person are unafraid to show their own sadness, but also to show that they are not overwhelmed by him or her (Parkes 1998). Eileen remembers with gratitude the friend who came round, sat and held her hand, and cried with her. She also recalled going back to her job as a headmistress and even though the staff had not known what to say, some had come up and put their arms round her. As Parkes reminds us, touch can be as healing as words: 'the quiet communication of affectionate understanding [which] can be conveyed as well by a squeeze of the hand as by speech' (1998: 175). This may be particularly so with suicide, when conventional words of sympathy can be more difficult to express.

Some newly bereaved survivors had reacted to the shock by being frantically busy; others, however, had found themselves almost totally unable to function on a practical level, and friends and neighbours who came round, took over the day-to-day housekeeping such as cooking meals, and generally assisted with preparations for the funeral had been parti- cularly welcome. Francesca could recall 'a wonderful sense of just being looked after . . . because normally it is me who does the looking after'. Apart from the fact that this sort of practical help provides positive support to survivors, it also offers a role to friends who feel less comfortable with the listening role described above.

As this chapter has already mentioned, other people will sometimes refer to the victim in ways which are hurtful to survivors. As Pam commented, 'Outsiders tend not to think too highly of people who have taken their own lives.' Because this does tend to happen, survivors can find it especially helpful to know that other people had loved and valued the person and that they would be missed. Although Maureen had been hurt by some of the comments made after Paul's death, when so many people felt they wanted to come and say goodbye, it was a healing experience:

> When I went [to the undertakers] on the day of the funeral I was so overwhelmed . . . and so proud of him . . . All those friends going to visit him and all those people queuing up to go in and say their last goodbye, you know, to touch him and kiss him . . . I was really touched, really proud of him . . . and it took the hurt away because I felt proud of him. I think that helped.

Survivors of suicide need to feel that they can face other people, and that friends will be there to support their grieving. They need the opportunity to talk about the death and the person who died, to express painful emotions, including possible anger or guilt. As this chapter has shown, though, facing the world is not always easy; survivors have their difficulties – and so do those around them. Both need to be aware of this, and as Kast has suggested: 'We must learn again to find ways to mourn with one another' (1988: 18).

Chapter 12

Looking for support*

I needed some help totally removed from the family . . . I felt safe with [a GP-based] counsellor. (Ursula)

If I could just have talked with somebody else, just to somebody else that it had happened to, just to say how much I blamed myself and they could say, 'Well everybody feels like that, you know. I felt like that, and it's not your fault.' (Jennifer)

Earlier studies of the impact of suicide have suggested that with self-inflicted deaths: 'the coping mechanisms of the bereaved . . . are especially likely to be thrown into disarray' (Shepherd and Barraclough 1979: 67). But while subsequent research has modified the view that suicide bereavement is necessarily always a catastrophic event (Clark and Goldney 2000), survivors may still look for support outside their own family and social networks.

The people interviewed for this book had found help from a number of different sources including: general practitioners and other members of the primary care team, volunteer bereavement counsellors, other non-specialist counsellors, psychotherapists, psychiatrists, social workers, clergy, and other survivors.

Help from 'outsiders' such as bereavement counsellors should not supplant the support of family and friends because 'the care of the bereaved is

---

* The survivors in this book were interviewed in the late 1980s, since when specialist help for bereaved people has become more widely available, from both voluntary organisations and professionals (Parkes 1998). However, specialist help for suicide survivors remains very patchy. Some bereavement services are well informed about the particular issues likely to arise in suicide bereavement and some professionals also have relevant knowledge and experience, but this is by no means universal. Newly bereaved survivors can still find it difficult to get the help they need, so although Chapter 15 provides a more up-to-date picture of support services, this chapter has been retained. It is also retained as part of this second edition because the survivors' experiences of looking for and using support are an integral part of their stories.

a communal responsibility' (Parkes 1998: 197). After her brother's suicide, Jane had supportive friends who were 'able to sit and listen and receive it, and not be embarrassed or frightened'. She remembers one evening in particular when she was with two friends: 'I started to cry a lot, and they didn't try to stop me or even make me talk; they quietly got on with things and let me cry, and in the circumstances it was extremely helpful . . . it's acceptance really.' Nevertheless, she also went to see a psychotherapist who helped her deal with particular aspects of her loss.

Marris suggests that 'the stranger' can sometimes more easily support the bereaved in working through and resolving their grief:

> A stranger, who understands grief in general and stands in an acknowledged therapeutic role, can probably give more support to the working out of grief itself . . . this support is in a sense impersonal, it does not threaten to pre-empt the personal resolution of the crisis . . . it offers reassurance that the crisis is natural, that it will find a resolution in time.
>
> (1978: 153)

Survivors need to find their own solutions, their own way through their grief. Even friends who are good listeners can sometimes be tempted to put forward their own solutions, but as Staudacher says, 'counsellors don't want to "fix" you' (1988: 221).

Support in the early stages

Whatever the events leading up to the death, and however much warning survivors may have been given, when the suicide actually happens it is still likely to be a major shock for those who were closest to the person who died. In the days immediately after the suicide, survivors encounter many strangers, including the police and other emergency services, the coroner's officer, and undertakers. While they can support survivors through providing appropriate information and explanations (Clark and Goldney 2000), their main roles are not generally supportive (though their interventions may be experienced as helpful and therefore supportive by some survivors).

It has been suggested that survivors can benefit from help being available in the first twenty-four hours, to offer what Resnik (1972) has described as 'psychological first aid'. Survivors are likely to be shocked and dazed at this point and any attempt to help them explore feelings would be inappropriate and even potentially harmful. What may be helpful, however, is having someone in a supportive role who can assist the survivor with decisions such as whether to view the body, what kind of funeral to arrange and how and what to tell other people about the death.

Immediately after her mother's death, Janice went to her local women's counselling and therapy centre where she was able to see a counsellor in their drop-in service. This helped her deal with the immediate issue of whether to go and see her mother's body. The undertaker was advising her not to, and her sister told her she thought it pointless; by talking it through with someone who was not involved, and who could look at the situation objectively, Janice was able to make her own decision, rather than going along with what everyone else was telling her to do. There are a growing number of walk-in centres which offer immediate help for a range of different problems, and although they tend to be based in major centres of population they are a potential source of immediate help for survivors.

Some survivors will contact their general practitioner at the time of the death or shortly afterwards (see pp. 141–142), although getting this help is not necessarily easy, as Carol discovered. The morning after her son's suicide, she rang the surgery requesting a home visit but was told by the receptionist this was not possible and she must come down to the surgery if she wanted to see a doctor. Even when she explained the reason for her request, she was still told a home visit was out of the question, and an appointment was made for her to attend the surgery. It was only after she failed to keep the appointment that her doctor finally came round to the house.

Finding and using support services

Support from relatives and friends often tails off after the first few weeks, but as the shock begins to wear off, and the intense feelings of grief start to emerge, this may be the point at which some sort of external support is needed. Whether survivors are able to find the support they need can depend on a number of different factors, including the availability of appropriate services, how well services are publicised, the kind of referral systems which operate, and the length of time people have to wait to be seen.

Carol had been given the local contact for Compassionate Friends by her general practitioner, and her vicar had told her about CRUSE, but most of the survivors who were in touch with CRUSE or Compassionate Friends had stumbled upon these organisations by chance, either through reading about them in newspapers or magazines, or by hearing them mentioned on radio or television.

After Caroline's suicide, Robert and his wife eventually managed to get in touch with other parents, but they only discovered the Compassionate Friends' Shadow of Suicide (SOS) network (see Appendix 1) by chance, and they had already given up scouring the telephone directories when their daughter Nicola happened to come across the address at her place of work.

Robert and his family found the help they needed in the end because they persisted, but as he says: 'unless you are articulate enough to seek help, then there's no machinery that will follow [you] up'. As he pointed out, though, survivors are in contact with various officials such as coroners and the police who could make this sort of information available. Getting hold of information was often a haphazard process; there was no system whereby survivors routinely received information about organisations they might want to contact either immediately or at some future point.

Some survivors were very clear that they wanted support specifically from fellow survivors; they saw them as the only people who could possibly be of any help to them. After her brother took his own life, Jane really wanted the chance to talk to other people who had been through this particular sort of bereavement; ideally she wanted to meet other sibling survivors. Both her parents had already died, and seeing a bereavement counsellor was not something she felt would be particularly useful; she felt she knew enough about bereavement in general; as she said, 'I'd had lots of it'.

Carol, who had been given contacts in both CRUSE and Compassionate Friends, initially went to see a general bereavement counsellor, but felt this had its limitations:

> I didn't feel that she had shared the same experiences, and I don't think that without shared experience that they can give the help that's really needed. They can be a listening ear but not the sort of listening ear that understands, and I think that's something that you do need in the early stages, [but] whether it's just me, I don't know.

Survivors can find it difficult to accept support from people who have not been through the same experience. They may feel they do not deserve to be alongside other bereaved people; as one parent said, 'they would probably think that my child *chose* to die', almost implying that the survivor's grief is also self-inflicted. Survivors who are blaming themselves for the suicide may feel unworthy of other people's care and support. The sense of being different and set apart from other people may convince survivors that they should remain apart, particularly if they think other people may be blaming them anyway. Finally, if survivors are in a support group with other bereaved people, they may feel inhibited from talking about the more shocking aspects of the suicide.

Although only a minority of survivors will need help from mental health services, they may be reluctant to approach services if they feel these services have let them down so badly. Relatives may feel bitter and disappointed, with services which they see as having contributed to the person's death. Although she never sought help for herself, nine months after Patricia's death Francesca admitted: 'All my anger is towards the hospital, and still is . . . I don't think I've plumbed any depths of anger towards Patricia yet . . . it's all gone to the hospital.'

Survivors may have very real doubts as to whether services which seemingly failed to help their relative can possibly help them. After her son's suicide Carole asked her GP to refer her to an NHS psychiatrist and after a wait, during which she saw a private psychotherapist, she had five sessions with a psychiatrist who specialised in bereavement. But despite this, she still feels that, after what happened to Jon, she now has little real faith in psychiatry. She also saw Jon's psychiatrist once after the suicide, but when it came to the second appointment, she decided not to go:

> He had told me that he did not think Jon was depressed, that he showed no obvious signs of depression at their last meeting. Why does a person kill themselves if they are not depressed? How far could I trust this man's judgement if he could make such a catastrophic error? How did he feel about it? Was Jon just a statistic to him? He didn't say.

Some survivors meet with the psychiatrist or therapist who had been treating the person who died although the reasons for these meetings are not always clear, and can be an uneasy and uncomfortable experience, as Carole discovered. On a more positive note, though, such meetings can provide both parties with the opportunity to talk together about the suicide; Francesca met four times with her daughter's psychotherapist to talk about Patricia and about what had happened.

When one of their patients dies, psychiatrists, psychotherapists, or other health care professionals also become 'survivors' (see Chapter 2), and their own feelings about the suicide may make it difficult for them to initiate contact with other family members. However, a recent study found that while eleven out of twelve families of psychiatric patients who had taken their own lives would like to have seen their relative's psychiatrist, in only one case were they offered that opportunity (Brownstein 1992).

Some survivors had found it difficult to get help because services were oversubscribed. Although Janice had been able to see someone at her local women's counselling and therapy centre on an emergency basis (see above), there was a waiting list for longer-term therapy, so she had to find a private therapist. It took Brian fifteen months after his wife's death to find the help he wanted. Although he feels he has benefited considerably from fortnightly sessions with a bereavement counsellor, he wishes he had been able to get this sort of help sooner.

Even when survivors have found someone who they hope will help them, they may discover that professionals can find it hard to cope with their own feelings about death: 'Even professional helpers . . . often defend themselves so thoroughly against the savage pain and anguish of loss through bereavement that they avoid facing it and are thus unable to support the necessary task of mourning' (Pincus 1974: 48). Marie, who is both a survivor and a trained psychiatric social worker, suggests that 'suicide is such a painful and difficult area, it is understandable that even the professionals seem to find it difficult to help'. When she returned to work after her husband's suicide, she found that, with one exception, if she started talking about Oliver's death, her social work colleagues would all melt away. As Parkes points out, although someone may have been trained in medicine, social work or counselling, this does not necessarily mean that they 'are well trained in the care of the bereaved' (1998: 180–1).

Experiences with general practitioners

Whereas in the past, the Church would often have been the main source of comfort and help, newly bereaved people are now more likely to turn to their general practitioner. Research has shown that recently bereaved people tend to consult their family doctor more often than prior to the death (Parkes 1998). Suicide survivors are no exception; most of the people I met had had some contact with their general practitioner, however fleeting, although the sort of help they had been offered varied considerably.

The average GP is likely to have one patient death by suicide every three to four years and a group practice with a list of 10,000 will have perhaps one suicide death annually (Wertheimer 1996). GPs vary in their approach to patients who have suffered a bereavement. A recent survey found that practices were divided about whether bereavement support should be proactive or reactive (Harris and Kendrick 1998). However, another study found that the GP was more likely to initiate contact if the death was unexpected and/or particularly traumatic (Sanderson and Ridsdale 1999).

According to Parkes, members of the medical profession are 'acquainted with the reality of death', and this, he adds, 'should make it possible for the bereaved to talk to them about this taboo topic' (1998: 192). However, by no means all GPs will be comfortable when faced with the relatives of a suicide victim. Many survivors sensed their GP's unease, and talked of how their doctor seemed unsure what to say; Heather's experience was not atypical:

> He just was hopeless, and he's a nice person and he just hadn't a clue . . . He came in. He was sorry. He sat in the garden, he had his case with him, and he offered us drugs, naturally, and we said 'What we want is help, we don't want drugs. Can you put us in touch with somebody who'll help us?' And he said, 'I don't know of anybody . . . the best thing you can do is talk to each other' and that was it. So we came a bit unstuck with the GP . . . he didn't give us any comfort or help.

Survivors were commonly offered medication by their doctor, although some people had already made up their minds, before visiting the surgery, that they did not want to take any drugs. Some time before her daughter's suicide, Pat had become dependent on tranquillisers, but had managed to wean herself off them – without a great deal of encouragement from her doctor who she described as 'a bit pill happy'. When she went to see him after Caroline's death, however, she found his approach more helpful:

> He said, 'I'm not going to give you any pills, because there are no pills for grief', and he was right really. It's something you've got to get through . . . He was very good . . . what he did say was 'My door is always open. You can come and see me whenever you want, any time, just come, the door is open.'

Very few of the survivors I met had used medication, except perhaps to help them get through the first few days. For people whose relative had died as the result of an overdose this was a particularly sensitive issue. Susan remembers the thoughtless advice she received after her husband's death, when well-meaning friends urged her to take sleeping tablets, even though they knew that Richard had overdosed on barbiturates.

But apart from medication, what sort of support can general practitioners offer to survivors of suicide? Are they able to offer counselling, or, if they lack the relevant skills, are they able to refer patients on to more appropriate sources of help? Do they hold up-to-date information on local or national bereavement organisations? The answer would seem to be, it depends on your particular doctor: Heather's doctor (see p. 141) had no idea where she could find help, but Carol was told about Compassionate Friends. When it comes to counselling, some survivors were fortunate in being registered with a practice which had a counsellor attached, but others had a doctor who they felt was not well equipped to deal with emotional problems.

Doctors, like others in the helping professions, can be the target of survivors' blame. At the same time, they may be blaming themselves for the fact that their patient committed suicide; all this can make the patient–doctor relationship somewhat uneasy, as Marie discovered. Although she felt that perhaps their doctor could have done more for her husband, she found herself reassuring him that he had done all he could, and telling him he was not to blame – when what she actually wanted to do was change to another doctor in the practice.

Use of counselling and psychotherapy

Although only a minority of survivors will seek out this kind of help, it can be an important source of support, and a means of working through some of the complex feelings and thoughts associated with suicide bereavement. The provision of counselling and therapy is gradually increasing, and, with the advent of 'advice' phone-ins on radio, more people are beginning to understand its potential benefits. In addition to counsellors and therapists who are trained to work with a range of problems, the number of bereavement counsellors is increasing, many working through local CRUSE branches.

As already mentioned, survivors may discover that family and friends have difficulty in offering adequate support; other people may be over-whelmed by their own feelings, or simply not be comfortable with talking about suicide. This can make it hard for survivors to find someone with whom they can share their feelings. A counsellor or therapist, on the other hand, can allow the bereaved to express their thoughts and feelings openly without the survivor having to worry about how the other person is coping; as Staudacher suggests: 'You can be allowed to feel the way you do – not talked out of it' (1988: 220). Christine, who started seeing a bereavement counsellor shortly after her husband's suicide, found it helpful to talk about Graham's death, 'and not feel it upset [him]. I mean, it still upsets my friends and relatives – and I can't really discuss it with them.'

The feelings of guilt commonly associated with suicide bereavement may be difficult to talk about with family and friends – who may have their own views on who was to blame anyway. The listening which a counsellor offers can enable survivors to explore their sense of guilt, and test the reality of those feelings in a safe and non-judgemental atmosphere (Worden 1991). Eileen, whose twin daughters had both taken their own lives, found that like many parent-survivors, she blamed herself continually for not having been a better mother. Sessions with a counsellor enabled her to reach a somewhat different perspective on her guilt and begin to recognise 'that every parent does what they feel best at the time'.

Survivors may feel that other people are holding them responsible for the death. Counselling can help survivors examine the validity of these feelings, to see whether other people really do see them as guilty or whether this is something arising from their own sense of culpability. After Brian's wife took her own life, he began to wonder whether his two grown-up sons perhaps held him responsible in some way for Judy's death, but did not feel able to discuss these thoughts with anyone. It was only when he started seeing a counsellor that he could explore this issue – and recognise that his guilt was unrealistic.

Non-communication between family members is not uncommon; after both of Marjorie's sisters had committed suicide, she became increasingly upset when her mother, Eileen, refused to talk to her about the twins and their deaths. After another member of the family had pointed this out to her, Eileen decided to seek help from a counsellor. This not only helped her to deal with her guilt, but enabled her to start talking with her surviving daughter about the twins' deaths. Counselling can help to re-open channels of communication which may have become blocked or distorted.

The sheer intensity of the survivor's feelings can be frightening – both for the survivor and for those around them. Counselling or therapy offers a setting in which the survivor can feel safe to face the sort of feelings which, elsewhere, may seem potentially overwhelming. As Ursula said at the beginning of this chapter, she needed to talk to someone outside the family and felt safe with a counsellor.

One way of dealing with potentially overwhelming feelings is to put a lid on them, pretend they do not exist. Melanie, who started seeing a counsellor two months after her husband's suicide, found counselling helped her get in touch with her buried feelings. 'Initially I was just so distant', she says, 'I don't think I could quite think it was real.' For Janice, sessions with a Gestalt therapist offered a direct means of getting in touch with her emotions. Although she found the Gestalt method rather confrontational, she felt it was right for her because, as she admitted, 'I'm very good at just talking and not letting the emotions out'.

Survivors are frequently coping people; that is how they see themselves, and how other people tend to see them too. The trauma of suicide can threaten anyone's coping strategies, but for someone who has always coped, acknowledging their own need for support can be difficult. Jane had been seeing a psychotherapist since her brother's suicide, but admitted that reaching the point of accepting that she needed help was not easy: 'I think my unconscious took me there because I needed it, but I went protesting.' Even after she started her therapy, relinquishing the coping role did not come easily:

> Once I was there it took me many many months to say 'I'm fed up with coping', to acknowledge that that was what I was doing . . . It kept coming out that I was really angry about being this coping person . . . out is coming all the anger that I've bottled up all those years.

In Jan's case, it was many years before she could begin to acknowledge that she no longer had to go on coping as she had done since her father's suicide when she was thirteen. Over the years, she has worked on many issues relating to her father's suicide, but during a recent osteopathy session, when her head was being cradled, she was surprised to find herself sobbing uncontrollably. It was only afterwards that she realised she could allow someone else to do the holding, and that she could let go. The child whose mother had died when she was ten, and whose father killed himself three years later had grown into the adult who, as she says, had always told the world, 'I'll manage, I'll show you, I'll do it all on my own.'

When the bereavement occurred in childhood, it can be as many as twenty or thirty years before the survivor finds help. But even adults may not immediately recognise their need for help. As Dunne points out, some survivors look for help straight after the suicide, while other survivors seek therapy only after many months or years of living with a host of unpleasant conditions and feelings (1987b: 196). Kevin and Jan, who experienced the suicide of a parent when they were children, both feel they have benefited from therapy as adults. In his mid-thirties at the time of interview, Kevin had been in therapy for the past year; twenty years after his mother committed suicide, when his sister had a major breakdown and attempted suicide, he realised that he needed to find help:

> My sister's illness triggered a lot of emotions in me . . . my life was becoming more and more intolerable because of the gap between thinking and feeling . . . You can actually only go on for a certain period of time not feeling . . . and it's a sense of me needing to move on . . . [to] grow and to become real and complete . . . and it's very difficult to actually get involved in relationships and be a real person if there are some major gaps . . . and bits which have been frozen for a very long time.

Kevin can acknowledge how much he has been helped by therapy, but he still resents the fact that it is something he has *had* to do. For Jan, too, it felt as though there was no real choice about entering therapy: she had to confront her past: 'It's a kind of blight that I know I have to deal with . . . It does feel for me about survival to have dealt with some of these issues.' For some people, the legacy of suicide can literally feel like a matter of life or death, of surviving or not surviving.

Self-help and mutual support

As Jennifer said at the beginning of this chapter, she really needed to talk to somebody who had been through a similar experience, but when she needed that, self-help or mutual support groups for suicide survivors were very thin on the ground.

A number of parent-survivors had established contact with the Compassionate Friends' SOS (Survivors of Suicide) network. The nature and level of contact with other parent-survivors varied but included: becoming members of Compassionate Friends and receiving their newsletter; being in touch with other parents by letter and/or telephone; meeting with another parent on a one-to-one basis; attending meetings locally; and attending the national gatherings of the Shadow of Suicide group which are held from time to time.

After their daughter's suicide, Robert and his wife had searched for help for some time before they came across the SOS network; Robert has vivid memories of Pat's first contact with another parent survivor:

> there was a sort of relief on her face, that she'd actually found someone, because so many people say, 'I know how you must feel', and really I wanted to hit them, and say 'You can't possibly know how I feel. There is no way you can know how I feel.'

As previous chapters have described, when one member of the family commits suicide, survivors may feel that their entire family is abnormal, stigmatised, and different from other families. Meeting fellow-survivors can often help families like this to see themselves in a less negative light. After her son's suicide, Heather attended a national gathering of SOS; for her this was:

> a real life-saver. I couldn't believe that all those people were so nice . . . and their children had died . . . I'd felt we must be a horrendous family to have had a child who could be so unhappy, but they weren't horrendous, so it followed that I wasn't.

Like a number of other parents, Heather had also been helped by reading Anne Downey's book about her son's suicide in which she describes her pressing need to find other people who had gone through a similar experience:

> you really believe for a while that you are the only one to whom it has happened. There is a great desire in the beginning to find someone else who has gone through this traumatic experience. It is an almost desperate searching as though you have some rare disease for which there is no cure . . . It does not seem to matter what state they are in so long as they are able to tell you that the same thing happened to them . . . You become one of the many instead of one alone.
>
> (1987: 93)

As she points out, survivors will be in different states, partly because everyone grieves in their own way, but also because some survivors will be further down the road. Pam, who, together with her husband, has supported many other parents in the ten years since their daughter's suicide, has found that newly bereaved parents can benefit considerably from meeting others whose loss was less recent. 'It's nice', she says, 'just to meet somebody who says "OK, we've been through it, and look, we're still alive, and I didn't think I would live through it."' This is one of the benefits of mutual aid: parents can act as support models for one another, and having been helped by less recently bereaved parents, many survivors appreciated the opportunity that SOS gave them to help other parents in turn. They wanted to be able to contribute something.

Like the experiences of some of those who were in therapy, meetings of survivors could also provide a setting where it was safe to acknowledge and talk about feelings which could not easily be expressed elsewhere. As Irene commented: 'People can say things they'd never say to the husband or wife or whoever's at home. [You] can admit to suicidal feelings which you can't at home.' This is borne out by Appel and Wrobleski who, from their involvement with support groups, have found that survivors 'can experience unconditional caring and support for the expression of whatever feelings may be plaguing them' (1987: 223).

Whatever the cause of death, the bereaved may question why the death happened and whether they could in any way have prevented it. Mutual support groups can provide a place where it is acceptable to air these thoughts and feelings, knowing that those who listen will understand why survivors need to do this. As Carol discovered: '[they] understood what I was going through . . . and why I was going through it . . . and the sort of search for the whys and the if-onlys'. Self-help and mutual support groups can provide a listening ear for the sort of searching which Carol was going through; but other survivors can also help them see that perhaps they do not need to go on shouldering responsibility for the death, and that anyone can miss what were understood to be clues or threats when it was too late. With the help of other parents, survivors can learn to be more self-forgiving, and more realistic about the limits of their responsibility for the death.

Some of the people whose experiences are described here felt very strongly that they would only join a group for others bereaved by suicide. On the other hand, Brian had found the experience of belonging to an ordinary bereavement group very supportive and helpful. In practice, there may be little or no choice.

Moving on

Bereavement is a process which people move through and, if all goes well, emerge from at some point; Chapter 14 will look at some of the ways in which survivors begin to come through their grief and pick up the threads of life again. One marker on the road to recovery may be when survivors decide they no longer need to be involved in a bereavement group. They can, to some extent, leave the world of the bereaved and rejoin the wider community.

Nancy was helped by Compassionate Friends, and she in turn has supported other parents. For the last few years she has been secretary of her local group, but now feels ready to relinquish her involvement, so has resigned from her post: 'It's time I moved on . . . one doesn't want to be a member for a long, long time . . . I no longer need to talk about Clare.'

For other survivors, a decision to stop seeing a counsellor or therapist is about feeling they are ready to move on. This does not necessarily mean that their grieving has come to an end, but the feelings are probably less intense, and occur less frequently. Janice decided to stop seeing her therapist about a year after her mother's death:

It was time for me just to get on with my life, but to be aware that I was still going to get upset, and if I did that was OK and I could cry, and I could be feeble sometimes about it, and I shouldn't just clam up about it.

Good support should offer help with the immediate tasks of mourning, but it should also equip the survivor to cope in the future, when grief re-emerges, as it inevitably will from time to time, even though the feelings will be less strong and less painful.

This chapter has been mainly concerned with the support offered by general practitioners, counsellors, therapists and fellow survivors. Earlier chapters touched on the role of other helpers, and in particular the clergy (Chapter 8) and the survivor's social network (Chapter 9). But although more fortunate survivors will find the help they need, this will not always be the case. Chapter 15 will look at some of the ways in which we may, in future, provide better support for survivors.

Chapter 13

Facing the feelings

There are lots of aspects that are exactly the same [as other bereavements], but there are also aspects that are different. (Ursula)

I thought he loved us too much to actually do that to us, because it's such a cruel thing to do . . . So you get all these dreadful mixed-up feelings, and it's a different sort of bitterness from somebody who dies of other types of disease. (Susan)

It's a relief because somebody like that, they're an emotional burden on you, you can't run away from it . . . she was a worry . . . I'd give anything to have her back, have her here, but that's not really the choice. (Dick)

'Grief', writes Parkes, 'is a process and not a state' (1998: 7), a psychological process which is characterised by phases: 'numbness, the first phase, gives place to pining and pining to disorganization and despair, and it is only after the stage of disorganization that recovery occurs' (1998: 7). Parkes' concept of phases or stages provides a useful framework for understanding the process of grieving, and it is unfortunate that it has been widely misunderstood. It is not a fixed sequence through which everyone who is bereaved must pass before they can recover. Neither is it a linear process: people may move back and forth. As Parkes makes clear, 'there are considerable differences from one person to another as regards both the duration and the form of each phase' (1998: 7). There are rarely distinct phases, and one may overlap with another. In the words of one survivor: 'Patterns they may have been, yet they were experienced as an onslaught of strange, extreme contradictory feelings' (Toop 1996).

The structure of this chapter, which describes emotions under discrete sub-headings, may assist the reader, but may also mask the reality of the survivors' experiences, which are often associated with the phase of 'disorganisation and despair'. Grieving is often chaotic; sometimes a single feeling will predominate, while at other times it can feel, as one survivor said, 'like a bag of every emotion under the sun'. Survivors may experience rapid and large mood changes (Clark and Goldney 1995).

It may appear odd to have a separate chapter about emotions, when so much of the rest of this book is also about feelings. Reactions such as guilt and anger have already been mentioned at various points so why another chapter? Up to this point, most of the discussion has been about the survivor's experiences in relation to the rest of the world: the public rituals of funerals and inquests, relationships with family and friends, and their contact with support services. This chapter is more concerned with aspects of grieving which survivors must go through on their own – in what Marris has called 'the ultimate privacy of grief' (1978: 153). As Pincus reminds us: 'without an ongoing interaction with [the dead person] . . . the whole painful and complicated process of separation has to be worked out entirely by the survivor alone' (1974: 46).

The survivor's inner dialogue

As survivors talked, their stories often took on the form of a dialogue, a questioning, a searching which they had undertaken alone, and were now recounting for the listener's benefit. It is the dialogue they are now unable to have with the other person. Frequently it seemed to represent the survivor's attempt to work through some of the particularly painful legacies of suicide – the guilt, the anger, the search for understanding. Susan's thoughts are typical of this sort of internal dialogue or, more accurately, a monologue:

> I could have forced him to have treatment, I suppose, but I chose to let him choose, and I suppose for that I might feel guilty, but I don't . . . but if I had realised he was going to commit suicide, perhaps I would have done; I mean, what happened was that I never thought that he would actually leave us like that – I thought that he loved us too much.

In that brief monologue, there are questions of power and control ('I could have forced him'), about freedom and autonomy ('I chose to let him choose'), about testing the reality of guilt ('I might feel guilty, but I don't'), about wisdom with hindsight ('had I realised'), a denial of the possibility of suicide ('I never thought he'd leave us'), and a sense of being rejected by the victim ('I thought he loved us too much'). As Marris has suggested: 'the process of grief seems to be the working out of conflicting impulses . . . [and] this conflict is crucial to an understanding of grief and mourning' (1978: 28).

Some survivors had written down their thoughts and feelings, sometimes in 'letters' to the dead person; Anne Downey (1987), for example, wrote her book *Dear Stephen* as a letter to her dead son. After her brother's suicide,

Jennifer also found writing helped her: 'I wrote down things simply because I wanted to at the time, and it got it out of my head.' Other survivors had expressed their feelings in poetry.

Writing can also be a means of reaching some understanding about the suicide death, perhaps drawing a line under the question 'why did this happen?' As Tim Lott says, in the final chapter of his book *The Scent of Dried Roses*, written following his mother's suicide, 'I have used it to work through some conclusions that I consider to be firm, to be final' (1997: 269).

Anthony Storr, in his book *Solitude*, suggests that the creative act of writing 'is one of the ways of overcoming the state of helplessness . . . a coping mechanism, a way of exercising control as well as a way of expressing emotion' (1989: 129), a point echoed more recently by Virginia Ironside (1996). For survivors of suicide, who may be experiencing extreme shock and horror, writing may be a means of exercising a measure of control over potentially overwhelming emotions. C.S. Lewis's book *A Grief Observed*, written after his wife had died from cancer, became a bestseller, but as he said, it was something he needed to do: 'partly as a defence against total collapse, a safety valve' (1966: 50).

Staudacher (1988) suggests there may be several potential benefits in keeping a journal or diary: because it is a private activity, previously denied aspects of the survivor's relationship with the victim can be safely expressed; constantly recurring thoughts when written down may lose some of their obsessive quality; and survivors may find they are recording thoughts of which they were not previously aware.

The same as other bereavements?

Comparative studies (see p. 23) suggest that there are particular themes and issues in suicide bereavement which while not necessarily unique are more common than among the bereaved in general. Certainly many of the feelings described in this chapter are likely to strike a familiar chord with other bereaved people. As Ursula said at the start of this chapter, though, it is both the same and different. This is echoed by Barbara Porter, founder of one of the first survivor support groups in the UK, who describes suicide bereavement as 'like other bereavements, but more so'.

Survivors of suicide may have certain things in common with several different groups of bereaved people; like those bereaved as the result of murder, for example, the death was sudden, untimely, and often violent. Robert described his daughter's suicide as a triple burden: 'the sudden death, the sudden death of a child, and the sudden death of a child by suicide'. Shneidman describes how: 'the person who commits suicide puts his psychological skeleton in the survivor's emotional closet . . . he sentences the survivor to deal with many negative feelings . . . It can be a heavy load' (1972: x).

Returning for a moment, though, to Parkes' (1998) phases of grieving. Survivors often seem to remain in a state of numbness which characterises the first stage of grieving for longer than many other bereaved people. Suicide deaths are sudden, and often violent, and prolonged shock is, therefore, a normal reaction. Brian, for example, described his mourning as 'dreadfully slow, with a numbness that must have gone on for nine months or a year'. Ursula also found getting through to the feelings took a long time: 'Although you know all these things, I don't think you really start feeling them for an awful long time.'

When the numbness wears off, however, there can be an intense period of grieving. Carol returned to her teaching job only a few weeks after her son's suicide; perhaps this stopped her from dwelling too much on what had happened, but it was six months later when her real feelings of grief emerged:

> for six months I'd cried, but not really cried, if you understand what I mean . . . I cried on the surface, but not properly crying, and I sort of survived and survived and survived, and it was a week in June . . . I completely went to pieces . . . I couldn't stop crying . . . It was almost as if the protective layer was coming off.

The intense guilt experienced by some survivors can make grief less easy to resolve than with other bereavements. It may take survivors a long time to work through their feelings of guilt and anger.

Guilt and the if-onlys

> The guilt doesn't go away. I don't believe it will ever go away . . . I keep rationalising and everybody says, 'Of course you're not guilty', but of course you are; well, I believe I am, because who else was supposed to sort it out, and decide that he needed help? (Heather)

> If only I'd phoned him up then, if only I'd forced him to speak to me when I met him . . . he said he felt terrible; if only I'd said to him, 'For heaven's sake tell me about it'; if only I'd forced myself. (Suzy)

Guilt is a common bereavement reaction (Worden 1991; Parkes 1998), but may be more prevalent when the death was a suicide:

> The bereaved may feel they contributed to the suicide and blame themselves for not having prevented it. They may feel they should have been totally in control of the deceased to the extent of being overly responsible for them. They may blame themselves for the poor

relationship . . . 'If only' is a common phrase used to describe acts which might have helped to prevent the suicide . . . Guilt may also be felt at the sense of relief created by the death.

(Clark and Goldney 2000: 473)

Feelings of guilt can be intense, as Carol found: 'I thought I was a wicked, evil woman who had brought Alan's death upon myself – that I was the reason for it. I was guilty, I was wrong . . . I thought I was evil, and I cried and cried.'

The survivor's guilt can take many forms, and focus on many different things, depending on the individual's circumstances, and the relationship they had with the dead person. Where the death was apparently out of the blue, survivors may blame themselves for not having noticed anything was wrong; if suicide was known to be a possibility, survivors may blame themselves for not being there to stop it happening. Whatever the guilt is about, the result may be an unending list of 'if-onlys'. Survivors like Janice can find themselves caught up in a constant and repetitive dialogue:

I think after the asking 'why' it was probably the guilt bit . . . going over and over and over it, again and again – the Friday night phone call, to her, and the fact that I hadn't gone down to see her when I said I was going, and that I'd put it off quite a few weeks, and the sort of irony of the fact that I'd written her a letter that arrived [after she died] – and just sort of blaming myself and thinking of what I could have done and if onlys – if only the GP hadn't retired, if only I'd sent her that present which I meant to and never did – or if only I'd been more generous with her and had her to stay more often.

If these 'if-onlys' could be cancelled, and the clock turned back, the dead person would return to life. Many people carry round these lists of 'if-onlys', and letting go of them can sometimes be difficult. In an unconscious attempt to punish themselves, survivors may live permanently with their guilt, convinced that that is what they deserve for having been a bad parent or husband or whatever and unaware that much of their guilt is unrealistic. After his wife's suicide, John embarked on what he describes as 'a kind of self-imposed exile' which lasted two years; he felt responsible for Averil's death, and even reached the point where he began to wonder whether he had actually wanted her to die. By deciding that they are personally responsible for the suicide, survivors are perhaps wanting to feel that they had some power over the person who died, believing that they were totally in control of them. As Carole eventually realised:

I think that's partly what the guilt is wrapped up in – that I want to take all the responsibility for Jon's life . . . in fact he passed beyond

my responsibility, and he had a wide circle of friends and other relationships which would have had just as much bearing on the outcome
as my relationship to him.

In situations like this, survivors are sometimes continuing a power struggle
which may have been happening before the suicide (see pp. 59–61). But as
Staudacher (1988) points out, the death is not within the realm of the
survivor's control or power.

Support groups or individual interventions such as counselling or therapy
can all provide an opportunity for survivors to examine how realistic their
guilt is (see Chapters 16 and 17). Staudacher (1988) suggests that friends or
relatives can also help the survivor with this task. Occasionally, the survivor
has reality thrust upon them, as Isabel discovered. A practising Catholic,
she regularly went to confession, where she would talk about her guilt over
Eric's suicide, until one day, nearly two years after his death, she suddenly
heard the priest telling her he was fed up with hearing about this, would she
please not mention it again because she'd done what she could, and as far
as he was concerned, that was the end of the matter!

While guilt is a common theme in suicide bereavement, not all survivors
will feel responsible for the suicide (Clark and Goldney 2000). When
Wrobleski (1986) questioned 158 survivors about their feelings of guilt, 34%
responded that they felt 'moderately guilty', and 39% felt 'very guilty'.
However, 14% claimed to feel no guilt at all, and the remaining 13% felt
only mildly guilty. Some families will feel that they did all they could.

Anger

> I was furious with her. I've never been so angry with anybody in my life
> until the day she died . . . How dare she leave me in this bloody horrible
> world . . . that she made wonderful for me . . . that she helped me to
> love in . . . and then she left me. How dare you do this? Why did you
> do it? (John)

Anger is a common respose to loss; it can stem from frustration or bitterness that the death was not preventable, or it can be the rage of abandonment (Worden 1991). Lukas and Seiden suggest that with suicide, this
anger can have three elements: 'It is a rage at being rejected, at being
abandoned and at being accused' (1987: 56). Such rage can be extremely
powerful, as Carole discovered:

> After the continual weeping in the summer came fits of rage. I threw
> my body around and grovelled in anguish. I took to hurling things
> around, and beating myself continually against walls. I would pound
> my fists into beds and pillows, screaming with rage.

The survivor's anger can have many targets. It may be directed towards others in the family, friends, health care professionals, God, oneself and the person who died (Tekavcic-Grad and Zavasnik 1992; Clark and Goldney 1995, 2000). Feelings of anger towards the deceased may be the most difficult point to reach, and when the death was suicide, maybe survivors try to protect not only themselves but their memories of the person who died:

> Grief's anger has to show its face to be assuaged . . . guilt is present already and anger can unearth yet more guilt . . . a violent death compounds the difficulty. Parallel to anger there surges a deep need to idealise the dead . . . [to] erect the statue of a saint in place of a flawed human.
>
> (Toop, 1996)

Although Carol and John (quoted above) were able to express their anger about other people, aggression can be difficult to even recognise, let alone accept and express. Anger may be repressed and denied. It may be considered unacceptable, particularly if survivors feel they are to blame in some way for the death. It has also been suggested that aggression does not easily fit into the usual image of bereavement. Tears, sadness, apathy and depression are the feelings more often expected in the mourner (Tekavcic-Grad and Zavasnik 1992: 66). Those with experience of running suicide bereavement groups have noted how anger may be avoided in the meetings (Tekavcic-Grad and Zavasnik 1992; Clark and Goldney 1995).

The person who died may be blamed for having cheated the survivor. After a friend's suicide, the poet Rilke (1957) wrote of feeling as if a door had been slammed in his face. Survivors may resent the fact that they had no choice in the matter, but it is they, and not the victim, who are left to cope with the aftermath. Susan recalls the bitterness she felt after her husband committed suicide:

> I did feel bitter at what he'd done . . . Why should he think that I was strong enough to carry on without him . . . and I really did resent what he'd done to his son. I mean, it was a dreadful thing to do, wasn't it . . . it sounds awful, as though one's a horrible person but I resented [his suicide] . . . it was sixteen years I'd supported him and this is what he's left me with.

Anger directed towards the dead person can leave the survivor feeling particularly guilty. After her daughter's death, Phyllis would find herself 'telling' Julie how the suicide had ruined her life, but then apologising. As Vollman and colleagues point out: 'in the event of suicide . . . anger towards a dead person is widely felt not to be legitimate, and is only experienced with great discomfort' (1971: 102). After her son's death, Heather also found it difficult to allow her angry feelings to emerge and she fluctuated between anger and sadness:

> He's left us in a real mess . . . and I think well, if he left us in a real mess, what kind of a mess was he in? He must have been in a worse mess, and I can't really be angry . . . We said at the beginning, if he was to walk back in that door we'd all let him have it . . . yes, we've been cross with him, but I feel more basically very, very sad for him.

Coping with anger can be difficult; survivors may oscillate between guilt and anger – unsure whether it is the victim or themselves they should be feeling sorry for, unsure who is to blame. Anger and guilt may become confused. Melanie spent much of the first year blaming herself for Ian's death, but then her feelings changed:

> I just wanted to scream how unfair it was . . . because I was the one that went away because I wasn't coping very well, and yet he was the one who killed himself; but it was typical of him in a way because he couldn't bear me to have any attention to myself so in a way, by killing himself, he gave himself a lot more attention . . . Ian had a lot of choices and he gave me no choice at all.

Allowing feelings of anger towards the suicide victim to emerge may be difficult, but resenting the rest of the world can also be uncomfortable. Since their daughter's suicide, Robert and Pat have found family celebrations particularly hard, because as Pat said: 'It's very difficult to join in their joys . . . We do get resentful at times because they seem to have everything, and we can't have that.'

Rejection and insecurity

> I could not cope with the idea that Jon really wanted to die, so I kept pushing it to the back of my mind. It was too much of a blow to my ego for me to think that a child of mine would want to die, that my love was not enough to keep him alive. (Carole)

> Hell is a sort of underground bog.
> There are no landmarks. In it
> Those we have loved and failed
> Turn their backs for ever.
>   'The Guide', U.A. Fanthorpe (1982)

Suicide can be experienced as a deep affront to the survivor. A powerful message from the person who takes their own life can be 'an implicit condemnation of the world left behind' (Hill 1995: 153). Indeed, Hauser suggests that: 'in every suicide, there is a component of rejection' (1987: 65). The person who takes their own life implicitly rejects life, but in doing so, rejects family and friends too (Silverman 1994–5). Feelings of rejection can be more common amongst suicide survivors than amongst those grieving other deaths, leading Reed to conclude that:

> Rejection is unique to suicide bereavement. The differing nature of the sudden death suggests that attachment loss in bereavement situations produces separation anxiety among accidental death survivors, but generates feelings of rejection among suicide survivors.
>
> (1998: 297).

Survivors have described this rejection as a slap in the face, a rebuke, an injury or an insult. If the relationship with the person who died had been difficult, the death may be seen 'as a malicious act with no opportunity for redress' (Clark and Goldney 2000: 473). If the survivor believes that the person chose to end their life, they can feel that the other person also chose to end their relationship. In the words of a widower: 'she chose to end our marriage' and a father described his son's suicide as 'a slap in the face'.

Some survivors will react angrily to the implied rejection, but others will feel that this somehow confirms that they are not lovable – not by the deceased, but not by any one else either. In Irene's case, the feeling that nobody cared about her led her to attempt suicide:

> I didn't care about the grief I was leaving because I didn't expect that there would be any. I thought we'd used it all up on Bill, and I didn't particularly care what anybody thought about me and yet . . . I needed somebody to tell me that I was worth it.

The possible effects of this lack of self-worth and damaged self-esteem should not be underestimated; it can lead survivors to cut themselves off from other people, and thus from potential care and support. Having been let down once, there may be a loss of trust in other people. However much they want and need support, the possibility of being rejected again may stop them from seeking out other people. As a widow wrote:

> I fear relationships and I fear never having a close, loving caring and sharing relationship again. I feel I have no more to give. If I could cut myself off from humanity I would. I feel somehow that I am not worthy, that I am not wanted.

However, discovering that you can still be part of a loving relationship can be very healing. Eileen remembers how good it felt when her surviving daughter told her how much she enjoyed her mother's love and attention; it helped to counter her feelings about not having been a good parent to the twin daughters who had both taken their own lives.

Suicide may also be experienced by survivors as a rejection of their coping and caring functions. They may be left feeling that they are wholly inadequate since whatever they did and however much they tried to help, even that was rejected, and was not enough to keep the other person alive. For Brian, who had supported his wife through three years of mental illness and suicide attempts, this was one of the most painful aspects of her death: 'You obviously weren't adequate as a person, you weren't providing a good enough life, a happy enough environment or whatever, to make a person's life worth living – and that I found very hard.'

It can be difficult for survivors to reach the point of acknowledging that however much they had done, perhaps this could never have been enough to keep the other person alive.

Parallels have been drawn between the reactions of the bereaved and people facing other types of loss including amputation of a limb (Parkes 1998). Although not exactly a 'rejection', for some survivors the suicide is experienced as losing a part of themselves, of undergoing an enforced amputation. This may occur with spouses – who have lost their 'other half' – and with parents who have lost the child who was a part of them before birth. After her son's death, Pauline described it as feeling: 'as if I was on a railway, and my leg had been cut off by a train, and I had to get up and there was no support, there's nothing, and you have to get up and go, and how can you?' Other survivors talked about feeling that they had 'lost a limb', or been 'cut in half', and of 'a great huge chunk of your life that has gone'.

Bereavement can engender feelings of intense insecurity. It can, Parkes suggests, 'undermine one's faith in the world as an ordered and secure place' (1998: 85). The survivor may feel that it is only a matter of time before something just as dreadful happens again – and if it does, the world can seem even more precarious. When she was seventeen, Bridget had to cope with two suicides within five months, when one of her sisters and then her father took their own lives. As a result, she says:

> I was really dangerously worried for everybody I was close to after that
> . . . [worried] that my brothers might kill themselves or be alcoholic . . .
> or my [other] sister would go mad . . . I was really terrified and always
> thinking that another bad thing was going to happen.

Although her fears have diminished over the seven years since the suicides occurred, Bridget's sense of insecurity remains; she still sometimes finds herself suddenly panicking about someone in the family, and will have to telephone them and reassure herself they are all right. This sense of insecurity can also make it hard for trust to operate in any of the survivor's relationships: 'they can't trust their world and the people in it ever to treat them fairly again' (Lukas and Seiden 1987: 38). As a result, survivors may hold back from other people because, as Maureen says, 'you're frightened to think too much of anyone in case [they are] gone again'.

Stigma and shame

> I felt as if I had leprosy – it's a terrible feeling . . . I wanted the ground to swallow me up. (Pauline)

Suicide survivors experience higher levels of shame than other groups of bereaved people (Silverman et al. 1994–5; Seguin et al. 1995a), although this reaction is not experienced by all survivors. Shame may be linked to the stigma of suicide, although it would appear that this is linked to the cultural and religious context in which the death occurred. However, shame can also be linked to the survivor's own feelings of guilt, blame and rejection, as well as the associations of suicide with mental illness (Clark and Goldney 2000).

Feelings of shame and the sense of stigma can be very powerful. As Miriam found: 'I felt I was sort of stained by an atrocity which had made me accursed . . . so that I felt I was a sort of pollutant.' The fact that her husband had committed suicide left Melanie feeling not only undeserving of sympathy, but different from other widows: 'I wasn't a proper widow, he hadn't been run over by a bus or had a heart attack.'

As Seguin and her colleagues (1995a) suggest, the survivor may feel humiliated and believe that the suicide has brought dishonour and disgrace on the whole family. The stigma of suicide and the survivor's 'spoiled identity' (Goffman 1968) can lead to isolation, to feelings of not being 'normal', of being an outsider and, in Maureen's case, of not even being a part of the human race:

> I look at my next-door neighbour, and I feel I am not one of you any more – I'm not a normal person any more. I'm different. I've got nothing in common with anybody, my whole outlook has changed, the way I live has changed and I feel alienated . . . as if I belong to a different planet, with my own kind . . . but I don't want to belong to people of this grief . . . I don't want to be with all of these sad people . . . even my friend, good as she's been, I'm not on the same wavelength any more.

As Goffman suggests, the stigmatised person can 'manage' their experience of stigma by seeking out others with a similar experience (1968). For survivors of suicide, a support group can provide a temporary refuge.

Relief

> We had years and years of listening to Patricia going round in circles –
> over and over the same ground – and sometimes I felt I was going mad,
> because it's such a circular thing, depression . . . and it was very
> wearing and very hard, so that's a relief, not to have all that . . . I
> wouldn't have wanted to have years and years more of her being
> depressed and living at home. (Francesca)

> I thought, well obviously he was in a lot of pain, and he's not in it any
> more. I sort of felt, he's safe now. (Christine)

Newly bereaved people can experience a sense of relief, especially if death
had been preceded by a long or painful illness. In these circumstances, relief
can be an acceptable reaction; the person is no longer in pain, everyone
feels relieved that that is the case, and they will often say so to each other.

Survivors of suicide may also feel relieved that the person who died is no
longer suffering and in pain, though their pain was emotional rather than
physical:

> For some families, the suicide becomes a means of resolving existing
> problems . . . Families who have struggled for years with a depressed
> individual and suicidal threats may experience relief after suicide as
> their family life has an opportunity to return to normal.
>
> (Clark and Goldney, 2000: 471)

This is echoed by Seguin and her colleagues (1995a) who interviewed
parents bereaved as the result of their son's suicide or accident; for some
suicide bereaved families, the death had had a positive effect 'due to the
calm that had come back into their lives from not having to worry all the
time . . . The suicide, as painful as it might be for all family members was
perceived as a relief from all the difficulties and suffering for themselves and
for their son' (1995: 493).

Andrew had looked after his wife through several years of her mental
illness and heavy drinking so when she committed suicide: 'There was
sadness – but really an overwhelming feeling of peace.' When someone
takes their own life, however, relief can be less straightforward than with
other deaths. Survivors may be uncertain as to whether they are relieved for
the person who died or for themselves. When her daughter took her own
life, Ursula was left with the feeling that perhaps it was a relief for Josie but
perhaps for the rest of the family too:

> It was something at the back of my mind, I'd been fearing. I'd been
> dreading [it] for a long, long while . . . and in a sense, as I pulled up to

the house and saw the ambulance, I almost hoped she was dead because she so desperately wanted to be; the thought of dragging her back so that she could attempt again was even more horrific than her being dead . . . It was a positive thing she did, a conscious decision . . . so in a sense, although I felt awful, there was also a tremendous sense of relief. Something that had been going on for years was over, and something else began of course that was just as difficult.

As Ursula recognised, what was to follow would not be any easier. It is rare for survivors to experience uncomplicated and unmitigated relief. Even when the survivor had expected to feel relieved, this does not always happen, as Janice discovered when her elderly mother died. Their relationship had often been troubled, and Janice had often thought her death would be a relief. Because her mother committed suicide, though, her feelings were more complicated:

> because of having to cope with the way she died I think it wasn't a relief – and I just missed her, I still miss her terribly, I miss the phone calls, I miss the letters, even though, when she'd been alive, sometimes I dreaded the phone calls, and sometimes the letters came through the letter-box too often.

When Solomon (1981) interviewed ninety suicide survivors, nearly a third expressed feelings of relief, but some also admitted to a sense of guilt about feeling relieved. Even when there is relief, the survivor can still want the person back, as Mark discovered after his daughter took her own life: 'Strictly within the terms of selfishness, life has been better which is a paradox, isn't it? My life is better, but of course I would rather have her here than not.'

Even if the survivor does not experience the suicide as a relief, there can still be a sense of confusion: who am I hurting for, and do I have the right to feel so hurt about what the other person did when they were in such pain? For Peter, the pain of Susie's suicide was mingled with a feeling that perhaps he was being selfish:

> There's an element of me that's very hurt and very angry with Susie for committing suicide, because I feel betrayed, I suppose, in some sort of self-centred way. But if that was the only option Susie felt she had, then I really have to come to terms with that for Susie, and it's no good just loving her for me. I have to love her for her . . . I don't think she accounted for how we might feel, but I don't think she was in a position to account for that – the desperation was absolute.

Unravelling these complicated and sometimes conflicting feelings can be hard work for the survivor.

Suicidal feelings

> For some reason I felt cheated when he committed suicide . . . I was the one who wanted to die, and for some reason I felt I couldn't do it because he'd beat me to it. (Irene)

> Certainly one goes through periods of almost taking your own life because you say, well, what's the point? I mean, that *was* my life. I didn't really see staying alive for the boys as being an issue . . . I couldn't see that they needed me; my life had ended almost with her life. (Brian)

Suicidal thoughts are common amongst the bereaved. They may represent a wish to be reunited with the person who has died, to complete unfinished business, or be linked to depression (Clark and Goldney 2000). Serious suicide attempts and actual suicides are less common (Bowlby 1985).

Conflicting views have been expressed in the past as to whether survivors of suicide have an increased risk of taking their own lives. Lukas and Seiden (1987), for example, suggest that the suicide rate among survivors is between 80 and 300% higher than for the general population although they do not provide any evidence for this view. McIntosh (1987a), on the other hand, reviewed fourteen studies of which only six found an above-average risk among family and friends of suicide victims.

A more recent study (Brent et al. 1996b) suggests that suicidal behaviour does run in some families. However, as Clark and Goldney point out, 'those bereaved by suicide may be an "at risk" group not so much because of the mode of death but because suicide identifies the vulnerable' (2000: 470). In other words, the suicide may occur in a family which before the death was already vulnerable because of the problems which were present such as mental illness, other losses and disturbed relationships between its members (see pp. 24–25).

For some survivors, suicide may be linked to punitive feelings. It may be seen as a means of retaliation, a way of 'getting even' and not allowing the deceased to have the last word: 'I'll punish you, for punishing me so dreadfully'. But the idea of suicide may spring from a desire to punish other people who the survivor feels were to blame for the death: 'I'll teach them a lesson they won't forget.' For yet others, there may be a sense that they are 'fated' to die by suicide (Worden 1991). Someone whose parent died by suicide may believe that they will not live beyond the age when their parent took their own life. A sibling may believe they will not live beyond the age when their brother or sister died.

During a radio programme on suicide, Colin Murray Parkes made the point that: 'to some extent, suicide has to be learned'. Sometimes the very fact that someone close to the survivor has committed suicide can make a previously impossible idea suddenly seem possible; the unthinkable can become thinkable. When someone in the family takes their own life, in the words of one survivor, 'It enters your bloodstream.' The person who died communicates to those left behind that this is a way of solving seemingly insoluble problems. By taking their own life, they have breached the taboo against the taking of life. For the survivor who has always assumed that 'life is for living', the deceased challenges that assumption and suggests an alternative reality. Ann could still remember something that happened to her fifty-two years previously, on the day her brother committed suicide:

> I was walking somewhere, I suppose going to my lodgings; I remember just pausing to cross the road, and a bus was just coming up, and the thought went through my mind – shall I just walk out? I had absolutely no feeling in me, and I thought to myself, well, I might just as well be under that bus . . . It was just the feeling that I'd lost all feeling for life really.

As Jane said, after her brother's suicide, 'It's a real option which it wouldn't be to a lot of people', a point echoed by Behrens, after the suicides of his brother Justin, and Justin's mistress: 'I've found out that suicide is infectious', he wrote. 'If you have suicidal instincts and somebody in your immediate circle kills himself, it's hard not to think, whether consciously or not, "He had the courage to do it – why shouldn't I?"' (1988: 194).

Survivors may see suicide as a way of being reunited with the dead person. Heather was never actively suicidal, but she remembers wanting to be with her son:

> In the beginning it upset me a lot that I couldn't commit suicide, because I wanted to go with Alastair, and I felt that I had to go with him . . . but I couldn't leave [her daughter], you see, that was my dilemma. That caused me a lot of anguish because I knew I couldn't go with him.

Even when survivors are not actually contemplating suicide, they can display a complete indifference to death. In a manner reminiscent of the Hiroshima survivors (see p. 22) who had experienced 'a jarring awareness of the fact of death' (Lifton 1969: 481), the idea of dying no longer seemed quite so alien. As Jennifer found after her brother's suicide, it was not that she actually wanted to die but more a sense that it really would not matter if she did. For Robert, dying would, he felt, provide a welcome release:

Death doesn't mean that much, it really doesn't. It would be a release
from the pain of grieving to be perfectly honest – not in the sense [of]
wanting to take your own life, but [it] wouldn't be nearly as painful as
it was before Caroline died.

Some survivors will behave in self-destructive ways. While not actively
suicidal, they may place themselves in dangerous or even life-threatening
situations. In the particularly cold winter following her husband's suicide,
Irene deliberately neglected herself, ending up with bronchitis and frost-
bitten ears: 'I was hoping to get pneumonia, to be honest. I was hoping that
I would be so ill that I would die.'

Other reactions

The pain and intensity of grieving can make survivors feel they are going
mad. At other times they may display the kind of irrational behaviours,
common in any bereavement (Worden 1991), which can be a source of
considerable distress. After her daughter's suicide, Pat twice found herself
driving away from petrol stations without paying the bill, leading her to
fear she might start shoplifting.

In some cases, survivors find rituals for coping with the loss which,
though they can be a positive way of coping with feelings, can seem bizarre
or even mad to themselves – and other people. Wrobleski describes how
'survivors have so-called crazy thoughts, ideas and actions which bewilder
and frighten them' (1984–5: 177); but apparently abnormal feelings can be
a normal reaction to a major trauma such as suicide bereavement. In the
months after her son's death, Heather continually wanted to buy things for
Alastair, so she would buy his favourite foods, take them up to the local
forest where he had died, and throw them around. It was something she
needed to do, and as she said, throwing Jaffa cakes around could also be
quite fun really! She was only worried in case anyone saw her doing this.

Physical reactions to bereavement have been well documented in the
general bereavement literature (e.g. Raphael 1985; Worden 1991; Parkes
1998) and for some survivors, the pain of bereavement was experienced
physically as well as emotionally; several people had suffered from severe
chest pains – perhaps the symptom of a broken heart? For Lois, this
physical pain was intense: 'Sometimes the pain has been so bad that I've felt
I would pass out. I've never had such pain as I've had from his death.'
Worden makes an interesting point about pain: *Schmerz*, the German for
pain, has, he says, a broader definition than the English term, and includes
'the literal physical pain that many people experience and the emotional
and behavioural pain associated with loss' (1991: 13).

Two of the survivors had experienced a complete lack of interest in
sexual activity in the months following the suicide. Parkes (1998) suggests

that a diminished sexual appetite is not uncommon during the early stages of bereavement, although this is not always the case and a heightened need to cling to someone can lead to increased sexual activity.

Few of the survivors I met had been prescribed some kind of medication, and those who did had generally used it during the very early stages. However, at least half a dozen people mentioned having been through a phase where they had depended fairly heavily on alcohol, usually in the months immediately after the suicide. Sometimes this was because they had decided that alcohol was preferable to medication. (Perhaps it is also a more socially acceptable 'drug' than pills?) Mainly, though, it was seen to offer possible relief, however short-lived, from the intense pain of their bereavement, as well as the possibility of sleep without recourse to sleeping pills.

In his book on grief counselling, Worden poses the question, 'When is mourning finished?' but suggests it is 'a little like asking how high is up?' (1991: 18). As Marie discovered, for the survivor of suicide, the tasks of mourning can be particularly hard to complete: 'it's too overwhelming, too much; there's too much in the way of feelings. It's just too awful, the whole thing, the feelings, the violence.' Later, though, she wrote:

> I am relieved to find my own life is calmer and the pain not so intense all the time – generally [I] feel more at peace with myself. Now I can recall [how] Oliver was able to speak of the happiest years of his life during our too-short marriage without being overwhelmed by a confusion of unhappy and guilt-laden feelings.

The lessening of pain, and the return of happy memories can be two markers on the road to recovery, and this is the subject of the next chapter.

Chapter 14

Finding a way through

> For Simon to commit suicide was almost beyond my endurance. Yet nevertheless, we do endure, and we do laugh, and we do go on contributing to our family and friends, and that, I suppose, is the miracle. (Lois)

> I count myself lucky in an odd sense, because I'm repairing damaged goods, and confident of being repairable. (Kevin)

In the weeks and months of their bereavement survivors may feel that they will never be able to live with what has happened. But gradually a way through may begin to seem possible. Two and a half years after his sister's suicide, Peter can look back and see how things have changed:

> It has got better, and it's got calmer, and life's gone on, and one finds one's way through . . . I don't believe you get over it, but I just think you learn how to accommodate it, and how to deal with it, and how to cope with it.

Of the fifty people I interviewed, over half had been bereaved for less than three years, some of these for less than a year – while one person had been a survivor for over fifty years (see Appendix 2). The number of years, though, does not tell the whole story: people move through the process of grieving at their own pace, healing takes place at different rates, and two people who have been bereaved for the same length of time will not necessarily be at the same stage.

Sometimes survivors can look back and see the different stretches of road along which they have travelled, recognising the points when they seemed to reach a new stage. Brian can recall three distinct phases in the two years following his wife's suicide:

> first of all it's deadfully slow . . . there's a numbness that must have gone on for nine months or a year . . . Then I think one comes out of the numb period, and that's hard too, because as you thaw, you think

more, and you realise, you question. Then I think . . . for me there was a degree of acceptance . . . [that] that's it, she isn't coming back; it's a phase of my life that has passed now. I've got to try and build something for the future.

In Ursula's case, the process of mourning was charted in a series of dreams which she had in the three years following Josie's death:

Initially I had several dreams where I was quite cross with her . . . not because of [the suicide] but reliving events in the past . . . and I've had one or two dreams of saying to myself, 'Gosh, what will she do now?' . . . But more recently I've had dreams, and she's been there and I've said, 'Oh, it's wonderful to see you', and yet I've known she's died . . . it's as if even whilst dreaming I've not allowed myself the luxury of pretending [she was alive].

Vivid dreams about the deceased are common (Parkes 1998), and a sequence of dreams of the kind Ursula described is not unusual. Kast (1988) suggests that this may be the means by which the unconscious is guiding the bereaved through the process of mourning. Ursula's dreams served a further purpose: they pointed to the inescapability of the fact of Josie's death. The suicide had happened, and the clock could not be turned back. For Jane, there was a realisation that her life had changed: 'There's one thing I do know, and that is that I will never be the same again.' And as Heather discovered, you have to learn to live with what's happened to you and once that is accepted,

once you realise that that's what you have to do, then you begin to do it. At the beginning, you hope that it will go away and that you'll be back to normal one day, but you won't . . . but you can learn to live with a different world and that's what I'm now trying to do.

In the midst of their grief, though, one of the things which comforted some survivors was the feeling that if they could cope with this – and survive – then they could cope with anything. It was not that they believed nothing terrible would ever happen to them again, but rather a sense that nothing could ever *feel* as bad; if disaster struck again they would be better equipped to cope with it. In Melanie's words: 'In a way it gives you a certain kind of strength, and I feel that whatever else happens to me, it wouldn't be so awful.'

Timescales of grieving

As already mentioned in Chapter 11, after a time, survivors may find that the victim is no longer mentioned; other people may assume that they are no longer grieving, and decide that it is best not to raise the subject. But there is no finite period after which the person will automatically pick up the threads of normal living again, and how people respond to the loss will depend on a range of different factors including the manner of their death (for example, anticipated, unexpected, violent, peaceful), their relationship with the person who died (for example, close, distant, warm, hostile, ambivalent), pre-existing family and social difficulties, and the amount and quality of available support.

Nevertheless, survivors can still find that after a certain time, others will expect them to have recovered. After her brother's suicide, Bushy Kelly wrote: 'somehow there is a belief that there is some magical date after which you are supposed to be normal, yourself again' (1989: 16). But survivors themselves may think they should stop grieving by a specific date. Janice had read somewhere that this was one year after the death: 'I was really impatient with myself, thinking it was time I got over this.' But, as she discovered, 'It was obvious that I hadn't . . . and that probably I think that's something that is sort of there for ever really.'

Staudacher (1988) suggests that the grief of suicide survivors will last longer than with other deaths and subsequent research has suggested that recovery sometimes may be slower (Farberow et al. 1992). While this is by no means always the case, suicide bereavement has certain features which can lengthen the process; survivors may become stuck in an endless and fruitless search for the definitive answer or answers to why the suicide occurred; or they may decide that they were responsible for the death and will punish themselves by continuing to grieve. As Shneidman found, in his work with survivors: 'some people offered help wished to maintain their suffering out of expiation. They felt they deserved punishment' (1975).

Feelings of numbness or 'blunting', with the bereaved person finding it hard to accept the fact that the death has occurred, usually last for anything between a few hours and a few days (Parkes 1998). Worden (1991) also refers to this state as lasting for a brief period of time. With suicide, however, survivors may feel numb for weeks or even months (see also Chapter 13). As Isabel discovered, though, 'At the beginning everyone comes round, and they think the bereavement is only going to last a couple of months, and [that you] will pull yourself together – and you're left stranded.'

The struggle towards acceptance

When the pain is bad, it's as bad as it ever was, and I still get on my knees and say 'why can't you come back?' – I mean, a totally illogical thing to say, but I still say, 'please, let her come back'. (Pat)

Acceptance was a word frequently used by survivors; it often seemed to hold the key to their recovery and survival. It meant acknowledging the finality of death, and recognising that they would not see or speak to the person again. All bereaved people are faced with this task of accepting the reality of their loss (Worden 1991), but for suicide survivors there were other aspects too: a need to accept the wounding that had occurred, and to work through some of the particular legacies of suicide (see also Chapter 13).

Being able to let go of the dead person can be particularly difficult for the survivor of suicide; there may be unanswered questions (see Chapter 6), and the survivor will cling to the hope of continuing a dialogue with the person who died; if the survivor feels guilty about the death, there may be hopes of a second chance, an opportunity for restitution. Whatever the reason, as long as the survivor refuses to accept that the person is not coming back, all their energies will be channelled in that direction (Worden 1991), and they may become stuck in their grieving, unable to move on; Heather realised the danger of this when, eighteen months after Alastair's death, she said: 'I want him back. That's bad; I want to let go of that – it's useless, a complete waste of energy, it wears me out.'

But letting go does not necessarily mean losing the person altogether but finding a new relationship with them. As Jean discovered, when the survivor can accept that the relationship in its previous form is no longer possible, a new feeling of closeness may emerge:

A lot of people said to me, 'You'll come to terms with it'. I thought, I can't possibly come to terms with it. They talked about acceptance. I do know she's dead now, and that took me a long time . . . to say 'she's dead and she's not coming back' . . . I had this mad feeling that the doctors were going to do something, that next week she [was] going to get better and come home . . . But I do know that she's dead now, and I have been able to feel her close to me which is something I didn't for a long time . . . I must have been angry with Anna or I couldn't understand her, because she was miles away from me. I thought, I'll never get close with you . . . and I do feel her close now.

Accepting that the person is no longer present in the physical sense can be a struggle, but it has been suggested that the survivor finding a new emotional or spiritual relationship with them can be an important contributor to recovery (Clark and Goldney 2000: 476).

Jean wondered whether her anger was possibly causing some kind of block, and getting these sorts of feelings into perspective may be a necessary task if the survivor is to emerge satisfactorily from mourning. After her brother's death, Jennifer questioned whether she could have done more to help Tim; should she have offered to sort out his business problems, she asked herself? She had known he was having financial problems and that people owed him money. Recognising and accepting the limits of her responsibility was an important stage in her recovery:

Twelve months later you begin to realise . . . how much you could have done, and how much difference it would have made anyway . . . You start to see things a bit more reasonably – that you can't possibly live someone's life for them . . . You start forgiving yourself a bit, because you can't do someone else's jobs for them unless they ask you to do them.

Survivors often talked in terms of learning to live with what had happened, of accepting that the hurts which had been inflicted would never really disappear. Pam described this as feeling one is 'bruised for ever'. For Pat, it is not expecting total happiness: 'We might experience happy times, but I can never be totally happy again because I've lost Caroline.' Similarly, John commented: 'I don't expect to be happy again, but I expect peace – and that's what I ask for now . . . as peaceful a life as possible and just [to] be content with what I have.' Perhaps these survivors had been able to accept what so many people find difficult today, namely that constant perfect happiness is a chimera.

Gains and losses

I think back on Alan as somebody who . . . brought the greatest joy into my life, the greatest pain into my life. He was my first child, and therefore the greatest joy I think any mother can have, and I think his death was the hardest thing, the greatest pain I've had to suffer. And he has also brought me the greatest understanding of what life is about. (Carol)

The way down is also the way up . . . Surviving a beloved person can become, at least for some, a time of growth and of becoming more fully human . . . [The survivor] may discover the values and capacities which he did not know of in himself.

(Seligman 1976)

No one chooses to be bereaved, and suicide bereavement can seem a particularly pointless and unnecessary loss; nevertheless, it can bring gains as well as losses. Drawing on her work as a psychotherapist with bereaved people, Kast suggests that recovery can sometimes depend on whether the survivor is able to see the possible gains:

I have observed that the sense of meaning . . . could be experienced, once they became aware of the fact that the death of the mourned one not only took a great deal away from them, but had also brought them a great deal.

(1988: 66–7)

Sometimes, what was lost or never achieved in the relationship with the person who died can be gained elsewhere, as Dick realised: 'Maybe I could have sorted things out more with Sally; then she was dead, and I couldn't . . . but I can do it with other people – I don't have to have that failure with everybody.' The fact that Sally had chosen not to continue with her life also made him more aware of the need to live his own life more fully: 'I was glad I was alive . . . it made me appreciate a lot of things I'd taken for granted before . . . Her death shook me up in terms of looking at my life.' Since Sally died, he has moved to a job he finds more worthwhile, has committed himself to a permanent relationship, and has become a father for the first time.

Staudacher suggests that, commonly, a survivor has less interest in social functions or materially oriented activities, and an increased interest in those areas of life concerned with human values such as love, compassion, assistance to others (1988: 49). This was reflected in comments made by a number of survivors who described how their attitudes towards other people had changed since the suicide. They talked of becoming 'more compassionate', of being 'more aware of other people's feelings' and of 'realising that other people are vulnerable'. Their own tragedy had made them more sensitive to the needs of those around them. Others described how the suicide had made them understand the relative unimportance of material objects, because as Carol said, 'people are important, not things, not possessions, and I think that it's important that you get this over to people – that they matter'.

Some survivors had decided to use their experiences in a positive way by supporting other bereaved people; in Suzy's case her decision to train and work as a bereavement counsellor was 'the bonus . . . of my father's death'. Some people had become counsellors with their local CRUSE groups, whilst others had become active members of the SOS network in Compassionate Friends. As Raphael points out, it is not unusual for people to become involved in bereavement support activities as a direct result of their own losses; our own bereavement 'allows us to empathise with the distress of others and to offer comforts and consolation' (1985: 404).

Existing relationships may be changed by the suicide too. When one member of the family dies, those remaining may become closer to one another. Ursula has noticed that, since Josie died, the rest of the family have become more caring of one another, because, as she says, 'I think it's up to us to make sure that there is something positive as an end result.'

Survivors may decide on major life changes. A switch of career – often into one of the helping professions – is not uncommon (Staudacher 1988). Since his wife's death, Brian has decided he will probably take early retirement from his job in the business world, and move into something involved with helping people. 'Material things', he reflects, 'have lost their value. Life itself – the quality of life – has taken on a much increased importance.'

Carole has also decided to leave teaching and retrain for a new career. Other survivors had taken up new hobbies and developed new interests.

Career changes of this kind can be part of wider change and growth which some survivors will experience as a direct result of the suicide. Ian's death has led Melanie to rethink her whole life – though as she says:

> it was a very hard way to find out. I think I've grown as a person in the last four years, because I've really had to sort out how I feel about a lot of things – not just his death, but our relationship, how I feel as a mother, what I'm going to do with my life; it's made me question an awful lot, whereas I'd just have stumbled on before.

Previous chapters have touched on some of the losses which stem from the one overarching loss of the person who died. Many survivors talked of a loss of security – of losing trust in the world, in other people, or in themselves:

> Personal disasters involve the personal experience of loss . . . They involve a loss of belief in the security of the personal and sometimes physical world, and in one's own immortality. These losses must be grieved in the adaptation to personal disaster.
>
> (Raphael 1985: 351)

Survivors talked of feeling 'less confident and less happy', of being 'more anxious and apprehensive', and of having 'a tremendous fear of rejection and a lack of confidence in handling life'. However, even losses can include elements of gain, as Francesca discovered:

> I've learned that I'm not queen of the world . . . I don't know it all. I'm not as good as all that. I think it's made me a little less pleased with myself than I was . . . I always felt I could do practically anything, and knew all about people . . . It's important too to know that I'm as vulnerable as the next person from time to time, and that's something I need to recognise rather than always being the strong person and able to cope with absolutely anything.

Memories

> When I think about him now, I think more about his life than dwelling on his death, although you're obviously aware of that even whilst you're thinking, because that doesn't go away . . . It's a step forward from the beginning, when all you can think about is the death. (Jennifer)

After the suicide, survivors will often mentally retrace the events leading up to the death. Where the manner of death was particularly violent, or if the survivor discovered the body, they may be obsessed with memories of what they saw or imagined. Even when this is not the case, in the early stages of bereavement, the dead person may only be remembered in the context of their suicide, and sometimes these painful memories will persist, as Pauline discovered: 'In the beginning it's all "that day", isn't it? I suppose I went over that for nine or ten months – well a year, I suppose. Now I'm beginning to think differently [but] it's still there, it comes back.' As Pam said, 'suicide fouls up the memories'. The survivor may feel that the act of suicide has negated or even destroyed everything that went before, including the happy times.

When Susan's husband committed suicide, it seemed to her 'as if he had destroyed everything that we had done and had together . . . and it was difficult to think of the good times'. These feelings about the death may have to be faced and worked through, though, before other – perhaps better – memories of the victim can emerge. Jane found that, although it took some time, she was eventually able to regain positive memories of her brother.

> In my mind, in my inner being, I have a picture of him . . . I think what I carry with me is a sense of his essential being which was very big in every sense, laughing a lot, very good-natured, and enjoying himself, and that's good . . . All the rest is over; [good memories] were hard to hold on to at first, they came and went, but the horror kept [them] away for a bit.

There may be other barriers; overwhelming feelings of grief and loss may need to abate before the good times can be recalled. Two years after his wife's death Brian was still unable to recall any of the happy times he and Judy had shared, and he wondered whether this was because there was, as he put it, 'still a kind of trapped grief there'. Persistent guilt may also cut the survivor off from happy memories, as Maureen found:

> I can remember him as a young man, and the laughs, sometimes the bad things, but I've shut out his childhood, I can't bear to think [about it] . . . I feel I didn't give him enough cuddles as a little boy but . . . as my doctor said, that's a normal thing to feel because you're trying to turn the clock back . . . so that I didn't tell him off and didn't smack him . . . So I find I can't look at photos of him as a child because it just tears me apart; if I see a little boy, a little ginger-haired boy, I just want to pick him up and bring him home and start again.

Strange as it may appear to others, survivors can sometimes find it easier to think about the difficult times; in that way the loss may feel more bearable, as Pam realised: 'I used to try and remember her when she was down and unhappy with herself and inside herself, and then I could understand perhaps, and I could live with her not being with us.' Three years after her daughter's suicide, Ursula still felt distant from Josie; she knew that Josie used to cuddle her, but she could not remember what that actually felt like, and she wondered whether perhaps remembering would be too painful.

Worden suggests that one of the signs of mourning coming to an end is when the survivor is able to think of the dead person – but without pain: 'There is always a sense of sadness when you think of someone that you have loved and lost, but it is a different kind of sadness – it lacks the wrenching quality it previously had' (1991: 18). Almost a year after her daughter's death, Francesca was beginning to recapture some of the 'rare moments of Patricia's happiness' – but they were mingled with sad memories.

A wasted life?

When someone takes their own life, the survivors can sometimes be on the receiving end of other people's criticisms of the person who died (see Chapter 11), but do survivors make these sort of judgements too? Do they see the victim's life as a waste, do they see the suicide as a wrongful act? Or do they place the dead person on a pedestal?

'Finding an image and a place in our lives for the people we have loved and lost', Parkes writes (1998: 71), is a creative aspect of grieving, and we tend to wish to hold onto the positive memories, creating an idealised image of the deceased. With suicide deaths, this can be more difficult with idealisation perhaps being overshadowed or completely overtaken by, to use Parkes' term, 'monsterisation'. If people grieving a non-suicide death tend to idealise at the expense of a more balanced image, maybe suicide bereaved people tend to adopt the opposite stance?

According to Worden (1991), suicide survivors often tend to have a distorted image of the dead person, seeing them as either all good or all bad. Certainly a tendency to idealise may sometimes contrast with the lack of self-worth often felt by people who take their own lives. Peter admits that perhaps he does rather venerate Susie but, as he sees it, she was 'a very remarkable person who just never understood how remarkable she was'.

Because of the traumatic and untimely nature of their death, the rest of the person's life, and particularly the more positive aspects, can be almost completely overlooked, but for some survivors it was important to recognise that their life had also included some significant achievements; Dick's sister, for example, had made an important contribution to the national campaign for lead-free petrol, and to him, Sally's life had to mean more than the mental illness which had overshadowed her last few years:

> I suppose I like to think of her . . . as all right. The later memories can overlie that, but we shouldn't forget that her life wasn't all awful . . .

the last five years probably were a lot of pain and suffering, but she did
have twenty-five years [before that], and I think it's something you can
lose sight of.

I was told about many different contributions which those who had died
had made to other people's lives: the doctor whose patients had found him
a deeply caring man; the researcher who had undertaken valuable work
with handicapped children; and the writer whose books had been well
received. Frances's contribution to others was particularly poignant;
because she was in a coma for some time before she died, her parents were
able to give permission for her organs to be used for transplant surgery.
Her death enabled others to live.

Survivors talked of ways in which the person had enriched their own
lives; Brian's wife, Judy, had taught the family to share her love of art and
music; she had also taught Brian how to fold fitted sheets! In Andrew's
case, his wife had worked in order to support him through medical school,
enabling him to train for the career he had always wanted to pursue and
which has been such an important part of his life. One of the most touching
tributes came from a survivor whose aunt had committed suicide. She
wrote:

> In my teens I was gawky and incoherent, unbearably shy and lacking in
> confidence. I was small and undersized and mousy. My aunt Dorothy
> was blond, tall, and voluptuous and articulate. She did, however, the
> most important thing for me. She made me feel I was attractive and
> worth listening to.

The funeral can be an opportunity for celebrating the person's life and their
achievements, but not all survivors had felt able to contemplate the idea of
celebration so soon after the suicide. Josie was cremated on Christmas Eve
and Ursula had not even been able to face people coming back to the house
afterwards. Three years later, though, she decided she wanted to celebrate
Josie's life and organised a gathering of family and friends, 'to celebrate
Josie and her uniqueness', because, as Josie's father said: 'in her short life
she made her mark'.

Anniversaries

For many bereaved people, the thoughts and feelings experienced at the
time of the death may recur at the time of the anniversary; 'anniversary
reactions' are mentioned frequently in the bereavement literature (e.g.
Bowlby 1985; Raphael 1985; Parkes 1998).

But for many survivors, the time leading up to the anniversary of the
death was even more difficult than the day itself. Jennifer found the run-up

to Tim's first anniversary very hard: 'as we came up to the first anniversary it felt so big and awful . . . but the day wasn't as bad as the weeks before'; it felt almost worse than the time of the death itself, when she had been numbed by shock: 'you're not thinking straight anyway, and twelve months later . . . you're beginning to think again'.

Anne Downey's experiences suggest another possible reason for the overwhelming feelings of dread which often seem to precede the actual anniversary:

> there are now only twelve days to go before the first anniversary of your death . . . I cannot sleep at night and am in a terrible state of anxiety. I know what is happening. I am reliving all the events of those final weeks except that *now I know the outcome*. Because there is no way of changing anything, I feel like an observer tied in chains and unable to do anything.
>
> (1987: 90; my italics)

Her situation is reminiscent of the dreamer who, in the throes of a nightmare, cannot stop the dream by waking up.

For some survivors, anniversaries posed a particular problem because they did not know the real date when the death had occurred. When someone had been missing for some time, there was often only an estimated date, decided by the pathologist or the police. In some cases, survivors could accept that, but others were convinced that it was wrong, and so were left with the confusion of an 'official' date, and the date when they felt sure the death had occurred.

Although December and January are not peak months for suicide deaths in the UK, nearly a third of the fifty survivors I met had an anniversary which was around Christmas or New Year. At a time generally associated with celebration, these survivors faced a reminder of their loss, and for parent-survivors, the missing son or daughter at the Christmas table often felt particularly painful.

Where the suicide is carried out in anger, the victim may even choose a date they know will be especially hurtful to the survivors. Melanie's husband, Ian, had threatened to kill himself if she did not return by a certain date. When she refused, he carried out his threat in a way she now realises was deliberately intended to cause the most hurt possible – he killed himself on her birthday.

Survival

> I think now I've accepted her death . . . I think I have let go. At the time it didn't seem as though I'd ever be happy again . . . every

morning waking up was an awful struggle, to get out of that awful black pit every morning, but then, eventually, you find it's not like that and you can be normal again. (Nancy)

The Chinese symbol for 'crisis' is the combination of the symbols for both 'danger' and 'opportunity' (Jones 1987: 141). The Chinese recognised many centuries ago a concept and its application which others have more recently developed and labelled crisis intervention theory. 'Crisis', wrote Erikson, 'is a turning point, a crucial period of increased vulnerability and heightened potential' (1971: 96). Danger and vulnerability, opportunity and potential – are all evoked by and present in crises. Suicide bereavement represents a major crisis, but one from which the bereaved can emerge as survivors, and that, as Lois said at the beginning of this chapter, 'is the miracle'. But it also forces people to make choices; the bereaved person, Seligman suggests, 'may remain the victim of an irredeemable loss, or he may emerge from darkness into dawn and become the survivor' (1976: 135).

Living with the aftermath of suicide can mean having to accept that one has been badly wounded and that scars will remain – and may occasionally hurt. 'There is a sense in which mourning can be finished', Worden suggests, 'and then there is a sense in which mourning is never finished' (1991: 18). Three years after her husband's suicide marked a turning point for Melanie: 'I really thought, I'm all right basically; some things still hurt, but basically I'm all right.' Her bereavement had been particularly painful and difficult, but becoming a survivor meant choosing not to let Ian's final angry gesture ruin the rest of her life. Similarly, as Jan found, it is for the survivor to choose whether or not they will become a victim – like the person who died.

Okay, my life has been difficult and I've got to take responsibility for making it different, and that's a lot of my struggle – to see that as my responsibility, and not to expect other people to fix it, and not to be a victim – and I do struggle with that day by day.

No one goes round consciously seeking out suffering, and when the suicide occurs, the survivors may understandably seek an escape route from its aftermath; as Dick realised, though, escape is not always possible, and the impact of the death has to be faced: 'You've got to live with it, and however much you went out, or you drank, or you watched telly, or whatever you did . . . it was there. I think that was the most difficult thing.'

Feeling 'all right', 'learning to live with it', 'living with a different world', realising one day that you 'feel normal again' – each person discovers how to live with their particular loss. Some of the people in this book were still struggling to accept their identity as survivors; others had reached the point where they felt able to accept what had happened, and had incorporated the experience into their lives; they had learned that they could live with it – and still live. The pain had not always gone away, but they had become true survivors. In Seligman's words, they had become 'the prospective carriers of life and hope' (1976: 135).

Part 3

Responding to people bereaved by suicide

Chapter 15

Meeting the needs of survivors

Introduction

There are now many potential sources of help and support for the bereaved person. Depending on where they live and what they are looking for, they may be able to choose between specialist and non-specialist, volunteer or professional, medical or non-medical, religious or secular assistance (Parkes 1998). The number of local bereavement services is increasing and more professional trainings are incorporating modules on loss and bereavement.

Many of the fifty people I interviewed in the late 1980s had been able to find some help, but as their experiences suggest, it was not always adequate, timely or appropriate and they had many suggestions about how their own needs could have been met more satisfactorily. Since then, we have witnessed a modest growth in the number of self-help and support groups for survivors, and anecdotal evidence suggests that bereavement services are receiving more referrals from people mourning a suicide death. However, we still have a long way to go before a comprehensive range of support is routinely available to individuals and families bereaved by suicide.

Over the last decade, new research into the impact of suicide has added to our knowledge and understanding of the particular needs of those bereaved by suicide and how these might be addressed in ways which will promote a healthy outcome of grieving. The experiences of organisations supporting survivors are also valuable in contributing to our understanding of survivors' needs.

Part 3 has been expanded to take account of some of these developments. It is intended as a resource for the growing numbers of people who are being asked to offer assistance and support to suicide survivors, though it does not claim to be comprehensive. Two new chapters focus on longer-term help, namely groups for people bereaved by suicide (Chapter 16) and individual counselling (Chapter 17). This chapter outlines the range of potential needs among survivors which have been identified in the literature on suicide bereavement, and goes on to describe briefly the current sources of support and assistance in the UK. The following section discusses the survivor's immediate needs, particularly in relation to contact with the police, the coroner's court and the media. The chapter continues with an overview of the literature on two particular interventions in later bereavement: groups for survivors and counselling. The chapter concludes with a brief discussion of training for those who are in a 'helping' role.

What are the needs of survivors?

While any form of support must recognise and be sensitive to individual needs, findings from studies of people bereaved by suicide suggest that the survivor may need any or all of the following:

- information about the death from the police, coroner's office and medical practitioners (Clark and Goldney 1995, 2000);.
- an opportunity to view the body or have access to photographs (Clark and Goldney 2000);
- help and advice with practical and social matters, including financial issues (Shepherd and Barraclough 1979; Rogers et al. 1982; Morgan 1994; Clark and Goldney 2000);
- opportunities to talk about the suicide and express feelings in a supportive context such as a survivors group (Shepherd and Barraclough 1979; Rogers et al. 1982; Battle 1984; Morgan 1994; Clark and Goldney 1995, 2000; Hill et al. 1997);
- individual counselling or therapy (Shepherd and Barraclough 1979; Hill et al. 1997; Clark and Goldney 2000);
- support from local religious leaders (Shepherd and Barraclough 1979; Hill et al. 1997);
- the provision of factual information about suicide (e.g. motivations, dynamics, limitations of prediction of suicide) and the causes of mental illness which can help to alleviate guilt and place the suicide in context (Rogers et al. 1982; Battle 1984; Clark and Goldney 2000);
- assistance and support in dealing with relationships with people in the survivor's network of family, friends and work colleagues (Rogers et al. 1982);
- education about strategies for coping with grief (Clark and Goldney 2000).

Individual survivors will have different needs; sometimes practical information and advice will be sought, while at other times, they will want comfort and support. Survivors will vary in how they meet their needs. Some will find they are able to draw on their own inner resources for coping; they may also have the support of family and close friends. Others will decide they want help from people not directly involved in the suicide. Many will be supported by a combination of these coping strategies.

There is no single optimum way of providing support, but as a recent government report on suicide pointed out, assistance must be tailored to individual circumstances and preferences, it must be timely and offered in a sensitive manner:

> There is no single formula here. Those who offer help must be sensitive to the wishes of each individual survivor: inappropriate help, or that which is pressed too vigorously can be as distressing as providing none at all . . . a whole range of helping styles should be made available.
>
> (Morgan 1994: 123, 124)

Existing provision

The main sources of specialist help for suicide survivors currently provided in the UK are the following (and details of the organisations can be found in Appendix 1):

- self-help groups, mainly run by SOBS (Survivors of Bereavement by Suicide) or the SOS (Survivors of Suicide) network of The Compassionate Friends;
- facilitated support groups, usually run by bereavement services or other community-based agencies;
- individual counselling provided by local bereavement counselling services (mainly branches of CRUSE Bereavement Care);
- practical and emotional support including face-to-face meetings, telephone contact, information and advice, social events, conferences and other gatherings;
- written materials (e.g. Hill et al. 1997; Compassionate Friends 1998; Shannon 2000; Winston's Wish 2001);
- support for bereaved families;
- telephone helplines.

Despite the growth in support services, survivors can find it difficult to access help. Suicide generally throws the bereaved into disarray and 'the recently bereaved person', as Shneidman reminds us, 'is typically bereft and disorganised' (1993: 162). Particularly in the early days, the survivor's pre-existing coping and problem-solving abilities can be severely compromised. Shame and stigma can also make it difficult for survivors to ask for help and 'declare their need' (Morgan 1994).

To maximise the likelihood of survivors receiving appropriate and timely help where needed, those offering support must reach out to newly bereaved survivors in a sensitive manner, whether or not they choose to accept an offer of help. 'To change the legacy of suicide, the model for implementing the use of resources should be definitely pro-active, with resources seeking the survivors . . . [it should be] an active model of postvention rather than a passive one' (Campbell 1997: 336).

Even when survivors are able to look for help, discovering what is on offer can be a lottery. Information is generally not made available to survivors on a routine basis. Clear written information about both local and national resources should be routinely available in the kind of locations where survivors are likely to be found, including coroner's courts, GP surgeries and health centres, undertakers' premises, hospital accident and emergency departments, places of worship, crematoria and libraries. If survivors could take away a leaflet or pamphlet, they would then have the information to hand, should they subsequently decide they needed help.

Survivors should be able to choose the kind of support they receive if they want to talk to someone outside their own social network. For some people, a self-help group where they can meet people experiencing a similar loss may meet their needs. Others may not feel comfortable in groups and may prefer to see a counsellor or use more informal support such as befriending. In some cases, the survivor will feel more comfortable talking to someone they already know such as a member of the clergy, or their GP.

Meeting immediate needs

In the days following the suicide, survivors often have to cope with difficult and stressful experiences. In addition to dealing with police, coroner's officers and undertakers, decisions will usually need to be made such as whether or not to see the body, who should be told about the death, and what information should be given to other people about the manner of the death.

Some survivors may be able to cope with little or no external help and any interventions at this stage should always aim to reinforce people's existing networks of support rather than replace them. However, some people will need assistance in these early days, and if this is sensitive and appropriate, it can set them on the path of healthy grieving and adaptation to their loss. 'Postvention' (or 'preventive intervention'), as it is sometimes described in the literature (e.g. Shneidman 1993; Campbell 1996), can reduce the potential after-effects of trauma, and help to identify those survivors who may be particularly vulnerable. Assistance at this stage should not attempt to help survivors explore their feelings but help them make the kind of decisions outlined above.

Immediately after the suicide, those most directly affected will usually gather together, but family myths and secrets can easily develop if communication between survivors in these early days is distorted or non-existent. Talking honestly about what has happened may be painful but if faced, it can prevent the development of unreal or distorted perceptions about the event (though it is not always necessary or appropriate to go into details of how the person died (Clark and Goldney 2000: 16–17). If feelings can be talked about openly and shared with others, this can establish a pattern of mutual support, and may reduce the need for help at a later point. Communication which is as open and honest as possible can prevent the development of unhealthy or blocked mourning.

Regardless of whether survivors seek outside help at this stage, they will come into contact with a range of 'first responders' (Dunne et al. 1987), including the police and the coroner's officer, as well as undertakers, clergy and possibly the family doctor.

Immediately following the death, decisions have to be made about viewing the body. Undertakers will need sensitivity and understanding in handling what can be a traumatic and difficult experience for survivors. They should have the opportunity to view the body or at least spend time with the covered body if mutilation makes viewing inappropriate or impossible. If a decision is made not to view the body, it may be appropriate to ask for photographs to be taken. This can be helpful if survivors, either at the time of the death or subsequently, are wondering whether it is a case of mistaken identification and the body was not that of their relative (Clark and Goldney 2000: 17).

Chapter 8 drew attention to the importance of funerals and, as survivors studied by Van Dongen (1993) reported, how this ritual was conducted was crucial in maintaining the dignity of the family and the person who died. Clergy, or others involved with arranging and conducting funerals, can find it difficult to know how best to approach the family grieving a suicide death, but sensitivity, a non-judgemental approach and a willingness to listen are all important for survivors already anxious about how others will respond to them.

Some families where there has been a suicide death elect to hold a private funeral and that choice should always be respected. However, difficult as this can sometimes be, including a wider circle of people, such as friends or colleagues from work, can enable the immediate survivors to accept the support and concern of others. It also gives everyone the chance to say a proper goodbye and recognises that although immediate family may be most affected by the death, suicide can have a significant impact on others who have the known the person too.

The police

The police are usually among the first on the scene following a suicide death, although unlike the clergy or the GP who will perhaps offer support, their role is primarily to investigate the circumstances surrounding the death, in collaboration with the coroner's officer. They are not meant to be counsellors; their job is to give correct information in the proper way and, where appropriate, direct people towards further help (Hood 1998).

It is frequently a member of the police force who has to inform the nearest relatives about the suicide. They also have to obtain statements from relevant individuals and collect any further evidence required for the inquest. They may need to explain official procedures to the relatives; for example, families may be unaware that any suspicion of foul play needs to be ruled out (Hood 1998; Clark and Goldney 2000).

To carry out these tasks in ways which will minimise the survivor's distress, police need to be properly trained and well informed about relevant aspects of suicide deaths. This is not always the case, according to anecdotal evidence from survivors. Further evidence comes from within the force. A pilot study in Gloucester found that many officers were unclear about the role of the coroner's officer and did not know what support services might be available to survivors (Hood 1998).

Communicating unwelcome news is never easy, even for the most experienced professionals. It is difficult for both the bearer and the recipient, and as a senior police officer acknowledged: 'We are all human and people will still get it wrong sometimes.' Initial police training instructs new recruits in the technicalities of investigating sudden deaths, but may not prepare them well enough for coping with relatives. More training, particularly if it is not presented solely in a 'chalk and talk' format, could help the police develop greater awareness of the potential reactions of survivors, including the fact that anger and hostility may well be directed towards them. (For further discussion about training, see pp. 193–195 below.)

Some survivors have found contact with 'family liaison officers' in their local police force to be helpful, although this kind of assistance does not seem to be routinely offered to survivors. The police's media representative or media team can also help and advise relatives about handling press enquiries. Although some survivors strenuously avoid any contact with the media, others may want to do so and welcome support from the police.

The coroner's court

The coroner's officer is responsible for organising the removal of the body from the site of the death and arranging for the post-mortem to be carried out. It is also their role to keep relatives informed about matters such as where the body has been taken to, and they may advise families about any arrangements they need to make. The coroner's officer also liaises with the police, to ensure that all necessary investigations have been completed before the main inquest hearing.

A number of practical steps could be taken to ease survivors through the inquest procedures. From the experiences described in Chapter 7 and Biddle's (1998) study of the inquest system in relation to suicide death, it is clear that more could be done to ensure that what will often be a difficult experience anyway is as humane and unstressful as possible.

It would be helpful if newly bereaved survivors were routinely provided with written information about the inquest system and the workings of the coroner's court. A leaflet of this kind could explain why following certain deaths inquests are held and what the possible outcomes may be.

A leaflet about inquests should also include information about what actually happens in court so that survivors have some idea of what may take place on the day. This may be easier said than done. As Biddle (1998) discovered during the course of her research, many coroner's courts appeared to rely on discretion and improvision when it came to inquest procedures. Reform is urgently needed to introduce much greater standardisation: 'Many of the difficulties could be improved upon by structural changes to the system and a move towards a standardisation of rules and procedure . . . a protocol for dealing with the bereaved must be established' (Biddle 1998: 124).

Meanwhile, other practical steps could ease survivors through the inquest system. They should be able to make a prior visit to the courtroom or at least be given a floor plan. The coroner's officer should provide relatives with a clear explanation of their entitlements, including their rights regarding return of the suicide note and other property which may have been taken away. Relatives should also be told about their right to leave the courtroom at any point during the inquest, should they wish to do so (Biddle 1998).

These issues are not new. Recommendations have been made which could go some way to addressing the difficulties frequently encountered by survivors (e.g. Barraclough and Shepherd 1976; Morris 1976; Chambers 1989) but have been largely ignored. No reforms appear to be imminent, but the Home Office has recently commissioned research into relatives' experiences of inquests which, it is hoped, will lead to much needed reform at some future point.

The media

Only a tiny minority of all suicide deaths will feature in the national media, but reporting in the local media is much more common. The growth of local media, including freesheets delivered to all households and the increasing number of local radio stations looking for stories, makes it unlikely that the level of reporting on suicide deaths has decreased, although no recent studies have been undertaken.

Shepherd and Barraclough's earlier study of suicide reports in a provincial evening paper found that coverage was selective, with the deaths of younger people and the more violent suicides having a greater chance of receiving attention than 'non-violent and middle-aged suicides' (1978: 286). This is echoed over two decades later by Peter Steward, Press and Media Relations Manager with Norfolk Constabulary, who has found that 'newsworthy' suicides where there are interesting or unusual facts (if the person was well known, for example) are particularly likely to be reported.

Given this scenario, are the interests of the media and those of survivors necessarily incompatible, or can they 'work co-operatively in a way which is healing for the family, helpful for society, and still "sells newspapers"' (Dunne-Maxim 1987: 47)? Survivors often find media attention unhelpful and intrusive and would prefer to see the press barred from coroner's courts. However, if the issue of suicide never featured in the media, might this unwittingly convey the message that suicide is an 'unspeakable' topic, thus helping to perpetuate the stigma and secrecy which still surrounds self-inflicted deaths?

To increase the likelihood of reporting being accurate and possibly even having an educative function with regard to suicide, survivors can be encouraged to respond to media enquiries either directly or by asking someone to respond on their behalf. Finding reporters on the doorstep may be unwelcome and intrusive, but if survivors are able to talk to them, perhaps with a relative or friend on hand for support, this could possibly reduce the likelihood of inaccurate or distorted information being broadcast or published. It could also provide an opportunity for the family to inject a more positive focus. They might want to tell reporters about the positive qualities and achievements of the person who died, thus presenting a fuller and more balanced picture.

National and local self-help and bereavement organisations can also contribute to improving the media coverage of suicide. If they can establish personal contact with journalists and reporters, they may be in a better position to encourage feature articles and programmes which explore the issues involved in suicide in greater depth and in a more balanced way than news items. Those working with survivors can also provide informed comment about the impact of suicide, if called upon to do so.

Although it has been proposed in the past that representatives of the media should be excluded from inquests (Shepherd and Barraclough 1978), the coroner's court is an open court, so the press are free to attend (even though members of the public are rarely present). More recently, Biddle has suggested that 'coroners could be granted the power to restrict press activity by providing journalists with only minimal details and disallowing them access to the courtroom where the criterion of broadcasting a public hazard is not met' (1998: 124). Biddle also proposes that the deceased and their relatives should have the same protection and privacy rights as those currently applicable to victims and perpetrators of crime. In fact there is anedotal evidence that some coroners already try to ensure that only the necessary minimum of information is heard in court: forensic and pathology reports will not necessarily be read out in full, for example. This should be standard practice in all courts but without legislative change, is unlikely.

Public interest and private grief are perhaps rarely comfortable bed-fellows, but if survivors and organisations which represent their interests are willing to enter into a dialogue which could lead to more sensitive and accurate reporting of individuals' stories and suicide in general, this must be a positive development

Meeting longer-term needs

Not all survivors will require longer-term interventions. In some instances, the death may have been experienced as a relief for the survivors and the suicide as an acceptable solution for the deceased. Other survivors may find the necessary help and support from family and friends. Some, however, will seek help from external sources, possibly soon after the death, but often weeks or months later when informal support may have faded but the survivor is still very preoccupied with their grieving.

The main sources of specialist help are groups for survivors and individual counselling. This section reviews literature on these groups, and on counselling and therapy for people bereaved by suicide.

Groups for people bereaved by suicide

Although the number of groups in the UK is gradually increasing, provision is still woefully inadequate. An earlier postal survey conducted by the author (Wertheimer 1992) identified 17 groups which described themselves as either 'self-help' or 'facilitated'; eight years later, estimates suggest that this number has roughly doubled, although no up-to-date central database currently exists. Survivors often travel considerable distances to attend meetings, but the fact they are prepared to do so suggests that there is still considerable unmet need.

Descriptive accounts of survivor groups in a number of different countries have been published (although I have not been able to locate any accounts of UK groups). These accounts include: Hatton and Valente (1981), Wrobleski (1984–5) and Billow (1987) in the USA; Rogers et al. (1982) in Canada; Clark et al. (1993) in Australia; and Grad (1996) in Slovenia. There are also several reports of evaluations of survivor groups: Rogers et al. (1982), Battle (1984), Farberow (1992), and Constantino and Bricker (1996) and some of their findings are described here.

Rogers and her colleagues (1982) evaluated the first two years of the Toronto Survivor Support Program. Teams of trained volunteers met with individual families for eight two-hour sessions, each of which had a specific focus for discussion. Following these sessions, families were invited to attend four fortnightly groups with other survivors. The aim of these semi-structured group sessions was to build on the earlier sessions with families by considering ways of dealing with practical and psychosocial concerns.

Although the evaluators were aware that results could not be solely attributed to the programme's interventions, reactions were generally favourable:

- participants had found the programme most helpful in terms of getting the suicide in perspective, having a safe place to express feelings without being judged, and talking about the suicide;
- on the other hand, they felt they had made less progress with understanding and dealing with reactions outside the family, and finding and using social, emotional and practical help from others;
- after completing the programme, participants had reduced levels of obsessive–compulsive and phobic anxiety behaviours.

With Battle's (1984) evaluation of a survivor group in Memphis, participants completed questionnaires before and after attending the group, and survivors who had not attended the group were also asked to complete a questionnaire to help the evaluators understand more about why some survivors elect not to attend groups. Battle found that:

- most people joined the group about two months after the suicide;
- the majority (87%) of participants were female (and the majority of suicide deaths involved males);
- most participants attended for ten sessions or fewer;
- 61% of participants reported that they had been helped; 27% felt that the group could not help them further, even though they were still suffering; and 12% reported that they were not helped;
- group participants experienced more guilt about the suicide than the survivors who did not attend the group;
- with regard to the suicide and other events in their lives, the non-group attenders experienced less intense emotions (both positive and negative) than the group participants.

Groups run by the Los Angeles Suicide Prevention Center which are co-led by a mental health professional and a survivor (who has been through the programme and undertaken training) were evaluated in depth by Farberow (1992). Questionnaires were designed to measure the intensity of a range of emotions (e.g. guilt, shame and depression) within the first four weeks after the suicide, at the start of the programme and afterwards. Questionnaires were also completed by a control group consisting of survivors who had applied to join a group but did not attend or dropped out after the first session. The results led Farberow to conclude that 'the group experience had made a significant impact on levels of difficult unhappy feelings' (1992: 32):

- 92% of group participants had found the programme helpful;
- asked to specify how the group had helped, responses included: lessening the shock, greater awareness of own feelings; feeling more in control; and helped to face the reality of the loss;
- immediately after the death, the intensity of feelings such as shame, anger and anxiety, shame and guilt was more or less the same for participants and controls;
- when they joined the programme, particpants were experiencing more intense feelings of grief, shame and guilt than the control group (which may have affected the former's decision to attend the group);
- after completing the programme, the intensity of participants' feelings had reduced significantly, but apart from feeling less anxious, the intensity of the control groups's feelings did not show similar improvements.

Little is known about the comparative effectiveness of different types of groups, although a recent study by Constantino and Bricker (1996) which compared the effects of two nurse-led groups for widows bereaved by suicide – a bereavement group and a social group – found similarities and differences:

- both groups experienced an overall reduction in depression and distress;
- both groups experienced a significant reduction in feelings of despair, rumination and depersonalisation;
- there were no significant differences between the groups in terms of social isolation, feelings of loss of control, somatization and death anxiety;
- social group members generally showed significant improvement in social adjustment, but were less well adjusted with respect to their parental roles;
- bereavement group members experienced significantly reduced levels of hostility, anger and guilt, whereas these increased among the social group.

Although formal evaluations add to our knowledge about the impact of a particular type of intervention they can be unpopular with groups, because of concerns about confidentiality. In this case, less formal strategies are an alternative means of obtaining feedback including: debriefings at the end of meetings; follow-up telephone call after a member's first meeting; distribution of questionnaires at the meeting asking about the format of meetings; a postal questionnaire asking members about perceived benefits of the group (Clark et al. 1993).

There are still many unanswered questions regarding survivor groups which require further investigation and exploration. As Rubey and McIntosh concluded in their survey of US and Canadian groups: 'It is clear that the more we learn about survivor groups, the more questions remain' (1996: 358). If the growing number of groups are to provide effective support for people bereaved by suicide we need to look for some answers to the following kinds of questions.

- How soon after the death is it helpful for survivors to join a group?
- Is there an optimum number of sessions?
- Is there an optimum length and frequency for group meetings?
- Is it helpful if group meetings have some structure and what kind of structure might it be (e.g. invited speakers)?
- Are groups reaching the most vulnerable survivors or those who would achieve a healthy outcome to their grieving anyway?
- Are survivors best served by groups with similar kinship losses (e.g. parents or spouses)?
- What kind of training do group leaders need?
- Does the combination of a mental health professional and a survivor offer the most effective leadership for groups?

Counselling and therapy

There is anecdotal evidence that bereavement counselling services are receiving more referrals from suicide survivors than was previously the case, although the reasons for this increase are not clear. It may be related to greater coverage of counselling issues in the media, the growth in the number of counsellors and the fact that this type of help may be seen as more acceptable by the general public. It may also be the case that survivors feel less stigmatised so are more able to ask for help – but perhaps that is wishful thinking.

If more survivors are opting to see a counsellor, will this meet their needs? Several evaluations (cited by Parkes (1998)) have found bereavement counselling to be an effective intervention, but the outcomes of counselling or therapy with suicide survivors have not been specifically evaluated other than in reports of individual case studies. Literature on bereavement counselling includes various proposals about what might be helpful and what needs to be addressed. For example, it is suggested that counsellors and therapists:

- should reality test the guilt and blame, help correct denial and distortions, explore fantasies of the future, work with anger; and reality test the sense of abandonment (Worden 1991: 96–8);

- need to give permission for the existence and expression of anger; and enable the survivor to acknowledge the horrific nature of the death (Lendrum and Syme 1992: 35–6);
- may help the survivor to rationalise unrealistic feelings, particularly guilt, rejection and those arising from the suicide note, though they should adopt a cautious approach towards exploration of feelings of distress, because while this is usually therapeutic, the timing of such interventions needs skilled judgement (Clark and Goldney 2000: 18);
- need to be aware of particular clinical themes including the survivor's need to search for a reason for the suicide, the legacy of guilt, the alteration of social relationships as the result of real or imagined stigma, complex and often incomplete grieving, the erosion of trust in others, and the idea of suicide as a solution to the problem (Dunne 1987b: 193–207).

One of two psychoanalytic therapists have written about their work with individual suicide survivors. Barnett and Hale (1985) describe the case of a middle-aged man who started therapy during the year before he reached the age when his father had killed himself – a fact that the authors see as central to his decision to seek help. More recently, a volume on psycho-analytic approaches to working with trauma (Garland 1998) has included two case studies: Gibb (1998: 123–8) writes about aspects of her work with a woman whose adolescent daughter had committed suicide and Bell (1998: 168–80) includes a brief illustration of therapy with a woman whose sister had committed suicide over a decade earlier.

More attention is now being paid to the evaluation of different forms of counselling and therapy but at present we know little about whether particular approaches are likely to be more or less helpful to survivors of suicide. Despite this lack of knowledge, however, some survivors will choose to see a counsellor or therapist, which has implications for the training of both volunteers and professionals.

Training

It is not uncommon for survivors to state that *only* someone who has also experienced a suicide bereavement could understand them or be of any use to them. There are various possible explanations for this. They may want to meet people who have had a similar experience (even though no two bereavements will be the same). Some survivors are reluctant to seek help because they are afraid of being judged or blamed in some way. However, it may be that they have had contact with professionals or others in a 'helping' role who have not been particularly knowledgeable about the potential impact of a suicide death or may have encountered apparently unsympathetic attitudes. If survivors are going to 'declare their need' as

Morgan (1994) suggests, they need to feel confident that the person will be competent and well informed.

As McIntosh pointed out over a decade ago, people who have frequent contact with suicide survivors need training in order to to sensitise them to the issues. Many mental health professionals and other carergivers, he adds, often do not receive training which would help them deal with survivors (1987c). This is echoed more recently in a government report which suggested that professionals such as the police and the coroner's staff needed specific skills (such as how to break bad news) and appropriate training should be available for everyone faced with the task of helping survivors (Morgan 1994). Although training in aspects of grief and loss is more widely available these days, less attention has been paid to the particular issues raised by suicide deaths, which could perhaps be addressed within the wider context of bereavement following sudden and traumatic deaths.

The kind of knowledge and skills required will vary, depending on the context in which they need to be used. Police and coroner's officers, for example, will find it helpful to know something about the immediate effects of a suicide death, and possible sources of help to which they can refer people. A counsellor or therapist, on the other hand, is more likely to need an understanding of the dynamics of suicide and the possible impact of a suicide death on the survivor's identity and self-esteem.

It is beyond the scope of this book to include a detailed discussion of the content and delivery of training on suicide bereavement, though training materials need to be developed. Nevertheless, it is perhaps worth making a few general suggestions.

Training should always include opportunities for people to explore their own attitudes, beliefs and feelings about suicide. Without some degree of self-awareness, there is a danger that they will, unintentionally or otherwise, display attitudes which the survivor perceives as unhelpful. For example, if someone believes that people have the right to take their own lives, they may have difficulty recognising and acknowledging that survivors can feel angry and cheated.

Training needs to take account of the feelings stirred up when people are asked to focus on death, and on suicide deaths in particular, as this can affect people's ability to be helpful. Spending time with people who are grieving is often emotionally painful and draining, reminding us of our own mortality and the possibility of losing those to whom we are close. Suicide deaths can also be a painful reminder of 'failure' including, at times, our professional shortcoming or failings.

It is not uncommon for people to arrive for a workshop on the impact of suicide believing that these bereavements are completely different from other bereavements. Although training needs to address the particular dimensions of suicide bereavement, it should always be placed in the broader context of loss and bereavement and training should help people to recognise the commonalities.

Factual information about the legal procedures involved in potential or actual suicide deaths, notably the role of the police and the coroner's officer and the workings of the inquest system, could also usefully be included in training programmes.

Where and how training about helping suicide survivors is delivered will obviously vary, but my experience of running workshops and similar events suggests that it is particularly important to try and create an environment which feels safe enough for people to explore the issues. In addition, because training is often a one-off event, trainers need to help participants be realistic about what can be learned within a two-hour session or even a day.

To return to the issue of survivors and non-survivors in helping roles. Some survivors do go on to support others bereaved by suicide and they can offer a great deal, perhaps leading groups, or counselling with their local bereavement service. Accounts of projects which use survivors who have undertaken a training programme before becoming volunteers have found their input to be very positive (e.g. Rogers et al. 1982; Farberow 1992; Clark et al. 1993). Training can provide opportunities for survivors to explore any unresolved issues in their own bereavement and acquire the necessary skills for running groups or counselling.

Finally, initial and continuing opportunities for training are important, but so is ongoing support, whether through informal debriefing or more formal supervision sessions. Working with suicide survivors is often very draining; good listening is hard work and being alongside people in pain can be very painful. Whether helping in a volunteer or professional capacity, support mechanisms need to be in place to avoid burn-out and a consequent high turnover of helpers. Support is not a luxury; it is a necessity.

Chapter 16

Groups for people bereaved by suicide

When I spend time with others who are struggling with their loss, I will experience the frustration of knowing that I cannot change their loss into non-loss. As I see my loss reflected in how they are talking about theirs, I can see their pain and in helping them to bear their pain, I can begin to bear my own. I then see the pain and grief for what they are, and in naming the pain and grief, I can become more free.

(Maxwell 1994)

Introduction

As this quotation suggests, a group can help the bereaved person to move on. In confronting and sharing their grieving, they can begin to be free themselves from the world of loss. Yet, Maxwell adds, 'We are less familiar with groups for the bereaved, partly because we see bereavement as a very private affair, something to be worked through on our own' (1994).

Drawing largely on published material, the previous chapter (pp. 181–95) described the current provision of survivor groups in the UK and elsewhere and what is known about their effectiveness from the very few evaluations which have been undertaken. The aim of this chapter is to provide a more detailed introduction to suicide bereavement support groups and share the experiences of some existing groups. It draws on the work of a number of experienced facilitators in the UK, as well as the author's own experience of co-leading a suicide survivor group. In order to maintain confidentiality, contributions are quoted anonymously.

The terms 'leader' (or co-leader), and 'facilitator' (or co-facilitator) are used interchangeably in this chapter, reflecting the fact that both these terms are used in existing groups. In practice, those running groups are likely to be facilitating *and* leading at different times. Facilitation brings to the fore the idea of a shared experience, where, at different times and to a greater or lesser extent, everyone has input and everyone takes responsibility for what happens in that group. The facilitator's role is to help that process along. At other times, a leadership role will be more important – in opening and closing the group, for example, or in intervening when the group seems stuck or is avoiding painful issues.

The remainder of this chapter addresses the issues which anyone thinking about starting a group needs to consider:

- What can groups offer survivors?
- What does leadership involve?
- How do you go about setting up a group?
- Training, support and supervision for leaders.
- Leaving the group.

What can groups offer survivors?

Reducing isolation

As described elsewhere, survivors often feel very isolated – 'outsiders', who are set apart from other people. The survivor may feel they are the only one this has happened to and that no one else could possibly understand their plight. As group members begin to get to know one another, however, and the group begins to gel, 'I' often becomes 'we' and 'us'. Being part of a survivor group can lessen the sense of aloneness:

> I felt so alone with the stigma – it was comforting to know I wasn't the only one in the world.

> I felt like an alien until I met others in the group.

Erving Goffman's work on the nature of stigma (1968) describes how the stigmatised individual needs to seek out and meet with others similarly marked. The individual with a 'spoiled identity' can find others who will help him feel normal, despite his self-doubts:

> The first set of sympathetic others is, of course, those who share his stigma . . . some of them can provide the individual with . . . a circle of lament to which he can withdraw for moral support and for the comfort of feeling at home, at ease accepted as a person who is really like any other normal person.
>
> (1968: 31–2)

As the survivors quoted above are saying, being part of a group provides a sense of belonging at a time 'where they may feel unable to establish a belongingness to ordinary human beings' (Menzies Lyth 1989: 254). The survivor of suicide may even feel they are different from others who have been bereaved; as one woman said to the group: 'I am not a proper widow.'

Although many people who attend suicide bereavement groups have family and friends around them, there are survivors who are literally on their own and for whom the group can be an invaluable lifeline.

> One of our group members lost her father through suicide and her mother died six weeks later. With no brothers or sisters or other relatives, she felt totally abandoned and wondered how she would ever 'pick up the pieces' again. Sensing that her loss was almost more desperate than their own, group members were very supportive. By the time the group had ended, she was able to say that the group had given her the courage to get on with her life again.

By joining a suicide bereavement group, the survivor is also forced to acknowledge that the death *was* a suicide when he or she may have been finding it difficult to accept this, and hoping that another explanation could be found.

Publicity material for survivor groups generally emphasises that the group is a place 'where you will meet other people who are experiencing the same type of loss' or 'meet others with a similar loss'. Knowing that other people have been through a similar experience helps the group to gel more rapidly than might otherwise be the case; its members can embark on the shared task of working through their grief. At the same time it is important to recognise that group members can unwittingly collude with one another in ways which reinforce the survivor identity ('How could anyone out there possibly understand us?'), and hence their set-apartness. One of the group leader's tasks is to challenge this, an issue to which we return below in the sections on leadership and leaving the group.

When members are sharing their feelings and experiences, it is important that the group is able to allow for and work with difference. The group has to struggle with this in the same way that many families do following a death. Individuals in the group will have their own particular ways of reacting and coping with their feelings and can be a source of friction if differentness is felt to threaten the group's cohesiveness.

Sharing feelings and experiences

As the experiences of survivors in Part 2 illustrate, sharing feelings with others in their usual social networks could be difficult. As one person told their group: 'I feel safe to cry here, but nowhere else.' Talking about feelings in the family can arouse unbearable anxieties. As Farberow (1992) suggests, one of the survivor groups' major contributions has been the provision of support through the sharing of mutual experiences, problems and losses.

While the experiences and feelings of suicide survivors are not unique, the horror of these particular deaths can make it difficult for people to relate the details of the suicide with others. But in the group, as one leader described it: 'anything can be said without others expressing shock or horror'.

> A widow bereaved by suicide can feel unable to say 'my husband shot himself' when she may be the only one with such an experience. Attending a survivor support group gives a forum to say how the individual ended his or her life without the person feeling that they are 'under the microscope'.

> With sharing comes the knowledge that you are not alone; that you are not going mad.

Discovering that another person in the group has similar feelings can make something rather frightening seem more bearable.

> It can be very simple things, like hearing that someone else had hardly slept for weeks when they thought they were the only one . . . and they'd thought they were going off their head.

In the group, the survivor can speak about the 'unspeakable' which might otherwise be unaddressed and therefore not faced and worked through. This may not happen immediately; it may take some time before the person can begin to talk about the circumstances of the suicide and allow feelings to emerge.

> At the first meeting, Jim introduced himself and told the group that his wife had committed suicide three months ago and he was finding it difficult to cope. He seemed reluctant to say anything more about what had happened and the facilitators did not press him to divulge anything further at this stage. It was some weeks before he was able to talk about the day he had found her hanging in their spare bedroom. He had not been able to bring himself to go into the room since then, but had also been trying to suppress his horror about what he had seen.

As well as talking about the death that has already happened, survivors may share with others in the group the fears of their own self-destructive feelings or their anxiety that other family members will go on to kill themselves because suicide is now seen as an option.

The fact that others in the group may have similar feelings and experiences can make it easier for someone to share these, but where they are very traumatic, the group can also find it hard to listen, particularly if what is being said stirs up uncomfortable or distressing feelings in the listener. One way of dealing with this is for people to move quickly into problem-solving mode ('Best to try and forget about it'; 'You must just try and put these things out of your mind'). While helping the person find their own coping strategies may be appropriate at some point, the danger here is that the group may, without realising it, be giving the message 'We can't bear to think about what you also find unthinkable'.

Alternatively, the group may deal with anxiety-provoking material by joking and laughter. Laughter *can* have a place in the group. It can be cathartic. It can give the message 'it's okay to laugh again', but leaders need to be aware when it is being used as a collective defence against painful feelings. When someone recounts an anecdote which provokes laughter, leaders may also need to draw the group's attention to possible underlying feelings.

> Mary told the group about a social event she had been to in the previous week. She found herself in a group arguing lightheartedly about the pros and cons of sliced bread. Irritated about what she felt to be a banal conversation, she had walked off to another part of the room. The group responded with sympathetic laughter. Anita then recounted how she had recently lost her temper with a customer in the greengrocer's where she worked who had complained about a mouldy carrot. Her story provoked further laughter. When this subsided, one of the leaders wondered aloud whether Mary and Anita were perhaps angry about having to cope with the aftermath of a suicide while other people didn't. Maybe it was difficult to be angry in the group.

When one person in the group expresses anger towards the person who died, the rest of the group can become frightened as they are presented with the possibility that they too harbour aggressive feelings. To avoid this, and particularly in the early stages of a group, survivors will frequently resort to 'sanctification', earnestly assuring the rest of the group that their spouse or son or daughter was perfect in every way. However, when people begin to trust one another, one person expressing their anger can make it easier for other group members to follow suit.

> A father bitterly described [how] he felt his son's suicide was intended as an insult to his parenting. This helped others to recognise and ventilate their own pent-up feelings. A widowed member of the group then talked about her anger at her husband for cheating her out of the rest of her marriage and for causing her so much hurt.

> A man who joined the group following his son's suicide was extremely aggressive towards the rest of the group and used language which

seemed designed to shock them. They in turn found this difficult but managed to cope so that he did not leave. One week, when he was unavoidably absent, they talked about his behaviour and realised that it had actually helped. They had realised how they also felt angry and could now express those feelings without the group falling apart. Although never an easy group member, the next week he was welcomed back by the others.

Although one person's overt anger can allow others to express similar feelings, at other times, the group may be paralysed. At this point, one of the facilitators may need to intervene, perhaps by asking whether others in the group perhaps feel the same.

Mutual support

Like any self-help group, the survivor group enables its members to give and receive support from one another. Offering support can be a very positive experience, enhancing the self-esteem of survivors who often feel that the support they tried to give to the suicide victim was inadequate, useless or rejected.

At the same time, leaders may notice that an individual always seems to be supporting the rest of the group but does not ask for space in the meetings to talk about their own experiences. This may be appropriate in the case of someone who has been in the group for a long time and has worked through many of their issues. But when someone referred to the group says the main reason they want to attend is because they feel they have 'a lot to contribute', this needs further exploration. Dealing with other people's distress can be much less painful than facing one's own difficulties.

Normalising feelings and self-perceptions

When reactions to the suicide are intense and distressing, the survivor may believe they are going mad, or that their feelings are very 'abnormal'. At the same time, they may find it impossible to share this with family or friends (who may also be afraid that the person is 'going mad'). Not feeling 'real', having flashbacks or recurring images of finding the body, having sleep problems and strange dreams in a half-waking state, can all be difficult to talk about with other people.

Support groups can be valuable in helping the bereaved person to understand that their feelings of intense emotional pain are normal, and that however 'abnormal' they feel, what they are going through is a normal process (Wrobleski 1984–5; Clark and Goldney 2000) As one group leader noted:

> Their feelings are so intense that it is a comfort to know that others feel
> equally strongly the fear of madness, isolation and anger.

Hearing that others have similar feelings and reactions can seem to 'normalise' the experience. Providing information about typical reactions to a suicide death may also lead survivors to conclude that their apparently 'abnormal' feelings are, as one person described it, 'normal reactions to an abnormal event'. Although not all groups will do so, there are some whose aims include 'education in grief management' and an 'understanding of the grief process' (Clark et al. 1993).

Distorted self-perception is by no means uncommon amongst suicide survivors. However, meeting others similarly bereaved can, as one group leader pointed out, 'also allow survivors to see that they are not "odd", "bad" or "strange"'.

> A woman who felt it was her fault that her partner had died by suicide
> commented that 'since being part of this group, I can rationalise my
> anger and guilt and realise how these are normal feelings. I feel an inner
> peace with myself now and know my partner was the one who made
> the decision to end his life'.

A preoccupation with negative thoughts and feelings is common amongst survivors but being part of a supportive group can also enable people to tap into more positive feelings such as sympathy and warmth towards others and to feel less trapped in a cycle of negative and often self-punishing feelings.

> At the end of her first group meeting Jo said, 'I feel as though I've been
> let out of prison'. Although at the next meeting, she admitted that the
> relief had not lasted, she felt it had given her hope for the future.

Role models of survival

When a recently bereaved person joins a group, they may be unsure whether they will ever be able to live with what has happened. If the group is one which people can join (and leave) at any time, membership is likely to include people less recently bereaved, so the meeting provides a forum where they can learn from the longer-term bereaved. 'It was only after going to the group that I realised that it was possible to survive the suicide of a son as there was living evidence across the room' (Clark et al. 1993: 28).

The benefits are mutual, as the group can acknowledge and affirm the progress of the less recently bereaved. However, occasionally there will be members of the group who seem to have become stuck:

Angie joined the group two years after one of her daughters had committed suicide by taking an overdose. She had recently stopped seeing her counsellor but felt that a group might be helpful and she wanted to meet other survivors. At her first meeting, Angie told the group about the recent separation from her husband, her continuing eating problems and how she still wondered whether Tina had accidentally overdosed. She became very distressed and both facilitators noticed that some more recently bereaved group members began to look rather upset. Perhaps they were wondering if they would still be as distressed as Angie two years down the road. The facilitators decided to wait and see what happened next. After a brief silence, one of the group started talking about something different. After two further meetings of the group, Angie sent a message saying that she had decided to return to counselling.

Protected time and space

As Martin told the group one day 'This is *my* space and time'. After his wife's suicide, Martin was struggling to look after their four children, who included a three-year-old and a daughter who had just started at university but was wondering whether to give this up and take her mother's place. All the children needed his attention but Martin was also struggling to hold down a part-time job and he had little time for himself. A group can be a refuge, even an escape at times, but it can also offer a space where the survivor can face their thoughts and feelings without worrying about protecting other people. To do this, though, the group needs to feel safe and be effectively led.

Leading survivor groups

The aims of survivor groups vary and the roles and functions of leaders will reflect this. With a *self-help* group whose broad aims are to provide the opportunity for survivors to share experiences and feelings in a mutually supportive way, leadership roles may include handling enquiries from potential members, welcoming people as they arrive, and opening and closing the meeting. During the meeting, the leader may at times participate as a fellow survivor and share their own experiences.

The other main type of group which has developed in the UK (and elsewhere) is a *facilitated support group*, often with two leaders (see below), one of whom may have personally experienced a suicide bereavement. Although these groups have similar aims to the self-help group, they often have a more 'dynamic' function, with leaders playing a more active role in terms of keeping the group on task and trying to ensure that the group does not collude in avoiding difficult areas. Groups of this kind are often time-limited (see below), which keep individuals focused on working together and can create an energy which aids and fuels the group process.

Survivors and professionals as leaders

Anyone wondering whether to start a group has to think about who will run the meetings, deal with the other tasks involved in setting up the group and keeping it going. Are survivors the people to do this or would it be helpful to involve others such as bereavement counsellors or mental health professionals? There are no easy or straightforward answers, no right or wrong ways of going about this. In some cases, survivors have found that the only way they can get a group going is to start one themselves. Nevertheless, if survivors are running groups, there are issues which need to be thought through, not least because of their potential impact on the group. For any survivor considering leading a group, Dunne (1992a: 102) suggests that addressing these kinds of questions may be helpful.

- Can I cope with the inevitable stresses which running a suicide bereavement group will involve?
- Am I ready, in terms of having 'processed' my own loss sufficiently, so that I am able to help others process *their* losses?
- Am I offering to do this because my experience of belonging to a group was positive and I would like others to have the chance of that too?
- Do I now see myself as an expert on suicide bereavement who can advise others – or can I recognise that I am only an expert on my own loss?
- Is there unfinished business? Am I offering to do this because my guilt makes me feel this is something I *should* do?
- Do I have the time and energy to learn how to run an effective group?

If someone has processed their own loss to the point where they do not need to talk about their own experiences in the group, then they are more free to decide whether to do so at some point because it might help the group in some way. These are not always straightforward decisions.

> Lisa, a survivor of her husband's suicide, co-led a group with a counsellor. In the early sessions she shared her own experiences extensively. This kept the conversation going and by talking about herself maybe it encouraged others to start sharing their losses. On the other hand, it did not allow for any silences, when participants' painful feelings could begin to surface and eventually find expression.

As this chapter has already discussed, survivors often feel set apart or different, believing that only other survivors can understand what they are going through or be of any use to them. This does not mean that non-survivors cannot lead groups – they already do – but it is an issue which the group may need to address. Members may directly confront the non-survivor leader in quite an attacking way, or, as a 'non-survivor' who leads groups has discovered, it may be less overt:

> There is often an implicit questioning. Are you going to be able to cope with us? Can you bear to listen to us? Can you hold this all together if we fall apart? It's as though they need the reassurance that their emotions will be validated.

In practice, when someone asks one of the leaders, 'Are *you* a survivor' this can open up discussion on important issues. How *do* group members feel about people who have not been bereaved by suicide? How do they think other people may see them? How do they feel about mixing with other people at the moment?

In practice, groups can benefit from being co-led by a survivor and a professional, as Farberow found when evaluating the Los Angeles Survivors-After-Suicide Program:

> It is our strong impression that most benefit is found by using a professional and a survivor as co-leaders. The two serve overlapping but very different and necessary functions. While it was generally the professional to whom members turned for information and security, it was to the survivor-facilitator that they most often turned to share their feelings.
>
> (Farberow 1992: 33)

This view is echoed by Clark and her colleagues, who set up and ran a group in Australia. Leadership was shared between a counsellor and support workers, the latter being survivors who had not only 'healed in their grief' but had gone on to successfully complete a grief management training programme:

> We have found it helpful for a counsellor who has not been bereaved by suicide to work with the group at meetings to provide objectivity and direction and to back up the support workers.
>
> (Clark et al. 1993: 165)

A trained counsellor or other professional can also handle difficulties in the group (see below), making a referral to alternative sources of more specialist help, for example.

Having two leaders or facilitators can have other benefits.

- If one leader is absent, this means the group is still able to meet with the second person.
- Tasks outside the group such as planning meetings and taking referrals of new members can be shared.
- During meetings, leaders can take turns: one person interacting more directly with members, while the other person can take more of a back seat and observe what is going on.
- If a group member leaves the room in distress, one person can remain with the rest of the group, who may also be quite vulnerable at this point, while the second person can support the temporarily 'absent' member.
- Perhaps most importantly, there can be shared debriefing afterwards (as well as more formal supervision, see below). As one person said after she became the group's sole leader: 'I miss the chance to talk while we're washing up the coffee cups.'

Roles and tasks of group leaders

Keeping the group on task

Attending a group will often feel like a lifeline to survivors but at the same time they may, understandably, try and avoid the inevitable pain and distress of their loss. As these facilitators explained:

> My difficulties are with the group's somewhat contradictory attitudes: 'We want a group so much we want it practically for always' against 'We don't really want this group to be too heavy, meeting too often, bringing back the pain'. My challenge is the thought 'Is enough work being done, particularly when people suddenly express a desire to go to the pub'.

> We sometimes find we are having to go back to basics – reminding the group what we are doing and what the group is for . . . you've got to keep at the centre otherwise the group can go off at a tangent.

Even when members are apparently 'on task', the facilitator may still need to redirect the group. For example, people may be getting bogged down with fruitless searching for answers to 'why', while sidestepping other issues needing to be addressed. When the group is only meeting for a fixed number of sessions, this is particularly important (though awareness that the group has a limited life can mean that its members engage with the issues more quickly than might otherwise be the case).

Acting as gatekeeper

As 'gatekeeper' or 'custodian' the group leader fulfils a number of tasks. Depending on the way in which the group operates, this can include being responsible for opening and closing meetings at the agreed times and, where necessary, reminding members of other 'ground rules' such as notifying the group if they are unable to attend a meeting.

Group leaders may also need to ensure that confidentiality is maintained, although how this operates in practice will vary. Some groups ask their members not to contact one another between meetings. This avoids 'secrets', where one member divulges something to another member which is not then shared with the rest of the group.

Gatekeeping can also necessitate watching out for vulnerable members and making sure that everyone is given the chance to speak at some point in the meeting – even if they choose not to do so. Knowing that there is someone 'in charge' can also reassure participants that if they begin to talk about their experiences, things will not fall apart. In the words of one facilitator: 'there's a sense that someone is minding the shop for safety'.

Feeling safe is important if survivors are to be able to risk sharing very personal issues with the rest of the group. At the same time, facilitators have to tread a fine line, trying to ensure that the group is safe enough for self-disclosure but not so safe that it becomes cosy, with discussion kept at a level where no one confronts difficult issues such as anger. Leaders may have to challenge the group when this happens.

Modelling behaviours and interventions

One way in which leaders can encourage participants to share with the rest of the group is by modelling appropriate language and behaviours. For example, if the group is resorting to euphemisms about death, the leaders can deliberately use more direct language such as 'suicide', 'dead' or 'killed himself', thus communicating to the group that it is not particularly helpful to deny what has happened by using ambiguous language.

The leader's interventions can model ways of responding which are more likely to be helpful and can act as a reminder of any ground rules the group may have adopted (but forgotten) such as not interrupting, helping people formulate their own strategies and solutions rather than giving advice, acknowledging and respecting differences and not monopolising the group.

Handling difficult situations

All groups have their difficult moments, but unless the leader intervenes and helps the group look at what is going on, people may leave the group prematurely because they cannot cope, or in the case of a 'difficult' member, the group may subtly – or not so subtly – reject them. Experienced group leaders (e.g. Wrobleski 1984–5; Dunne 1992b; Clark et al. 1993) suggest that survivor groups can be faced with one or more of the following scenarios.

- The survivor with an 'evangelical' approach who has a solution for all problems (including other people's as well as their own).
- The compulsive advice giver who can't allow the other person to develop their own solutions.
- The 'competitor' who attempts to establish hierarchies of grieving – 'my loss is much bigger or worse than your loss'.
- The survivor who monopolises meetings, wanting the group's attention for longer than may be appropriate
- The 'help-rejecting complainer' who demands advice from everyone but always responds with a 'yes but . . .'
- The group member whose anger is such that it threatens to destroy the group and its cohesiveness.
- The individual who requires more specialist help than the group can provide, perhaps because of pre-existing mental health problems or other difficulties.

Although this could begin to sound like a list of personality types, it may be more helpful to view them as situations requiring some kind of intervention. Otherwise there is a very real danger that individuals will have the degrading experience of being categorised and as Dunne points out, people may not necessarily behave like this all the time (1992b: 22).

Each of the situations described above will require some form of intervention from the leader which addresses the individual's needs as well as those of the group. Someone constantly monopolising the group *may* need individual counselling in addition to, or instead of, the group. Suggesting other kinds of help is not a sign of the group's failure but can be a reminder of what the group is for – that it is not offering therapy, for example. It also reminds the group that there are limits to what it can provide for others, often a particular difficulty for suicide survivors if they feel they did not do enough for the person who died.

When someone constantly asks for help and constantly rejects it, other members may respond by offering different advice, only to have that rejected again. The group leader can help to break this frustrating cycle by reminding everyone that giving advice doesn't help people develop their own problem-solving capacities.

Sanctioning differentness in the group

This issue has already been touched on but is revisited at this point because leaders may need to tackle it directly. People are meeting together because they have had to deal with similar situations. They may all have had to deal with police, coroner's officers and the media, for example. However, their experiences of these encounters will almost certainly vary widely. One person may have found the inquest very helpful, someone else may have found it only added to their distress. Individual experiences with the same GP or psychiatrist can be very different. If the group is finding it difficult to deal with this because differences feel too threatening, the leader may need to step in and remind the group that different people react differently – and that that is okay; the group is not going to fall apart as a result.

Setting up a survivor group

The pressure to start up a group quickly can be considerable.There may be survivors knocking at the door wanting help *now*. The traumatic nature of suicide bereavement can create an atmosphere of crisis: 'This thing has got to be dealt with immediately because if it isn't something dreadful is going to happen.' (It already has, of course.) In addition, if potential leader(s) are feeling very anxious about the prospect of running a group, they may be tempted to get started without adequate preparation, in which case the group may quickly fold or turn out to be less helpful than might otherwise have been the case. The experience of those who have been facilitating survivor groups in the UK for some time suggests that thorough preparation can take a year or more depending on the individual circumstances.

Certain preparatory tasks are essential, including finding a venue, planning how to publicise the group, deciding whether to assess people before they come to the group, agreeing on the timing, length and frequency of meetings.

Funding is also a consideration. Although most people currently leading survivor groups are working on an unpaid voluntary basis, and meetings are often held in a venue which they can use free of charge, funding will be needed for supervision, publicising the group, and administrative costs such as postage and telephone calls.

It is also important to think in advance about whether the meetings will be structured in any way: whether any written information will be made available in the groups, for example, or whether speakers will be invited on some occasions. In practice, most facilitated groups do not set formal agendas, although the leaders usually try and ensure that before the group ends certain issues have been addressed (e.g. being told about the suicide, viewing the body, funerals, inquests, and anniversaries).

Before some of the practicalities are sorted out, however, decisions need to be made about two key areas:

- Who will the group be for?
- Will the group run for a fixed number of sessions or not?

Who will the group be for?

'Anyone who is a survivor of suicide' might seem the obvious answer and if the group is the only local resource for survivors, then the decision *may* be to open the group to all comers. But will this include teenagers? Is the group going to cater for very recently bereaved people? What about people asking to join who were bereaved several years ago and looking for help? If prospective group members are also having individual counselling, will they join the group or will it be suggested that they join after they have finished the counselling? There are no 'right' answers to these questions but these experiences from group leaders highlight issues which might need to be considered:

> We decided eventually not to take very long-term survivors as we found they were addressing very different problems [from the more recently bereaved] if, three or four years after the suicide, they were still stuck.

> We have found that very recently bereaved people are not usually ready to join the group; they are often still in shock, not able to express themselves and not able to bear other people's distress. We've found that four to six months after the suicide works well.

> We only accepted people referred from professional or voluntary bodies such as CRUSE, Samaritans, social workers and GPs. Prospective group members were then contacted by phone which enabled us to form some idea of their suitability for group work.

> We have had members of the same family using our service [of groups which meet for eight sessions] but not in the same group. We have found that without other family members present, people feel more free to express themselves.

Time-limited or open-ended?

Survivor groups in the UK are usually either:

- open-ended, with people joining and leaving at any point (sometimes referred to as 'slow open' groups) and usually meeting monthly or sometimes more often;
- closed groups which run for a fixed number of sessions, with everyone joining at the same time; meetings may be weekly or fortnightly but sometimes more widely spaced to enable members to digest and consolidate learning from the previous session.

Each model has potential benefits and disadvantages which anyone considering setting up a group needs to think about, although sometimes they may have to opt for one over the other for practical reasons (e.g. leaders are not able to commit themselves beyond a fixed number of sessions).

Potential advantages of open groups:

- survivors can join at any point in the life of the group;
- people can attend for as many or as few sessions as they choose;
- it may be easier to establish a group of a viable size.

Potential disadvantages of open groups:

- each session can be like a first session when new members attend;
- constantly changing membership can make it more difficult to establish a climate of trust and safety.

Potential advantages of closed (time-limited) groups:

- easier to develop group cohesion, allowing deeper issues to be explored;
- regular attendance promotes trust and facilitates self-disclosure;
- because the group has a limited life, members may work harder;
- facilitators can have a 'breather' between groups.

Potential disadvantages of closed time-limited groups:

- it can be difficult to recruit sufficient numbers to start at the same time;
- some people may feel unable to wait for the next group to start;
- the number of sessions may not be sufficient for some survivors.

Thinking about and talking through the kind of issues raised here also provides an opportunity for leaders to get to know each other, find out what makes the other person 'tick', start forming a picture of what it will be like to work together and talking about possible points of friction or disagreement about how particular issues might be handled in the group.

> You've got to get to know each other – to learn something about the other person's background. You've got to be able to give each other support – and be able to have a shared experience in the group.

There will be times when co-facilitators will handle the same situation very differently. Talking about possible differences before the group starts can help to ensure that differentness enriches rather than threatens the group.

This preparation time also enables new leaders to reflect on how they feel about running the group. All sorts of issues may emerge. Will I be good enough? Do I know enough? Suicide has not touched me personally so am I perhaps afraid that being alongside survivors will be contagious? My own experience of suicide bereavement was ten years ago, but is the group going to bring it all back?

Training, support and supervision for leaders

In the UK, there is no specific training and supervision for people leading suicide bereavement groups and no guidelines on training. However, experienced facilitators have found it essential to have some knowledge and experience in the areas of bereavement, suicide and group work. With two facilitators working together, individual skills and experience could be pooled and were often complementary.

Group leaders have often had experience of working with CRUSE and/or the Samaritans and some have had previous experience of running groups. In some instances, an inexperienced group leader (who had some background knowledge of bereavement and suicide) worked alongside an experienced facilitator in an 'apprenticeship' model. There was also an emphasis on continuing development by regularly attending relevant workshops, courses and conferences.

Running a suicide survivor group is usually demanding, and though it can be extremely rewarding, it can also be very stressful. Many of those currently leading groups expressed the view that regular supervision was essential and they welcomed the input from a 'third party' who could give them other perspectives on their work as well as offering support. Informal debriefing with one another after group meetings was helpful but external supervision allowed for more reflective exploration and for feedback from an objective standpoint.

Leaving the group

This chapter would not be complete without a mention of endings, whether in a time-limited group with a defined end point which is known from the first meeting, or in an open-ended group where, hopefully, individual members leave when they are ready. Suicide survivors meet in a group because they have experienced a traumatic and difficult ending of an important relationship, so 'good endings' in the group matter. People attending survivor groups will often form strong bonds with one another; and separating can be a painful reminder of how bonds were severed with the person who took their own life. At the same time, it is important to remember that 'the point of coming to a group is to be able to leave the group' (Wrobleski 1987: 8). What may be initially a place of refuge should also be part of a transition (Parkes 1998).

> The group is there to help people come to terms with their loss . . . to enable people to work through their grief and move on.

Open-ended groups allow survivors to move at their own pace. Someone can stay as long as they need – but sometimes it can be difficult to leave. The group may be a safe place where the survivor feels understood. The outside world may seem rather daunting. However, the group should be a transitional place. It may be a stepping stone to other groups and relationships, a time-limited surrogate family for survivors, a temporary support group where temporary alliances and friendships are common, as various survivor group leaders have described.

Time-limited groups offer a different, sometimes more intense, experience with a defined ending for its members. People join, knowing that an ending is in sight from the first session. However, six or eight sessions may not be sufficient for some people. Depending on the resources of the organisation (and some groups were run with minimal organisational backing), this can be addressed in a number of ways.

- Survivors are offered a 'repeat' next time the group is run, if the leaders feel this would be helpful.
- People are directed to organisations which can offer individual counselling.
- A one-off follow-up meeting is held to check out how people are managing and provide an opportunity for leaders to get some feedback about the group.
- A 'second-tier' programme for the longer-term bereaved which might include social events as well as educational and personal development activities, the latter partly aimed at supporting survivors who have gone on to become support workers (Clark et al. 1993).
- Booster groups for people who have attended the regular survivor groups in the past, which enable 'veterans' to check out their progress with one another and share disappointments and successes (Dunne 1992c).
- Former group members keeping in touch informally by telephoning or writing to one another.

Just as each person's grieving is unique, so each person's experience of belonging to a group will be different, and what they contribute to and take out of the group will vary. Some will go away having gained a great deal from the experiences, others less. Sometimes one person's experiences will enrich the whole group.

A young woman joined the group after her brother had hanged himself. During the lifetime of the group, she became pregnant. For other group members, this became a powerful symbol of commitment to the future and new life.

Finally, it is not only survivors who gain from being part of a group.

Being part of a group lets the members realise they are not alone with their pain and allows them to accept and live on. Group facilitators learn from the group too by being part of their painful journey. It's a privilege to have been part of that journey.

Chapter 17

Counselling people bereaved by suicide*

The person who commits suicide puts his psychological skeleton in the survivor's emotional closet . . . he sentences the survivor to deal with many negative feelings.

(Shneidman 1972: x)

The therapist plays the role of witness and ally, in whose presence the survivor can speak of the unspeakable.

(Herman 1994: 175)

Introduction

Suicide bereavement is often 'an unspeakable loss' (Worden 1991: 96), and because death through suicide falls into the unthinkable category, 'we tend to deny the unthinkable' (Lendrum and Syme 1992: 34). For the survivor, communication with others can be difficult at best and sometimes impossible. Yet the impact of the death and its meaning for the bereaved individual need to be faced if the survivor is to move on. Counselling can offer a place – a safe space – where the unspeakable may be spoken and the unthinkable thought about with another person. It offers the survivor the chance to work through the particular legacy of a self-inflicted death and hopefully find meaning in what can often seem to have been a meaningless act. The breakdown in communication with others in the survivor's life can begin to be repaired in the counselling relationship.

* This chapter is based mainly on my experiences of counselling people bereaved by suicide and also draws on relevant counselling and psychotherapy literature, but I have endeavoured to make it as accessible as possible so that it may be read not only by counsellors and therapists, but by others who may be wanting to understand more about the sometimes complex emotional legacy of suicide and how they can most appropriately and helpfully respond to survivors. I have included numerous vignettes to put some kind of 'clothing' on the psychological concepts and, hopefully, bring them to life. However, I have deliberately said very little about how I have worked with these issues since individual counsellors and therapists will have their own ways of working.

Of course not all survivors will seek, or need, counselling or therapy, but some will. Bereavement counselling services are receiving an increasing number of referrals from people whose lives have been directly affected by suicide, but counsellors working in other settings will also encounter survivors whether the suicide was recent or occurred many years ago.

Some people may seek counselling in the weeks immediately following the death. Others will only approach a counsellor months later. They may seem to be 'back to normal'; they are managing to work, perhaps even starting to socialise again, but behind the apparent normality, they are struggling with distressing thoughts and feelings. Yet others will have seemingly 'adjusted' to the suicide, but years later will seek help for apparently unrelated problems. Only during the counselling will unresolved issues around an earlier suicide bereavement emerge.

> A, a woman in her early twenties, contacted the local bereavement counselling service a month after her mother's suicide. She was extremely distressed, felt she was to blame for the death, and in the last few days had started cutting her arms and legs. She wasn't sure if counselling would be any use, but said she was desperate for help.
>
> M had come home from work one day to find that his wife had hanged herself in their bedroom. Almost a year later, M was drinking heavily in order to get to sleep and still having frequent nightmares about finding J's body. His sales job meant he was mostly out of the office and his colleagues generally assumed he had got over the death. He sometimes met up with old friends, but his wife was not usually mentioned. At the first session, he told the counsellor he was scared of crashing his car or cracking up.
>
> V, who was in her late twenties, went to see her GP, complaining of depression and problems with her boyfriend who was threatening to break off the relationship. The GP referred her to the practice counsellor. During the initial session, when the counsellor was asking about her past, V mentioned in passing that when she was eight her mother had committed suicide. She also mentioned that she and her older brother were sent to boarding school three months later. She recounted this in a rather matter-of-fact way and did not seem aware that her current relationship difficulties might be linked to this early loss.

Each client's journey in counselling will be unique, just as their loss is unique, and counsellors and therapists will work from particular theoretical orientations. However, the themes discussed below are offered as landmarks which counsellor and client may encounter along the way. Although there is now a fairly substantial literature on bereavement counselling, little attention has been paid to working with the specific issues which may arise in counselling suicide survivors, issues which though not unique to suicide bereavement are often more prevalent.

The psychological legacy of suicide

Suicide is complex and multi-faceted, and the act of suicide is a multi-dimensional event. In Shneidman's words:

> No single learned discipline is sufficient to explain any individual suicidal event . . . biological, cultural, sociological, interpersonal, intrapsychic, logical, conscious and unsconscious, and philosophical elements are present, in various degrees, in each suicidal event.
>
> (1993: 3)

This is echoed by Hawton, when he writes of how: 'suicide is usually the tragic end point of various possible pathways, influenced by mental ill-health and psychological, socio-economic, familial, interpersonal and genetic factors' (1998: 156).

The counsellor's awareness of these multiple dimensions or pathways is important, but it is the *interpersonal* element which is likely to dominate the counselling and which, together with the impact of the traumatic nature of suicide, is the focus of this chapter. Suicide is usually a solitary act, but, paradoxically, it deeply involves others. The person who takes their own life is making a powerful statement about life and about their relationships. In rejecting life, they are also rejecting those who were a part of it. Suicide is perceived as the only escape from an intolerable situation and, by implication, others are seen as unable to offer any solution which would make life worth living.

Working as a group therapist with survivors, Battle was able to observe 'the psychodynamics of people who commit suicide as those dynamics reflect themselves in the survivors' (1984: 52). These survivors, he concluded, reached a number of 'unstated understandings' or hidden messages about what the suicide victim was saying:

> When the suicide says 'I can't handle the problem', he is also saying . . . 'You can't handle the problem either' . . . The suicide says 'I need no more people to love outside of myself, therefore I reject you' . . . Insofar as suicide is an attempt at mastery and control . . . the suicide is saying, 'My death is preferable to my trying to work out my problems with you or through you; therefore you and I are terribly distant' . . . The suicide is saying by his act that the hated situation or person is more important to him than his loved ones or the affection and dependency that he had upon them.
>
> (1984: 54)

It is not difficult to discern the implicit aggression in some of these statements. This is vividly described by Campbell and Hale who suggest that,
although sadness and pessimism are commonly present in suicidal individuals, it is important to recognise 'the violence inherent in the suicidal act
. . . an act aimed at destroying the self's body and *tormenting the mind of
another*' (1992: 288; my italics). Not surprisingly, Hale and Campbell point
out, this view of suicide is commonly resisted by relatives, as well as by many
professionals. No one wants to feel that they are the object of another's
aggression, even if it is an unconscious attack, but the sadistic nature of
suicide is undeniable 'if we have the opportunity to observe the way it
relentlessly dominates the inner life of the survivor' (Barnett and Hale 1985).

When a man kills himself on his wife's birthday or on the birthday of one
of his children, there is an undoubted attack on the surviving spouse and
family (the hidden message being 'I'm making sure you will never be able to
enjoy your birthday ever again because now it is the anniversary of my
suicide too'). As Hillman points out, the shadowy aspects of suicide include
elements of aggression, revenge and hatred (1976).

The person who takes their own life escapes from psychological pain, but
one of the most striking features of suicide bereavement is the way in which
their unbearable feelings are passed to the survivors. The 'psychache'
(Shneidman 1993), the shame, guilt, humiliation, anger, loneliness, angst
and other emotions associated with suicidal states frequently become the
survivor's legacy. It is as though the person who died is saying, intentionally
or otherwise, 'I want you to know what it feels like to be me'. Thus, as
Shneidman (1972) suggests, the suicide victim passes on his psychological
'skeletons'.

As already touched on in Chapter 2, the person bereaved by suicide has
experienced a traumatic event. Survivors may be driven to seek help from a
counsellor or therapist because they are experiencing distressing thoughts
and feelings commonly associated with trauma: repeated vivid recall of the
event, flashbacks, intrusive images and thoughts, nightmares and sleep
disturbances, increased anxiety and vulnerability, guilt and regret, anger
and blame, and shame. Symptoms of post-traumatic stress disorder (PTSD)
may be part of the picture (Worden 1991; Lendrum and Syme 1992; Archer
1999). Survivors may have repeated flashbacks about finding the body, or
violent dreams about the person dying.

Shneidman suggests that sudden death can be viewed as a 'disaster'.
Drawing on the professional literature on conventionally recognised disasters, he cites a number of reactions commonly found among survivors of
both collective and individual disasters including: an impaired capacity for
self-love, traumatic loss of feelings of identity, and psychic closing-off or
numbing (1993: 166–7).

Increasing attention has been paid in recent years to the psychological
impact of collective disasters such as the Omagh bombing or the Dunblane

shootings. There is much greater recognition of the effects of these traumatic events on the survivors. As a result, more professionals, including counsellors, are being trained to identify and work with symptoms of post-traumatic stress disorder.

Alongside this, there is a growing awareness of the needs of people experiencing individual and private 'disasters', including those bereaved by suicide. The work of Garland and her colleagues at the Tavistock Clinic's Unit for the Study of Trauma and its Aftermath (Garland 1998), for example, is furthering our understanding of the meaning of trauma from a psycho-analytical perspective and ways of working with this.

The psychological legacy of suicide is rarely straightforward and frequently painful. Like others who are bereaved, the survivor faces the pain of separation from the deceased, the forfeiture of a shared future and the sadness of grief. But suicide brings additional issues to the fore. Counsellors need to be aware of these other dimensions which can include shame, guilt, anger and questioning why the suicide occurred. They can be difficult issues for survivors to acknowledge and if the counsellor is unaware of them, there is a danger that they will remain unaddressed and therefore not be worked through.

Suicide is one of the most extreme manifestations of 'acting out': action becomes a substitute for feelings which cannot be thought about or talked about. The person who takes their own life has not been able to think or talk about their problems, and may well have belonged to a family where feelings were not talked about and problems were not discussed in order to find possible solutions or coping strategies. If the survivor comes from the same family, the counsellor needs to be aware of this and help the client find a voice so that, unlike the person who died, they can find a way of talking about and processing their feelings.

Themes and issues in counselling

Getting started: engaging the client in the counselling

It would be easy to assume that the many distressing emotions associated with suicide bereavement would lead the survivor to readily engage in counselling. Like most clients, they will claim to be seeking relief from unwanted thoughts and feelings and hope that counselling – and the counsellor – will offer that. But at the same time, there are issues which can make it difficult for the survivor-client to really engage in the counselling and allow a therapeutic alliance to develop.

The client who comes to counselling following a traumatic suicide bereavement may be desperately seeking help but unsure if the counsellor can really help them. There often seems to be an implicit message: 'If I'm not coping with this awful event in my life (with possible sub-text: "and no one around me seems to be coping with it either"), how on earth can I expect that you are going to be able to hear all this, let alone help me.' There will often be a need to test out the counsellor.

As Ingham (1998) suggests, at the start of therapy, individuals are often very preoccupied with the therapist's capacity and will try to find out about their strengths and weaknesses, their limits and their capabilities. For the person who has experienced a significant trauma, he concludes, 'this may be especially the case . . . where the therapist's or indeed any listener's, task of being open to and partially identified with an experience that the patient finds unthinkable, and at the same time thinking about it, is testing, and sometimes so in the extreme' (1998: 100). The suicide survivor may believe that they will be 'too much'. They may be extremely watchful, wondering whether the counsellor will be able to bear what they find so unbearable. The traumatised survivor may fear that their story will traumatise the counsellor too so that she becomes unable even to listen, let alone be of any use to them.

Suicide survivors often find it difficult to be around other people. They may feel tainted by the suicide, as though the death has contaminated them in some way. Shame is commonplace and can lead survivors to isolate themselves from others. This can make it difficult for the survivor to engage with the counsellor, even when they are also wanting help with managing their distress.

Suicide survivors can echo the ambivalence of many of those who seek counselling or therapy: 'I want you to help me look at these problems – but I don't want to look at them (and maybe you can just take these nasty feelings away)'; 'I want to change, but change is really frightening, so I'd really prefer it if things remained the same (even if they are very difficult)'.

> P, who was in her thirties, came to counselling following the suicide of her brother to whom she had been very close. During the first session, she described how it felt as though D's death was on the other side of a big wall. She felt this helped her to cope with what had happened. P talked a great deal about how sad she felt and frequently cried in the sessions, but any other emotions seemed to be absent from the room. The counsellor wondered whether P was avoiding more difficult or negative feelings and several weeks later suggested that P might begin by looking over the wall. P then told the counsellor that she could see 'rejection, anger and abandonment'. The sessions continued but the counsellor began to feel that P was 'sitting on the fence', or the wall, when it came to any deeper exploration of her feelings. Shortly afterwards P phoned to say that she had decided to end the counselling.

In some cases, the survivor-client may have spent months or years trying to persuade the other person to seek help for their problems but to no avail and the culmination of their efforts has been the suicide. Now it is the survivor who is having to seek help. The upshot can be a client who feels they are there under duress.

> B's daughter had taken her own life, following several years of mental illness and two 'unsucccessful' suicide attempts. In the second session, B told the counsellor that she was coping and that she was okay; she gave the impression that she had only come to counselling because her GP had suggested it and she didn't want to offend him. Although B spoke in a rather calm manner, the counsellor was aware of feeling rather angry herself. When the counsellor asked B how she felt about seeing a counsellor, B said rather emphatically: 'It's [her daughter] that should be doing this. *She* should be sitting here, not me.'

For some clients, fears of dependency can make it difficult for them to engage with the counsellor. Survivors have often seen themselves as the 'copers' or 'carers', the ones on whom others, including the deceased, depended. But now, as Battle suggests, the survivor faces 'the same predicament as the one from which [the suicidal person] has escaped – helplessness' (1984: 53). In a strenuous attempt to ward off these unwelcome feelings of helplessness, the survivor-client may find ways of trying to control the counselling itself.

> S started weekly counselling following her husband's suicide, but after the first few weeks, she asked to change to fortnightly sessions. The counsellor attempted to explore this with her and S said that she didn't feel able to cope with weekly sessions. Although S reluctantly agreed to continue the weekly sessions she frequently cancelled so she often only came fortnightly.

> H began arriving ten to fifteen minutes late for her sessions. After this had gone on for several weeks, the counsellor decided to raise the issue. H said she didn't see what the fuss was about, but was sorry to keep her waiting. At the end of the following session, when it was time to stop, H told her the clock must be wrong. The next week she queried the fifty-minute session, saying she thought they were supposed to meet for an hour. All this led the counsellor to speculate about the reasons why H was behaving in such an apparently controlling manner. Maybe she needed to re-assert the control she felt she had lost when her partner had killed himself. Perhaps she was trying to find ways of mastering her sense of helplessness.

The survivor may decide to look for counselling hoping it will help them, but if the person who died had had counselling or therapy, they may be deeply sceptical about whether it can really be of any use, whether it can really make a difference and whether change is really possible.

The rejection inherent in suicide leaves many survivors struggling with low self-esteem and feeling undeserving of help from others. A reluctance to seek out support in their own networks can be enacted in the counselling too. As one survivor told his counsellor at their first meeting: 'I'm sure there are other people who are more deserving of your help than I am.' In bereavement counselling services, where clients are generally seen free of charge, survivors may feel they are less deserving of help than those bereaved through non-suicide deaths.

Survivors who have decided – however unrealistically – that they were responsible for the death may well feel undeserving of help or understanding from other people. If the suicide was their fault then why should they expect any understanding or sympathy from others? Survivor-clients may not always express these feelings directly, but may subtly attempt to get the counsellor to reject them – thus confirming what they 'know' to be true.

> R had started counselling, following her husband's suicide when he had left a note which she felt blamed her for his death. Although the counsellor felt they had made quite a good start, R began to make somewhat disparaging remarks about the counselling room and the neighbourhood, although the comments were usually made in an apparently lighthearted manner. After several sessions, the counsellor became aware of her own wish to retaliate in the face of these attacks. She also realised that maybe that was precisely what R wanted, as that would confirm R's feeling that she was not worth anyone's concern.

Survivors will often defend themselves against very painful feelings, and counsellors need to understand this and be aware when it is happening in sessions. Resorting to intellectualisation is not uncommon. They may talk about what has happened in a rather dissociated manner. The survivor whose relative has had a long-standing involvement with mental health services often acquires some knowledge of psychiatric terminology and familiarity with psychotropic medication. Words like 'psychosis', 'deliberate self-harm' and 'SSRIs' may trip off the tongue. Counsellors need to be aware of this when it constantly occurs in sessions.

> L started seeing a counsellor after her younger son had killed himself. In the early sessions, she talked at length about the time leading up to V's suicide, his increasingly bizarre behaviour, her attempts to get help and her discovery of his body. Listening to this, the counsellor felt she was sitting in on a 'case' presentation but at the same time was aware of her own mounting anxiety. She wondered if L was projecting into her

the horror and panic which she was unable to allow herself to experience. At the same time, the counsellor realised that L may have been unconsciously attempting to communicate to the counsellor the powerful and frightening feelings V's death had evoked.

People who kill themselves may bequeath unbearable feelings to survivors, but, as though engaging in a rather macabre game, a survivor may attempt to 'pass the parcel' to the counsellor in a desperate attempt to ward off their own unbearable feelings.

Why: puzzlement and perplexity

The particular questioning of suicide survivors in counselling can be more, or less, useful, depending on the purpose it serves. As Dunne suggests:

> Surviving suicide establishes in the survivor a perpetual need to search for both physical and psychological clues as to the reason for the suicide. This search may be quite conscious and represent an obsessional need to review the events prior to the death, or it may be less overtly evident, manifesting itself in a generalised attitude of vigilance and suspicion.
>
> (1987b: 200)

Searching for answers *can* have a positive purpose. It may represent an attempt to reach some kind of closure on a painful event and put a stop to the endless, repetitive questioning. The survivor can move on, even if this means accepting that they do not have all the answers and may always have an incomplete picture. If searching for answers to 'why' enables the survivor to develop a satisfactory account of the death which they can live with, this will contribute significantly to a healthy resolution of their grieving (Clark and Goldney 2000).

Although not the sole prerogative of those bereaved by suicide, 'why?' is a key issue for survivors and unless the counsellor is vigilant, one which can dominate the counselling to the point where other important issues remain unaddressed. The counsellor needs to be aware of the different ways in which this searching can appear in sessions.

Looking for the answers to 'why' may be the (conscious) reason why the survivor has decided to go to see a counsellor. There may be a hope – however unrealistic – that the counsellor will provide the answers.

> During the first session, E told the counsellor he was coming to see her because he'd heard that she was an 'expert' on suicide and thought she would be able to help him. He'd seen another counsellor just after his father's suicide six months ago, but had left after two sessions because

he felt that the counsellor lacked the necessary knowledge or under-standing about his bereavement. The counsellor wondered whether there were other reasons why E had left the previous counsellor. Was it too soon after the death? Did E find the counselling too painful? And what did he want from an 'expert'? Would E expect her to provide an explanation for his father's suicide?

Continued and endless searching can postpone or prolong the grieving. Someone may spend a great deal of time in counselling sessions going over and over the events around the time of the suicide in an attempt to re-write the 'story' and produce a diffferent version: perhaps one that does not include suicide. The aim of this searching can be to reinforce denial, almost as if by producing a different version the other person won't really have died or at least will not have died by their own hand.

Survivors may also attempt to engage the counsellor in a dialogue about 'why'. The client talks about suicide in a rather unemotional manner and the person who died is hardly mentioned. This rather rational, intellectual search may serve to prevent the emergence of painful feelings – feelings which may include a fear that unless the 'answers' are found (or preferably *the* answer), then someone else in the family is going to kill themselves too.

A common question is 'Why did my relative commit suicide? What was going on in their head at the time of their death?' Here the survivor may be attempting to initiate (or continue) a dialogue which the suicide victim has abruptly terminated by the act of suicide. Or it may be seen as an attempt on the part of the survivor to achieve mastery or control over an event which may have left them feeling anything but in control. Trying to get inside the suicide victims's head may be an attempt to regain control.

> After his sister's suicide, W became increasingly preoccupied with trying to understand what had led to P's death. He had not seen his sister for several weeks before the event and found her death totally inexplicable and meaningless. In an attempt to find the answer, he travelled to the place where the death had occurred, and sat in the car where P had killed herself.

The chaotic, complex and rapidly changing emotions commonly experi-enced by the survivor can be very frightening. Although there is never a single reason why a person takes their own life, for the survivor, the urgent need to find an answer – *the* answer – may represent an attempt to contain those seemingly uncontainable feelings.

For some survivors, searching can be an attempt to avoid feelings of guilt. It is as though they are saying: 'If I can find a reason why they died, a reason "out there", someone who I can hold responsible for the death, then maybe I will be able to stop blaming myself.' As Dunne (1987b) suggests, however, although searching may be a way of avoiding guilt, the search may result in increased guilt.

Guilt and self-blame

Alvarez writes of how 'suicide effortlessly promotes guilt' (1974) and together with the 'why?' is often a dominant issue in the counselling. Surviving suicide can leave 'a legacy of inexorable guilt' (Dunne 1987b: 200). This may be directly expressed in self-blame and shouldering responsibility for the death – 'If only I'd done this . . . if only I hadn't done that . . .'

Feelings of guilt can surface with any bereavement ('I could have done more'; 'Why did I do that'; 'Why didn't I do [such and such]') but for some suicide survivors, the guilt can be particularly intense, long-lasting and difficult to resolve. A young woman graphically described her feelings of guilt and self-hate in the counselling sessions following her mother's suicide saying: 'I'm a selfish bitch'; 'I'm a spoilt brat'. It can be the predominant problem for some survivors (Battle 1984: 51) and the overriding reason why they seek counselling or other help.

Guilt 'can arise from the sense that the deceased blamed the survivor for his or her misery' (Dunne 1987b: 201). Suicide may become the only means of escape from this persecutory guilt, the only means of freeing oneself, but guilt is then passed on – part of the survivor's 'legacy':

> The ultimate intention of suicide is often to project this unbearable guilt . . . It could be formulated as follows: 'It is not fair that it should be I who carry this guilt. As you have not understood me nor helped me to free myself from it, I am killing myself so that you will have to bear it now'.
>
> (Grinberg 1992: 108)

Survivor guilt can be triggered by individual as well as collective disasters (see p. 22) and the survivor of suicide may believe that he or she has survived at the cost of another person's life. Survivor guilt can have many dimensions.

> The survivor feels guilty about being alive when others have perished. This is the more intense if the survivor feels he has, or actually has, done less than he might have done to help others . . . He feels guilty about abandoning people for whom he should have cared, even if he could not really help.
>
> (Menzies Lyth 1989: 249)

When death occurs after a period of illness, relief that the deceased is no longer suffering physical pain is generally considered acceptable. With suicide deaths, relief can be more complex. Relief is often about cessation of emotional pain, but survivors may also be relieved that the dead person is no longer making demands on them; they are freed to get on with their own lives. This in turn can create further guilt, making it hard for the survivor to acknowledge these feelings. Counselling can provide opportunities for expressions of relief, which can be an important element in grief recovery.

Suicide survivors may come to counselling in the hope that the counsellor will free them from an overwhelming sense of culpability and, aware of the survivor's pain, the counsellor may be tempted to respond by swiftly exonerating them, urging the client to stop blaming themselves. The upshot of this can be that the client feels neither heard nor understood. At this point they may terminate the counselling, or they may return to the issue, hoping for a different response from the counsellor. So how can the issue of guilt be addressed in the counselling?

Worden suggests that 'the counsellor can help because guilt yields itself up to *reality* testing' (1991: 45), though he acknowledges that this may take more time in the case of a suicide survivor (1991: 96). If, as Worden suggests, guilt is often irrational and inappropriate, then he suggests that the client may obtain a sense of relief through the counsellor's questioning: 'You say you didn't do enough, but what did you do . . . and what else? And what else?' Clark and Goldney also suggest that 'Counselling may be helpful to assist the person rationalise unrealistic feelings, particularly guilt' (2000: 18). While this 'reality testing' approach *may* be effective or helpful for some people, with other survivors, intense guilt persists, requiring a deeper exploration of its meaning for the individual.

Survivors may feel that because all their efforts to keep the other person alive ended in failure, this can only mean that they are useless and incompetent. One way of dealing with these painful feelings and the shame they engender is to project them onto the counsellor.

> K talked bitterly about how stupid she had felt at being unable to stop her husband taking his own life because she had always managed to sort out crises before. She left the session in some distress. The follow-ing week she sat down and, sounding rather angry, said she thought she should stop coming to counselling. She'd expected it would help her feel better but if anything she felt worse and thought the counselling was no use. The counsellor's initial reaction was to wonder whether counselling *was* helping K but remembering how the previous session had ended felt that this attack on her competence was perhaps related to K's need to disown her painful feelings of helplessness.

Guilt may not always be consciously experienced. It can appear in the survivor's dreams as the following vignette illustrates:

N's brother, S, had a long history of severe depression and his problems had often dominated family life as they were growing up. Following her brother's suicide, N had the following dream. She is standing by a well. Looking down, she sees S at the bottom of the well. He is calling to her to rescue him. N is rooted to the spot. She knows she should try and pull him out but is unable to do so. In counselling, she was able to acknowledge that S's death had in some ways been a relief – but that she also felt guilty for having survived.

Guilt may be the suicide victim's legacy, but where someone clings to that bequest, it can be an attempt to regain control, thus fending off feelings of helplessness and rejection. The unspoken script may go something like this: 'If *I* was responsible for this death, then however bad that makes me feel, it's preferable to feeling powerless. At least I can escape from feeling out of control. I don't have to acknowledge that they chose to walk away from me.'

T came to counselling following her partner's suicide for which she blamed herself. The first few sessions were dominated by T telling the counsellor how guilty she was because she knew she could have saved him. Although the counsellor's instinct was to try and help T understand that she was not responsible for her partner's death, she realised that T maybe felt unable at this point to face her partner's rejection of her.

Survivors of trauma can become preoccupied with a wish to rescue others (Gibb 1998) and people bereaved by suicide may become caught up in trying to stop other people taking their own lives, perhaps feeling that *this time* they can succeed – even though the traumatic death has already occurred.

Several months after her son's suicide, one of Y's acquaintances, who knew about the suicide, mentioned to Y that she sometimes felt suicidal herself. Although Y did not know this person well, she became very involved with supporting her. The counsellor was aware that Y was still finding it hard to cope with her son's death and suggested that maybe she did not have to look after someone else when she was still struggling herself. Y reacted angrily to this at first, but was then able to admit her fear that if she did not intervene, another person might take their own life.

This desire to rescue others may have a genuinely reparative element, but can also be a way of projecting the survivor's own unbearable feelings onto others (Gibb 1998). By directing their attention towards rescuing other people, it is those others who become the ones in need of rescue, not the survivor.

With some survivors, counselling sessions become bogged down by a litany of 'if only I had done such and such' or 'if only I hadn't done such and such'. It is as though by constant repetition, the survivor hopes to turn the clock back and cancel out the suicide – the defence of 'undoing' which Freud described as an attempt 'to "blow away" not merely the *consequences* of some event . . . but the event itself' (1936: 33; italics in original). Helping the client recognise what is happening can enable them to move towards accepting that the suicide cannot be 'undone' – an acceptance that is often painful and difficult for the client to reach.

For young adults, the suicide of a parent at the point when they are leaving home and beginning to establish a life outside the family can be a considerable source of guilt. A normal move towards independence, which may evoke a degree of guilt in any young person, becomes magnified when the suicide is seen to convey a message that the parent could not tolerate the separation.

> O, a woman in her early twenties, was seen for counselling shortly after her father had taken a fatal overdose. A year before his death O had left the small town where she grew up and started work in a large city some distance away. Things had gone well, she was enjoying her new career and had made new friends. Her father's death left her not only bereft, but extremely guilty. She told the counsellor that she believed he would still be alive if she had stayed at home. However, when the counsellor asked what else had been happening in the family, she began to talk about her father's serious financial problems, an impending court appearance, and her mother's recently diagnosed health problems. Eventually she was able to see that there were probably a number of different factors which had led her father to take his own life.

The survivor's identity

Bereavement of any kind will involve changes in self-concept, when 'the old self [is] no longer appropriate for the changed circumstances' (Archer 1999: 89). Writing of the impact of major disasters, Menzies Lyth suggests that 'Survivors are likely to experience an identity crisis: "I'm not the person I was, but who am I?" . . . The shattering of the familiar external world, shatters the internal world that gives identity' (1989: 250, 251).

This sense of a shattered internal world is echoed in the way suicide survivors may describe their situation to the counsellor: 'my world has fallen apart' or 'the bottom has dropped out of my world' . . . familiar phrases which, despite sounding rather clichéd, represent the survivor's attempt to communicate something of their panic, their unbearable anxiety, a belief that their world is falling apart – and maybe that they fear they will fall apart or lose their mind. The counsellor's role in containing the client's feelings will be critical. The survivor may feel totally uncontained, as though 'there is no functioning part of himself or others that can help him put himself back together again' (Menzies Lyth 1989: 251).

> D, whose partner had recently committed suicide, arrived saying that she felt she was 'going crazy' and wanted to be admitted to hospital immediately. The counsellor thought maybe D wanted to be somewhere where she would feel safe and where other people could deal with the feelings which were 'sending her crazy'. The counsellor wondered if that would help, while also being aware of her own anxiety about coping with this situation. At the same time she was concerned about what might happen if she did not accede to D's request. By the end of the session, D said she was feeling less agitated but asked for the counsellor's telephone number. Although clients in the organisation for which the counsellor worked usually did not have access to their counsellor's private phone number, in this instance the counsellor felt that D perhaps needed to have this but would probably not use it – which was indeed, the case.

The survivor may, as in D's case, demand hospitalisation, wanting a *place* which will physically contain them and stop them from falling apart or 'going mad'. More commonly they may want medication to deaden or take away their distressing feelings. However, what the client is really seeking in this situation 'is a form of holding such as a mother gives to her distressed child' (Casement 1985: 133). The counsellor needs to create a sense of safety where the survivor can feel secure enough to confront the feelings of unsafety engendered by the trauma of the suicide.

The framework in which the counselling or therapy takes place will be important. The counselling room, the frequency and duration of sessions, arrangements for breaks and (where applicable) payment of fees, and agreements about any contact between sessions, need to be as clear and consistent as possible. 'Secure boundaries', as Herman reminds us, 'create a safe arena where the work of recovery can take place' (1992: 149). Having these explicitly understood boundaries may be particularly relevant to survivors, because the suicide victim has, in a very real way, broken boundaries and overturned taboos.

The containment which the counsellor and the counselling framework offer will also help the suicide survivor negotiate the transition that all bereaved people face. How the survivor is able to rebuild their internal world will depend to some extent on their pre-bereavement identity. If their internal world was one which felt supportive and safe, and the external world was generally experienced as reasonably supportive and predictable, despite these assumptions being severely challenged by the suicide, the survivor may find it easier to negotiate the transition.

At times of transition, the individual is between two places. The past is past and the future is not yet visible, so it is not all that surprising if survivors do everything in their power to hold on to the past, or construct a future pattern which attempts to maintain the previous identity. At least these are known.

> Six weeks after his wife's suicide, Z told his counsellor: 'I just want everything to go back to normal, or at least to be as normal as before, even though I know it won't be the same.' He realised things could not be the same as before, but at the same time, he was resisting the idea of a changed future.

For some survivors, the suicide will be experienced as an insult or 'narcissistic injury' (Kohut 1986). An image of the self is destroyed or severely compromised by the suicide victim's seeming rejection of them. The parent whose child has died by suicide may, as one person described it, 'not really feel like a parent any more, or only half a parent', even when there are surviving children. The belief in oneself as a competent provider for the family is severely challenged.

For some survivors, an important part of their identity is about rescuing, caring and coping. Their own needs may be denied, enabling them to avoid feelings of dependency because neediness is projected onto others – including the suicide victim.

> C told the counsellor how she had spent a great deal of time looking after her boyfriend who suffered from severe depression. On several occasions, she had managed to dissuade him from attempting suicide, but while she was visiting relatives one weekend, he drowned himself in a nearby river. The counsellor acknowledged how much C had done to try and keep him alive to which C responded that she often felt like Florence Nightingale with all the looking after she had done. She sounded rather proud and pleased about this but then sat silently looking rather troubled. C arrived the following week deeply depressed, saying she had been crying a great deal since the previous session. She realised that all her previous boyfriends had been rather needy types and maybe she enjoyed being a rescuer. In the following weeks, she talked to the counsellor about her anger towards friends. As she said: 'No one thinks about my needs'.

A person bereaved by suicide who has always felt strong and powerful is faced with a situation in which they now have to grapple with feelings of powerlessness. However strong and able they believed they were, they have been unable to prevent the suicide. Shame is central to the experience of suicide (Seguin et al. 1995a) and in the counsellor's presence, the survivor may struggle with feelings of embarrassment and shame about their needs.

> Q started counselling following a friend's suicide but admitted that the idea of getting help for herself was very difficult to accept. As she told the counsellor in the first session, 'I really had to swallow my pride to come here'. She continued to feel very exposed in the counsellor's presence and any tears were always quickly wiped away. Q would also cancel sessions when she was feeling particularly upset and distressed, admitting that she did not want the counsellor to see her distress.

> During the third session, G told his counsellor that he disliked vulnerability, adding angrily that he had never anticipated being a client. The counsellor felt that underlying G's anger was a tremendous fear of being vulnerable and needing to depend on others. She was therefore not surprised when G wrote after two further sessions, saying that he did not plan to return. G's anger may also have had something to do with the fact that he never settled the bill for the sessions.

The survivor-client who believes that dependency on others is dangerous or threatening can present difficulties for the counsellor. The client's 'defensive self-sufficiency' (Casement 1990) can leave the counsellor feeling frustrated and useless as their attempts to be helpful are rejected again and again. As Dunne (1987b) points out, the suicide survivor may fear the possibility that if they allow themselves to depend on the counsellor, they may be rejected, thus symbolically re-enacting the suicide victim's implied rejection of their relationship with the survivor. Unless the counsellor is aware of this possibility a struggle may ensue, with the counsellor making ever more strenuous attempts to reach out to the client, who in turn retreats even further behind their defences.

Counsellors need to be aware of the actual or perceived stigma experienced by many suicide survivors – the acquisition of a 'spoiled identity' (Goffman 1968) and the impact of this on the counselling relationship. One strategy for managing this spoiled identity is to seek out others with similar experiences. This is echoed by Menzies Lyth, who suggests that associating and identifying with others who have had similar experiences may offer a sense of belonging, even though this may have other less positive effects (1989: 253–4). How might this be played out in the counselling?

Unless the counsellor has disclosed her shared identity as a fellow survivor, the client may adopt a sceptical or even hostile stance towards her. The counsellor is, after all, one of the 'normals' (Goffman 1968) who does not bear a stigma and a part of that other group who the client feels are 'pointing the finger'. Being cast in this role can be uncomfortable, with the

232 A Special Scar

result that the counsellor tries her best to be the understanding, accepting, non-stigmatising 'nice guy' and the issue of the client's stigmatised identity is not addressed.

Suicidal ideation

Thoughts of suicide, however fleeting, are not uncommon among the bereaved; it may offer the possibility of reunion with the person who has died and an escape from the pain and sadness of loss. When the death was a suicide, however, there is an added dimension. As one survivor described this: 'It's as though suicide enters your bloodstream.'

The person who has taken their own life creates a path down which others may tread. That can be a terrifying prospect. In the words of one survivor: 'It's as though he has forced *his* reality onto me.' Through the act of suicide, the person who dies makes a statement that life is not sacrosanct. The suicide survivor may have to face not only their own suicidal thoughts but the fear that other people touched by the death may share these feelings. All this can evoke enormous anxiety which the survivor feels unable to share with family or friends because this would almost certainly create further distress – and anger – amongst people who may be already highly vulnerable.

Survivors may talk openly about feeling suicidal, they 'can't go on', 'they'd just like everything to stop', but counsellors also need to be alert for clues and oblique references in sessions. Survivors may be behaving in ways which, though not overtly suicidal are, nonetheless, self-destructive. They may be abusing alcohol or drugs. While the outcome may not be instant death, it can be an attempt to achieve the oblivion and the cessation of emotional pain sought by the suicidal person.

Dunne (1987b) states unequivocally that the issue of suicide must be openly addressed in therapy or counselling with suicide survivors. This can be testing for counsellors. They may find themselves going into 'rescue mode', sidestepping the client's very real feelings of despair or anger without addressing the underlying issues which are leading the client to consider suicide as an option. If the counsellor is unwilling to enter into this arena, the survivor's self-destructive feelings will remain unaddressed with the danger that these feelings will be acted out rather than talked about.

The counsellor or therapist has to recognise and contain their own anxieties in order to help the person make sense of the fear that they are being drawn towards suicide. They have to be in touch with the client's powerful feelings while still being able to think about the meaning of those feelings (Cooper 2000). Regular support and supervision, and where appropriate, collaboration with other professionals, are essential for counsellors and therapists working with people who are suicidal (Richards 2000).

The dead person has shown that there is a means of escape from intolerable mental pain and that suicide is the way to solve apparently insoluble problems. Reporting on her research into therapists' experiences of working with suicidal clients, Richards writes:

> The therapist describes how the patient saw her sister's actions as creating a path for her. 'The patient talks about almost an inevitable way in which she is going to repeat her older sister's behaviour . . . when she is at her most bleak and most despairing, she feels that her sister's behaviour, as it were, creates a path or solution to a state of despair that she gets into.'
>
> (Richards 1995)

The survivor may believe that they are fated and that self-destruction is inevitable, even if it is not what they consciously desire. Worden (1991), for example, has written about working with a group of young men whose fathers had killed themselves: and all of whom believed that suicide would be their fate.

Sometimes this fatedness is linked to an anniversary or birthday. Barnett and Hale (1985) describe the case of a middle-aged man who entered therapy in the year before he reached the age at which his father had killed himself, leading them to conclude that this could be seen as a means of obtaining a safe passage up to and through that birthday. Although the man sought to differentiate himself from his father, this seemed to be contradicted by his implicit statement that he was very like his father and would kill himself when he reached his next birthday. As Grinberg suggests, precipitating factors in suicide can include: 'a particular suicidal attitude often based on an identification with someone who has committed suicide in the past' (1992: 110).

For survivors struggling with extreme feelings of guilt, suicide can be seen as a means of escape. The suicide victim's unbearable guilt can then be handed on to others. Anger towards the deceased which cannot be allowed to surface into consciousness, may be directed towards the self and expressed through suicidal ideations, threats and thoughts (Tekavcic-Grad and Zavasnik 1992: 67).

> F's older brother had committed suicide. As children they had been very close and F painted a rather idealised picture of her brother in the counselling sessions. Despite the manner of his death, F seemed to feel that he could do no wrong and said that if anyone was to blame it was her. When her sadness and despair became acute, F began talking about her own suicidal feelings and the counsellor wondered if this represented an attempt to be reunited with her brother. However, when F said emphatically that if she died 'then the score would be even', this

led the counsellor to consider whether in fact F wanted to punish her
brother for abandoning her.

Survivors of suicide may embark on counselling unsure whether they will
survive their loss, but unlike the person who took their own life, they can be
helped to see that, unlike the person who died, they do have choices –
including the choice to live.

Anger

For the suicide survivor, angry feelings can be extremely frightening, not
least because of the aggressive and sadistic nature of the act of suicide. A
survivor of his son's suicide was surprised to hear himself telling the
counsellor: 'If he were to walk in the door right now, I'd kill him.'

Survivors will find ways of blocking out their anger towards the person
who died. The anger may be directed towards themselves or others or may
be somatised and only experienced through physical symptoms. Counsellors need to find ways of helping the client acknowledge and express their
aggression. It has even been suggested that unless survivors can recognise
their anger and vent their aggression, the grieving process will be incomplete (Tekavcic-Grad and Zavasnik 1992).

Anger may be buried, safely hidden from the survivor's consciousness,
but may begin to surface in their dreams, albeit in a disguised form.
Tekavcic-Grad and Zavasknik (1992) relate the following dream which
while not directly expressing the dreamer's anger, nevertheless has an
extremely aggressive content:

> A woman whose daughter died by suicide a year ago, visits the
> cemetery once or twice a day and finds this comforting. In the dream
> she goes to the cemetery and finds the grave has been damaged. There
> are traces of horse shit everywhere and the gravestone had been torn
> down. She is in shock and feels devastated.

Counsellors can sometimes find they are listening to what can feel like an
endless litany of angry complaints from the survivor, directed towards
others who they feel were responsible in some way for the death. Whether
or not the anger is justifiable, while it remains targeted at other people 'out
there', it can also defend the survivor from their anger at being rejected and
abandoned by the person who died who may, in turn, be idealised to the
point of sanctification.

If the survivor is able to begin expressing their anger towards the person
who died, this can still be difficult if they then feel guilty about their anger.
If the person had been very distressed or disturbed, the survivor may find it
hard to allow their anger to emerge. 'How can I be angry with them when

they were obviously so unhappy?' Angry feelings may be at odds with feeling that the person who died is now 'at peace'.

When the survivor admits their angry feelings, there may be a fear that the hatred will block out any loving feelings. The counsellor may need to help them accept that these very different feelings can co-exist – that anger does not need to wipe out more positive feelings.

Endings and recovery

Grieving is a process which has no clear end point. An anniversary, hearing a piece of music, experiencing another loss – these and other events can re-activate feelings about the suicide. Nevertheless, the counselling will finish at some point. For the survivor-client, the ending may stir up feelings about the relationship which was severed by the suicide. This time, however, it is different. The survivor can (usually) decide when the counselling relationship will come to an end and how that ending is experienced.

There is no single path of recovery from suicide bereavement but as Herman suggests, because hopelessness and isolation are the core experiences of psychological trauma, 'empowerment and reconnection will be the core experiences of recovery' (1994: 197). The counsellor or therapist cannot 'cure' the survivor but they can support them in being the authors of their recovery. The social isolation and disconnection from the world so frequently experienced by suicide survivors can be replaced by relationships of trust with others.

Reaching a point in the counselling where the survivor feels able to move on will be different for each person, but counsellors may find it helpful to think about the following questions. Has the survivor been able to give up searching for reasons why the suicide occurred? Are they able to live with whatever conclusions they have reached? Have they been able to face and acknowledge the traumatic nature of the death? If they were experiencing flashbacks, nightmares or other effects of trauma have these stopped or reached a manageable level where they occur very rarely? Can they talk about the person who died, but with less distress than at the start of the counselling? Do they have memories of the person which include both good and bad times? What are their relationships like with other people? Are they finding social activities easier? Do they feel that they have accepted what has happened and is there a sense that their life is moving on?

Working with survivors is challenging. Because a suicide death enters the room, the counsellor is confronted with the fact that as professionals *and* human beings we are not always able to prevent the death of another. Counsellors need to be aware of their own attitudes towards suicide and to have explored these in their personal and professional development, as well as in ongoing supervision. Where this does not happen, the counsellor may unwittingly allow their own feelings and attitudes to affect their responses to clients.

Counsellors who are themselves survivors of suicide may feel they have 'processed' this, but issues can still resurface and it is important to be aware of this possibility. Otherwise they may withdraw and become emotionally distant from the client – or offer inappropriate reassurance.

Because the emotional legacy of suicide can seem so overwhelming, the counsellor may find that they have to contain those unbearable feelings until the client is able to look at these. As Grad suggests, the counsellor must hold 'a dark and painful part, which is placed in the therapist's custody and contains all the ambivalent feelings about the deceased and which should be forgotten as soon as possible' (1996: 138).

Counsellors will need a robust attitude if they are to accept survivors' frequent projections of their anger, anxiety, guilt, hopelessness and other distressing emotions. And when the client is able to take these back and can begin to think with the counsellor about these feelings, the counsellor must be able to tolerate the intensity of the survivor's grief. When the counsellor can allow herself to hear the survivor's story and remain in touch with her own feelings, both counsellor and client may begin to think about what has happened. Hopefully, the survivor will be able to find a place for what has been lost and incorporate that event into their life.

Postscript

Perhaps inevitably, a book of this kind can only begin to open up such a huge topic. Even given the opportunity to revise the first edition, I am aware that gaps remain. Some matters have not been dealt with, and others have only been touched on briefly.

Just as there are gaps in what I have written, gaps exist in services too. Survivors may read this book but where will they go for help? If they are lucky, they will find someone to whom they can tell their story, someone who can listen and help them begin to make sense of a death which at first may seem senseless.

Suicide is a complex problem and there is rarely a single reason or a single path which leads someone to take their own life. For the survivors there is also no single route to recovery. Each person's grief will be unique and each will find their own ways of surviving the loss and moving on with their life.

This book is about one of the most painful losses a person may face, but I have endeavoured to show that it is an experience from which survivors can emerge not only changed, but stronger. The bereaved person can find new strengths and capacities, something positive can emerge, giving meaning to what is often seen as a meaningless death. The survivor may be more aware of the need to make something of their life which can be set against the 'wasted life' of the person who died. As Lily Pincus reminds us: 'There is no growth without pain and conflict; there is no loss which cannot lead to gain' (1974: 278).

Relevant organisations

British Association for Counselling and Psychotherapy (BACP)
1 Regent Place
Rugby
CV21 2PJ
Tel. 01788 550899
E-mail: bac@bac.co.uk
Website: www.counselling.co.uk

BACP can provide callers with information about counsellors in their local areas. The BACP Directory of Counselling Services across the UK is also available on the website (see above). Publications include information sheets on 'What is Counselling?' and 'A Client's Guide to Counselling and Psychotherapy'.

Centre for Suicide Research
Department of Psychiatry
Warneford Hospital
Oxford
OX3 7JX
Tel. 01865 226258
E-mail: crs@psych.ox.ac.uk

The Centre's programme of work aims, through research, to increase knowledge directly relevant to prevention of suicide and deliberate self-harm. Areas of concern include research into fatal and non-fatal suicidal behaviour; suicidal behaviour in young people; psychological, social and biological influences on suicidal behaviour; evaluation of strategies to treat and prevent suicidal behaviour; and investigation of the needs of people bereaved by suicide.

The Compassionate Friends
53 North Street

Bristol
BS3 1EN
Tel. 0117 953 5202.
    0117 953 9639 (Helpline: 9.30 a.m. to 10.30 p.m. daily)
E-mail: info@tcf.org.uk

The Compassionate Friends is a self-help organisation of bereaved parents and is open to parents who have experienced the loss of a child of any age and from any cause. The Shadow of Suicide (SOS) network can put parents in touch with others similarly bereaved. Pamphlets include: 'On Inquests' and 'After Suicide'.

CRUSE Bereavement Care
Cruse House
126 Sheen Road
Richmond
Surrey
TW9 1UR
Tel. 0870 167 1677
E-mail: info@crusebereavementcare.org.uk

CRUSE Bereavement Care is a national organisation offering help and support to anyone who is bereaved. CRUSE provides advice, counselling, befriending, groups where people can talk with others in similar circumstances, and information on practical matters for bereaved people. CRUSE has 180 branches across the UK. A list of local suicide bereavement support groups is available from the above address.

INQUEST
Ground Floor
Alexandra National House
330 Seven Sisters Road
London
N4 2PJ
Tel. 020 8802 7430
Fax. 020 8802 7450
E-mail: inquest@inquest.org.uk
Website: www.inquest.org.uk

INQUEST provides an independent, free, legal and advice service to the bereaved on inquest procedures and their rights in the coroner's court. It aims to raise awareness about controversial deaths, particularly deaths in custody, and campaigns for the necessary changes to improve the investigative process, increase accountability of state officials and avert future deaths.

Jewish Bereavement Counselling Service
PO Box 6748
London
N3 3BX
Tel. 020 8349 0839

The service offers counselling and support to bereaved members of the Jewish community. People are visited in their own homes by trained voluntary counsellors. The service operates mainly in North and North West London.

Lesbian and Gay Bereavement Project
Tel. 020 8455 8894 (Helpline 7.30–10.30 p.m.)

The project offers support and advice to anyone bereaved by the death of a same-sex partner or friend.

London Bereavement Network (LBN)
356 Holloway Road
London
N7 6PA
Tel. 020 7700 8134
E-mail: info@bereavement.org.uk
Website: www.bereavement.org.uk

LBN is the forum for many of the bereavement counselling and support organisations in the Greater London area and exists to promote and support good working practices. LBN can refer those seeking bereavement support to their nearest provider.

Nafsiyat
278 Seven Sisters Road
London
N4 2HY
Tel. 020 7263 4130

Nafsiyat is an inter-cultural centre offering a range of psychotherapies to individuals from many different ethnic groups. The majority of its current users live in the London borough of Islington but referrals (including self-referrals) can be accepted from elsewhere. The centre is also able to offer consultation and assessment services to professionals in other services. Nafsiyat's service is offered free to those living in Islington and Camden and costed according to individual means for others. Referring agences will be charged at Nafsiyat's standard rates.

PAPYRUS
Rossendale GH
Union Road
Rawtenstall
Rossendale
BB4 6NE
Tel. 01706 214449

Established in 1997, PAPYRUS is committed to the prevention of youth suicide and the promotion of mental health and well-being. Aims include: increasing public awareness; encouraging research; seeking to influence local and national policy; encouraging the provision of appropriate support to parents/carers of suicidal young people; and offering suicde bereaved parents and carers contact with other organisations such as SOBS (see below) and Compassionate Friends.

The Samaritans
Tel. 08457 90 90 90 (national number)
    1850 60 90 90 (Irish Republic)
    08457 90 91 92 (textphone: UK)
    1850 60 90 91 (textphone: Irish Republic)
E-mail: jo@samaritans.org
Website: www.samaritans.org
Write to: Chris, PO Box 90 90, Stirling, FK8 2SA

The Samaritans is a nationwide charity, providing confidential emotional support to anyone in a crisis. The service operates 24 hours a day and 365 days a year. Samaritans can be contacted by phone, face to face visit, e-mail or letter. Telephone number of local branches can be found under S in the local directory; or on the website. Or phone the national helpline (see above).

Survivors of Bereavement by Suicide (SOBS)
Centre 88
Saner Street
Hull
HU3 2TR
Tel. 01482 610 728
    0870 2413 337 (Helpline)

SOBS is a self-help organisation which offers emotional and practical support in the following ways: telephone contacts; bereavement packs; group meetings (in some locations); conferences; residential events; information relating to practical issues and problems; one-to-one meetings and home visits (in some areas).

Winston's Wish
Gloucestershire Royal Hospital
Great Western Road
Gloucestershire
GL1 3NN
Tel. 01452 394377
     0845 20 30 40 5 (Family Line)
E-mail: info@winstonswish.org.uk
Website: www.winstonswish.org.uk

A service supporting bereaved children and young people, and their families, including those where a parent or sibling has died by suicide. Twice yearly residential events are run for families bereaved by suicide as well as ongoing support. The service publishes 'Beyond the Rough Rock: supporting a child who has been bereaved by suicide' 2001. The service covers the Gloucestershire area but offers a small number of places to families from other areas (where funding can be established). Winston's Wish is committed to helping people develop services for bereaved families throughout the UK. The Family Line offers support, information and guidance to all those caring for a bereaved child.

The people interviewed

Name of survivor	Age at time of suicide	Name of the deceased	Relationship of deceased to survivor	Victim's age at time of death	Date of suicide
Andrew	50	Gwen	Wife	47	1972
Ann	23	Giles	Brother	19	1936
Betty	58	Jonathan	Son	26	1985
Brian	50	Judy	Wife	48	1986
Bridget	17	Catherine	Sister	20	1982
	17	n.a.	Father	55	1982
Carol	47	Alan	Son	21	1985
Carole	46	Jon	Son	21	1986
Christine	42	Graham	Husband	35	1987
Colin	48	Helen	Ex-lover	40?	1979
David	39	Paul	Son	20	1987
Denise	4	n.a.	Father	25	1963
Dick	33	Sally	Sister	30	1984
Eileen	53	Sheila	Daughter	30	1976
	59	Donna	Daughter	36	1982
Francesca	57	Patricia	Daughter	29	1987
Frank	45	Josie	Daughter	21	1985
Harry	50	Frances	Daughter	22	1977
Heather	42	Alastair	Son	18	1987
Hilary	18	n.a.	Mother	48	1953
Irene	53	Bill	Husband	55	1984
Isabel	51	Eric	Husband	52	1977
Jan	13	n.a.	Father	58?	1963
Jane	37	Christopher	Brother	41	1984
Janice	40	n.a.	Mother	75	1986
Jean	52	Anna	Daughter	20	1987
Jennifer	29	Tim	Brother	30	1987
Joan	44	Lesley	Sister	42	1977

Name of survivor	Age at time of suicide	Name of the deceased	Relationship of deceased to survivor	Victim's age at time of death	Date of suicide
John	54	Averil	Wife	44	1984
Kevin	10	n.a.	Mother	42	1963
Liz	29	Tony	Brother	32	1984
Lois	48	Simon	Son	21	1987
Marie	61	Oliver	Husband	72	1985
Mark	68	Patricia	Daughter	29	1987
Martin	14?	n.a.	Mother	mid-50s	1950?
Maureen	39	Paul	Son	20	1987
Melanie	28	Ian	Husband	37	1984
Miriam	46	Ben	Son	20	1987
Nancy	53	Clare	Daughter	20	1980
Nick	30	n.a.	Mother	64	1983
Nicola	23	Caroline	Sister	20	1987
Pam	46	Frances	Daughter	22	1977
Pat	45	Caroline	Daughter	20	1987
Pauline	62	Michael	Son	40	1987
Peter	32	Susie	Sister	21	1985
Phyllis	45	Julie	Daughter	19	1986
Robert	47	Caroline	Daughter	20	1987
Susan	41	Richard	Husband	43	1973
Suzy	32	n.a.	Father	59	1985
Ursula	45	Josie	Daughter	21	1985
Wendy	31	n.a.	Father	74	1981

References

Alexander, V. (1987) 'Living through my mother's suicide', in E.J. Dunne, J. McIntosh and K. Dunne-Maxim (eds) *Suicide and its Aftermath. Understanding and Counseling the Survivor.* New York and London: W.W. Norton.

Alvarez, A. (1974) *The Savage God: A Study of Suicide.* Harmondsworth: Penguin.

American Association of Suicidology (1992) *Survivors of Suicide: Support Group Guidelines.* Denver, CO: AAS.

Andress, V.R. and Corey, D.M. (1978) 'Survivor victims: who discovers or witnesses suicide?', *Psychological Reports* 42: 759–64.

Appel, Y.H. and Wrobleski, A. (1987) 'Self-help and Support Groups: Mutual Aid for Survivors', in E.J. Dunne, J. McIntosh and K. Dunne-Maxim (eds) *Suicide and its Aftermath: Understanding and Counseling the Survivor.* New York and London: W.W. Norton.

Archer, J. (1999) *The Nature of Grief. The Evolution and Psychology of Reactions to Loss.* London: Routledge.

Asgard, U. and Carlsson-Bergstrom, M. (1991) 'Interviews with survivors of suicides: procedures and follow-up of interview subjects', *Crisis* 12, 1: 21–33.

Barker, A., Hawton, K., Fagg, J. and Jennison, C. (1994) 'Seasonal and weather factors in parasuicide', *British Journal of Psychiatry* 165: 375–80.

Barnett, B.R. and Hale, R. (1985) 'A singular form of death: some aspects of the psychological sequelae of the loss of the father by suicide', paper read at the International Psychoanalytic Congress, Montreal, Canada, July.

Barraclough, B. (1990) 'The Bible suicides', *Acta Psychiatrica Scandinavica* 86: 64–9.

—— and Shepherd, D.M. (1976) 'Public interest: private grief', *British Journal of Psychiatry* 129: 109–13.

—— (1977) 'The immediate and enduring effects of the inquest on relatives of suicides', *British Journal of Psychiatry* 131: 400–4.

—— (1978) 'Impact of a suicide inquest', Letter, *The Lancet*, ii: 795.

Barrett, T.W. and Scott, T.B. (1990) 'Suicide bereavement and recovery patterns compared with nonsuicide bereavement patterns', *Suicide and Life-Threatening Behavior* 20, 1: 1–15.

Battle, A. (1984) 'Group therapy for survivors of suicide', *Crisis* 5, 1: 45–58.

Behrens, T. (1988) *The Monument.* London: Sphere.

Bell, D. (1998) 'External injury and the internal world', in C. Garland (ed.)

Understanding Trauma. A Psychoanalytic Approach. London: Duckworth (Tavistock Clinic Series).

Bernhardt, G.R. and Praeger, S.G. (1983) 'After suicide: meeting the needs of survivors', paper presented at the Annual Convention of the American Personnel and Guidance Association, Washington, DC, March.

Biddle, L. (1998) 'On trial: the inquest system and bereavement by suicide', MA dissertation, University of Reading.

Billow, C.J. (1987) 'A Multiple Family Support Group for Survivors of Suicide', in E.J. Dunne, J. McIntosh and K. Dunne-Maxim (eds) *Suicide and its Aftermath: Understanding and Counseling the Survivor.* New York and London: W.W. Norton.

Black, D. (1998) 'Coping with loss: bereavement in childhood', *British Medical Journal* 316, 7135: 931–3.

Boakes, J. (1993) 'The impact of suicide upon the mental health care professional', in *Suicide and the Murderous Self. Understanding self-harm as a prelude to effective intervention.* Conference Proceedings, London: Department of Mental Health Sciences, St George's Hospital Medical School.

Bowlby, J. (1985) *Attachment and Loss, Volume III. Loss: Sadness and Depression.* Harmondsworth: Penguin.

Brent, D., Perper, J., Moritz, G., Friend, A., Schweers, J., Allman, C., McQuiston, L., Boyland, M.-B., Roth, C. and Balach, L. (1993a) 'Adolescent witnesses to a peer suicide', *Journal of American Academy of Child and Adolescent Psychiatry* 32, 6: 1184–8.

Brent, D., Perper, J., Moritz, G., Allman, C., Liotus, L., Schweers, J., Roth, C., Balach, L. and Canobbio, R. (1993b) 'Bereavement or depression? The impact of the loss of a friend to suicide', *Journal of American Academy of Child and Adolescent Psychiatry* 32, 6: 1189–97.

Brent, D., Moritz, G., Bridge, J., Perper, J. and Canobbio, R. (1996a) 'The impact of adolescent suicide on siblings and parents: a longitudinal follow-up', *Suicide and Life-Threatening Behavior* 26, 3: 253–9.

Brent, D., Bridge, J., Johnson, B.A. and Connolly, J. (1996b) 'Suicidal behavior runs in family. A controlled family study of adolescent suicide victims', *Archives of General Psychiatry* 53: 1146–52.

Brown, H. (1987) 'The impact of suicide on therapists in training', *Comprehensive Psychiatry* 2, 8: 101–12.

Brownstein, M. (1992) 'Contacting the family after a suicide', *Canadian Journal of Psychiatry* 37, 3: 208–12.

Cain, A.C. (ed.) (1972) *Survivors of Suicide.* Springfield, IL: Charles C. Thomas.

—— and Fast, I. (1972a) 'Children's disturbed reactions to parent suicide: distortions of guilt, communication and identification', in A.C. Cain (ed.) *Survivors of Suicide.* Springfield, IL: Charles C. Thomas.

—— and Fast, I. (1972b) 'The legacy of suicide: observations on the pathogenic impact of suicide upon marital partners', in A.C. Cain (ed.) *Survivors of Suicide.* Springfield, IL: Charles C. Thomas.

Calhoun, L.G., Abernathy, C.B. and Selby, J.W. (1982) 'The rules of bereavement: are suicidal deaths different?', *Community Psychiatry* 116: 255–61.

Campbell, D. and Hale, R. (1991) 'Suicidal acts', in *Psychiatry and General Practice.* London: Churchill Livingstone.

Campbell, F.R. (1997) 'Changing the legacy of suicide', *Suicide and Life-Threatening Behavior* 27, 4: 329–38.

Carstairs, G.M. (1973) Foreword, in E. Stengel, *Suicide and Attempted Suicide*. Harmondsworth: Penguin (revised edition with revisions).

Casement, P. (1985) *On Learning from the Patient*. London: Routledge.

—— (1990) *Further Learning from the Patient*. London: Routledge.

Cerel, J., Fristad, M.A., Weller, E.B. and Weller, R.A. (1999) 'Suicide-bereaved children and adolescents: a controlled longitudinal examination', *Journal of the American Academy of Child and Adolescent Psychiatry* 38, 6: 672–9.

Chambers, D.R. (1989) 'The coroner, the inquest and the verdict of suicide', *Journal of Medicine, Science and Law* 29, 3: 181.

—— and Harvey, J.G. (1989) 'Inner urban and national suicide rates. A simple comparative study', *Journal of Medicine, Science and Law* 29, 3: 182–5.

Chesser, E. (1967) *Living with Suicide*. London: Hutchinson.

Clark, S.E. and Goldney, R.D. (1995) 'Grief reactions and recovery in a support group for people bereaved by suicide', *Crisis* 16, 1: 27–33.

Clark, S.E. and Goldney, R.D. (2000) 'The impact of suicide on relatives and friends', in K. Hawton and K. van Heeringen (eds) *The International Handbook of Suicide and Attempted Suicide*. Chichester: John Wiley.

Clark, S.E, Jones, H.E., Quinn, K., Goldney, R.D. and Cooling, P.J. (1993) 'A support group for people bereaved through suicide', *Crisis* 14, 4: 161–7.

Cleiren, M.P.H.D., Grad, O., Zavasnik, A and Diekstra, R.F.W. (1996) 'Psychosocial impact of bereavement after suicide and fatal traffic accident: a comparative two-country study', *Acta Psychiatrica Scandinavica* 74: 37–44.

Cline, S. (1996) *Lifting the Taboo: Women, Death and Dying*. London: Abacus.

Colt, G.H. (1987) 'The history of the suicide survivor: The mark of Cain', in E.J. Dunne, J. McIntosh and K. Dunne-Maxim (eds) *Suicide and its Aftermath. Understanding and Counseling the Survivors*. New York and London: W.W. Norton.

Compassionate Friends, The (1997) *On Inquests*. Bristol: The Compassionate Friends.

—— (1998) *After Suicide*. Bristol: The Compassionate Friends.

Conley, B.H. (1987) 'Funeral directors as first responders', in E.J. Dunne, J. McIntosh and K. Dunne-Maxim (eds) *Suicide and its Aftermath. Understanding and Counseling the Survivors*. New York and London: W.W. Norton.

Constantino, R.E. and Bricker, P.L. (1996) 'Nursing postvention for spousal survivors of suicide', *Issues in Mental Health Nursing* 17, 2: 131–5.

Cooper, C. (2000) 'A matter of life and death', *Psychotherapy Section Newsletter* (British Psychological Society), September, 28: 19–29.

Davenport, D. (1989) 'A past and a future too', in T. Philpot (ed.) *Last Things: Social Work with the Dying and Bereaved*. Wallington, Surrey: Reed Business Publishing/Community Care.

Davis, C.G., Nolen-Hoeksema, S. and Larson, J. (1998) 'Making sense of loss and benefiting from the experience: two construals of meaning', *Journal of Personality and Social Psychology* 75, 2: 561–74.

Department of Health (1998) *Our Healthier Nation. A Contract for Health*, Cm 3852. London: DoH.

—— (1999) *Safer Services. A report of the National Confidential Inquiry into Suicide and Homicide by People with Mental Illness*. London: Department of Health.

Doka, K.J. (1999) 'Disenfranchised grief', *Bereavement Care* 18, 3: 37–9.

Downey, A. (1987) *Dear Stephen . . . A Letter Diary Written to Stephen By His Mother*. London: Arthur James.

Dunne, E.J. (1987a) 'A response to suicide in the mental health setting', in E.J. Dunne, J. McIntosh and K. Dunne-Maxim (eds) *Suicide and its Aftermath. Understanding and Counseling the Survivors*. New York and London: W.W. Norton.

—— (1987b) 'Special needs of suicide survivors in therapy', in E.J. Dunne, J. McIntosh and K. Dunne-Maxim (eds) *Suicide and its Aftermath. Understanding and Counseling the Survivors*. New York and London: W.W. Norton.

—— (1992a) 'How to start your own support group', in *Survivors of Suicide. Support Group Guidelines*. Denver, CO: American Association of Suicidology.

—— (1992b) 'The discussion phase of an SOS group meeting', in *Survivors of Suicide Support Group Guidelines*. Denver, CO: American Association of Suicidology.

—— (1992c) 'Themes and variations', in *Survivors of Suicide. Support Group Guidelines*. Denver, CO: American Association of Suicidology.

—— and Dunne-Maxim, K. (1987) Preface, in E.J. Dunne, J. McIntosh and K. Dunne-Maxim (eds) *Suicide and its Aftermath. Understanding and Counseling the Survivors*. New York and London: W.W. Norton.

——, McIntosh, J. and Dunne-Maxim, K. (eds) (1987) *Suicide and its Aftermath. Understanding and Counseling the Survivors*. New York and London: W.W. Norton.

Dunne-Maxim, K. (1987) 'Survivors and the media: pitfalls and potential', in E.J. Dunne, J. McIntosh and K. Dunne-Maxim (eds) *Suicide and its Aftermath. Understanding and Counseling the Survivors*. New York and London: W.W. Norton.

——, Dunne, E.J. and Hauser, M.J. (1987) 'When children are suicide survivors', in E.J. Dunne, J. McIntosh and K. Dunne-Maxim (eds) *Suicide and its Aftermath. Understanding and Counseling the Survivors*. New York and London: W.W. Norton.

Erikson, E.H. (1971) *Identity: Youth and Crisis*. London: Faber & Faber.

Fanthorpe, U.A. (1982) *Standing To*. Calstock, Cornwall: Peterloo Poets; *Selected Poems*. Peterloo Poets and King Penguin (1986).

Farberow, N. (1992) 'The Los Angeles Survivors-After-Suicide Program. An evaluation', *Crisis* 13, 1: 23–34.

——, Gallagher-Thompson, D., Gilewski, M. and Thompson, L. (1992) 'The role of social supports in the bereavement process of surviving spouses of suicide and natural deaths', *Suicide and Life-Threatening Behavior* 22, 1: 107–24.

Finney, A. (1988) 'When death haunts the track', *Independent*, 12 December.

Foster, T., Gillespie, K. and McLelland, R. (1997) 'Mental disorders and suicide in Northern Ireland', *British Journal of Psychiatry* 170: 447–52.

Freud, S. (1936) *Inhibitions, Symptoms and Anxiety*, trans. A. Strachey. London: Hogarth Press and the Institute of Psycho-Analysis.

Gaffney, D.A., Jones, E.T. and Dunne-Maxim, K. (1992) 'Support groups for sibling suicide survivors', *Crisis* 13, 2: 76–81.

Garland, C. (ed.) (1998) *Understanding Trauma. A Psychoanalytical Approach.* London: Duckworth (Tavistock Clinic Series).

Gibb, E. (1998) 'Dreaming after a traumatic bereavement: mourning or its avoidance?', in C. Garland (ed.) *Understanding Trauma. A Psychoanalytical Approach.* London: Duckworth (Tavistock Clinic Series).

Glass, C. (1995) 'Why?', *Daily Telegraph*, 7 October: 24–28.

Goffman, E. (1968) *Stigma: Notes on the Management of Spoiled Identity.* Harmondsworth: Penguin.

Gorer, G. (1965) *Death, Grief and Mourning in Contemporary Britain.* London: Tavistock.

Grad, O. (1996) 'Suicide: how to survive as a survivor?', *Crisis* 17, 3: 136–42.

—— and Zavasnik, A. (1998) 'The caregivers reactions after suicide of a patient', in R.J. Kosky et al. (eds) *Suicide Prevention: The Global Context.* New York: Plenum Press.

——, Zavasnik, A. and Groleger, U. (1997) 'Suicide of a patient: gender differences in bereavement reactions of therapists', *Suicide and Life-Threatening Behavior* 27, 4: 379–86.

Grinberg, L. (1992) *Guilt and Depression.* London: Karnac Books.

Guardian, The (2000) 'Alarm as jail suicides soar to new high', Alan Travis, 14 August 2000: 9.

Handke, P. (1976) *A Sorrow Beyond Dreams.* London: Souvenir Press.

Harris, T. and Kendrick, T. (1998) 'Bereavement care in general practice: a survey in South Thames Health Region', *British Journal of General Practice* 48, 434: 1560–4.

Hatton C. and Valente, S. (1981) 'Bereavement group for parents who suffered a suicidal loss of a child', *Suicide and Life Threatening Behavior* 11, 3: 141–50.

Hauser, M.J. (1987) 'Special aspects of grief after a suicide', in E.J. Dunne, J. McIntosh and K. Dunne-Maxim (eds) *The Aftermath of Suicide. Understanding and Counseling the Survivors.* New York and London: W.W. Norton.

Hawton, K. (1998) 'A national target for reducing suicide: important for mental health strategy as well as for suicide prevention', editorial, *British Medical Journal* 317, 7152: 156–7.

—— and Fagg, J. (1988) 'Suicide, and other causes of death, following attempted suicide', *British Journal of Psychiatry* 152: 359–66.

—— and Vislisel, L. (1999) 'Suicide in nurses: review article', *Suicide and Life-Threatening Behavior* 29, 1: 86–95.

——, Appleby, L., Platt, S., Foster, T., Cooper, J., Malmberg, A. and Simkin, S. (1998) 'The psychological autopsy approach to studying suicide: a review of methodological issues', *Journal of Affective Disorders* 50: 269–76.

——, Simkin, S., Deeks, J., O'Connor, S., Keen, A., Altman, D., Philo, G. and Bulstrode, C. (1999) 'Effects of a drug overdose in a television drama on presentations to hospital for self poisoning: time series and questionnaire study', *British Medical Journal* 318: 972–7.

Henley, S.H.A. (1984) *Bereavement following Suicide. A Review of the Literature* (CRUSE Academic Paper No. 1). Richmond, Surrey: CRUSE.

Herman, J.L. (1994) *Trauma and Recovery.* London: Pandora.

Hill, K. (1995) *The Long Sleep. Young People and Suicide.* London: Virago.

——, Hawton, K., Malmberg, A. and Simkin, S. (1997) *Bereavement Information*

Pack. For those bereaved through suicide or other sudden death. London: Royal College of Psychiatrists.

Hillman, J. (1976) *Suicide and the Soul*. Dallas, TX: Spring Publications.

HMIP (1999) *Suicide is Everyone's Concern*. London: HM Inspector of Prisons.

HMSO (1971) *Home Office Report on Death Certification and Coroners*. Cmnd. 4810. London: HMSO.

—— (1984) *Coroners Rules 1984. Statutory Instrument No. 552*. London: HMSO.

Holmes, J. (1995) 'When professionals fail: surviving the death of one's patient', in *Suicide and the Murderous Self; Hearing it and Bearing it*, conference report. London: Department of Psychotherapy, St George's Hospital.

Hood, P. (1998) 'Survival Strategies', conference report, Hull: Survivors of Bereavement by Suicide.

Ingham, G. (1998) 'Mental work in a trauma patient', in C. Garland (ed.) *Understanding Trauma. A Psychoanalytical Approach*. London: Duckworth (Tavistock Clinical Series).

Ironside, V. (1996) *'You'll Get Over It'. The Rage of Bereavement*. London: Hamish Hamilton.

James, K. (1988) 'Overdose of suicide', *Guardian*, 1 June.

Jones, F.A. (1987) 'Therapists as survivors of client suicide', in E.J. Dunne, J. McIntosh and K. Dunne-Maxim (eds) *Suicide and its Aftermath. Understanding and Counseling the Survivors*. New York and London: W.W. Norton.

Karpf, A. (1997) *The War After: Living with the Holocaust*. London: Minerva.

Kast, V. (1988) *A Time to Mourn. Growing through the Grief Process*, trans. D. Dachler and F. Cairns. Einsiedeln, Switzerland: Daimon Verlag.

Keir, N. (1986) *I Can't Face Tomorrow. Help for Those Troubled by Thoughts of Suicide*. Wellingborough, Northants: Thorsons.

Kelleher, M.J., Chambers, D., Corcoran, P., Williamson, E. and Keeley, H.S. (1998) 'Religious sanctions and rates of suicide worldwide', *Crisis* 19, 2: 78–86.

Kelly, B. (1989) 'In the face of death', *Open Mind* June/July: 16.

King, E. (1997) 'Suicide: perceptions, procedures and prevention. Is fear the key?', *Southampton Health Journal* 13, 12: 5–7.

Kingston, M.H. (1981) *The Woman Warrior: Memoirs of a Girlhood amongst Ghosts*. London: Pan.

Kohut, H. (1986) 'Forms and transformations of narcissism', in A.P. Morrison (ed.) *Essential Papers on Narcissism*. New York: New York University Press.

Lake, T. (1984) *Living with Grief*. London: Sheldon Press.

Leith, W. (1993) 'Trying not to talk about suicide', *Independent on Sunday*, 16 May.

Lendrum, S. and Syme, G. (1992) *Gift of Tears. A Practical Approach to Loss and Bereavement Counselling*. London: Routledge.

Lewis, C.S. (1966) *A Grief Observed*. London: Faber & Faber.

Lifton, R.J. (1969) *Death in Life: Survivors of Hiroshima*. New York: Vintage Books.

Litman, R.E. (1970) 'Immobilization response to suicidal behaviour', in E.S. Shneidman, N.L. Farberow and R.E. Litman (eds) *The Psychology of Suicide*. New York: Science House.

——, Curphey, T., Shneidman, E.S., Farberow, N.L. and Tabachnik, N. (1970) 'The psychological autopsy of equivocal deaths', in E.S. Shneidman, N.L.

Farberow and R.E. Litman (eds) *The Psychology of Suicide*. New York: Science House.

Lott, T. (1997) *The Scent of Dried Roses*. London: Penguin.

Lukas, C. and Seiden, H. (1987) *Silent Grief. Living in the Wake of Suicide*. New York: Charles Scribner's; republished Jason Aronson, Northvale, NJ: 1997.

Lyall, J. (1987) 'Too young to despair of life', *Independent*, 25 August.

McIntosh, J. (1985–6) 'Survivors of suicide: A comprehensive bibliography', *Omega* 16, 4: 355–70.

—— (1987a) 'Suicide as a mental health problem: epidemiological aspects', in E.J. Dunne, J. McIntosh and K. Dunne-Maxim (eds) *Suicide and its Aftermath. Understanding and Counseling the Survivors*. New York and London: W.W. Norton.

—— (1987b) 'Survivor family relationships: literature review', in E.J. Dunne, J. McIntosh and K. Dunne-Maxim (eds) *Suicide and its Aftermath. Understanding and Counseling the Survivors*. New York and London: W.W. Norton.

—— (1987c) 'Research, therapy and educational needs', in E.J. Dunne, J. McIntosh and K. Dunne-Maxim (eds) *Suicide and its Aftermath. Understanding and Counseling the Survivors*. New York and London: W.W. Norton.

—— and Kelly, L. (1992) Survivors' reactions: suicide vs. other causes', *Crisis* 13, 2: 82–92.

Malmberg, A., Hawton, K. and Simkin, S. (1997) 'A study of suicide in farmers in England and Wales', *Journal of Psychosomatic Research* 43, 1: 107–11.

Marris, P. (1978) *Loss and Change*. London: Routledge & Kegan Paul.

Maxwell, B. (1994) 'The role of groupwork in bereavement', paper read at AGM of London Bereavement Network.

Menzies Lyth, I. (1989) *The Dynamics of the Social. Selected Essays*. London: Free Association Books.

Mitchell, S. (1985) *The Token*. London: Futura.

Mooney, B. (1985) *The Anderson Question*. London: Pan.

Morgan, G. (1994) 'The relative's response', in R. Jenkins et al. (eds) *The Prevention of Suicide*. London: Department of Health.

Morris, A. (1976) 'Wanted: a coroner's welfare officer', *Community Care* 26 May, 20.

Nelson, B.J. and Frantz, T.T. (1996) 'Family interactions of suicide survivors and survivors of non-suicidal death', *Omega* 32, 2: 131–46.

Ness, D.E. and Pfeffer, C.R. (1990) 'Sequelae of bereavement resulting from suicide', *American Journal of Psychiatry* 147, 3: 279–85.

Nichols, R. (1981) 'Sudden death, acute grief and ultimate mourning', in O. Margolis *et al.* (eds) *Acute Grief: Counselling the Bereaved*. New York: Columbia University Press.

Observer, The (1999) 'The suicide journalist', 4 July.

Osterweis, M., Solomon, F. and Green, M. (eds) (1984) *Bereavement: Reactions, Consequences and Care*. Washington, DC: National Academy Press.

Perceval, D. (1994) 'Foreword', in F. Minnis *You're Better Off Without Me*. London: BBC Education.

Parkes, C.M. (1998) *Bereavement. Studies of Grief in Adult Life*. London: Penguin (3nd edn).

Pincus, L. (1974) *Death and the Family: The Importance of Mourning.* New York: Vintage Books; London: Faber & Faber (1976).
—— and Dare, C. (1978) *Secrets in the Family.* London: Faber & Faber.
Pritchard, C. (1995) *Suicide – the Ultimate Rejection. A psycho-social study.* Buckingham: Open University Press.
Range, L.M. and Niss, N.M. (1990) 'Long-term bereavement from suicide, homicide, accidents and natural deaths', *Death Studies* 14: 423–33.
Raphael, B. (1985) *The Anatomy of Bereavement. A Handbook for the Caring Professions.* London: Hutchinson.
Reed, M.D. (1998) 'Predicting grief symptomatology among the suddenly bereaved', *Suicide and Life-Threatening Behavior* 28, 3: 285–300.
—— and Greenwald, J. (1991) 'Survivor-victim status, attachment, and sudden death bereavement', *Suicide and Life-Threatening Behavior* 21, 4: 385–404.
Resnik, H.L.P. (1972) 'Psychological resynthesis: a clinical approach to the survivors of a death by suicide', in A.C. Cain (ed.) *Survivors of Suicide.* Springfield, IL: Charles C. Thomas.
Reynolds, J., Jennings, G. and Branson, M.L. (1997) 'Patients' reactions to the suicide of a psychotherapist', *Suicide and Life-Threatening Behavior* 27, 2: 176–81.
Richards, B.M. (1995) An exploration of the relationship between internal and external object relations and suicide, MA dissertation, University of Reading.
—— (2000) 'Impact upon therapy and the therapist working with suicidal patients: some transference and countertransference aspects', *British Journal of Guidance and Counselling* 28, 3: 325–37.
Rilke, R.M. (1957) *Requiem and Other Poems,* trans. J.B. Lehman. London: Hogarth Press.
Rogers, J., Sheldon, A, Barwick, C., Letofsky, K. and Lancee, B. (1982) 'Help for families of suicide: survivors support program', *Canadian Journal of Psychiatry* 27, October: 444–9.
Rubey, C.T. and McIntosh, J. (1996) 'Suicide survivor groups: results of a survey', *Suicide and Life-Threatening Behavior* 26, 4: 351–8.
Rudestam, K.E. (1987) 'Public perceptions of suicide survivors', in E.J. Dunne, J. McIntosh and K. Dunne-Maxim (eds) *Suicide and its Aftermath. Understanding and Counseling the Survivors.* New York and London: W.W. Norton.
—— (1992) 'Research contributions to understanding the suicide survivor', *Crisis* 13, 1: 41–6.
Sacksen, C. (1999) 'Siblings bereaved by suicide. An exploration of the experiences of some siblings in England', MA dissertation, University of East Anglia.
Samaritans, The (1996) *Challenging the Taboo: Attitudes towards Suicide and Depression.* Slough: The Samaritans.
—— (1997) *Media Guidelines on Portrayal of Suicide.* Slough: The Samaritans.
—— (1998) *Listen Up. Responding to People in Crisis.* Slough: The Samaritans.
—— (2000) *Information Resource Pack 2000.* Slough: The Samaritans.
Sanderson, E.M. and Ridsdale, L. (1999) 'General practitioners' beliefs and attitudes about how to respond to death and bereavement: a qualitative study', *British Medical Journal* 319: 293–6.
Seguin, M., LeSage, A. and Kiely, M. (1995a) 'Parental bereavement after suicide and accident: a comparative study', *Suicide and Life-Threatening Behavior* 25, 4: 489–98.

—— (1995b) 'History of early loss among a group of suicide survivors', *Crisis* 16, 3: 121–5.

Seligman, E. (1976) 'On death and survival', *Harvest* 22: 135–7.

Shannon, P. (2000) *Bereaved by Suicide*. London: Cruse Bereavement Care.

Shepherd, D.M. and Barraclough, B.M. (1976) 'The aftermath of a parental suicide for children', *British Journal of Psychiatry* 129: 269–76.

—— (1978) 'Suicide reporting: information or entertainment?', *British Journal of Psychiatry* 132: 283–7.

—— (1979) 'Help for those bereaved by suicide', *British Journal of Social Work* 9: 67–74.

Shneidman, E.S. (1969) 'Prologue' in E.S. Shneidman (ed.) *On the Nature of Suicide*. San Francisco: Jossey-Bass.

—— (1972) Foreword, in A C. Cain (ed.) *Survivors of Suicide*. Springfield, IL: Charles C. Thomas.

—— (1975) 'Suicide', in A.M. Freedman, N.L. Farberow and R.E. Litman (eds) *Comprehensive Textbook of Psychiatry, Volume II*. Baltimore, MD: Williams and Wilkins.

—— (1979) 'Help for those bereaved by suicide', *British Journal of Social Work* 9: 67–74.

—— (1982) *Voices of Death: Personal Documents from People Facing Death*. New York: Bantam Books.

—— (1993) *Suicide as Psychache. A Clinical Approach to Self-Destructive Behavior*. Northvale, NJ: Jason Aronson.

Silverman, E., Range, N. and Overholser, J. (1994–5) 'Bereavement from suicide as compared with other forms of bereavement', *Omega* 30, 1: 41–51.

Simkin, S., Hawton, K., Fagg, J., Whitehead, L. and Eagle, M. (1995) 'Media influence on parasuicide: a study of the effects of a television drama portrayal of paracetamol self poisoning', *British Journal of Psychiatry* 167, 6: 754–9.

Smith, B.J., Mitchell, A.M., Bruno, A.A. and Constantino, R.E. (1995) 'Exploring widows' experiences after the suicide of their spouse', *Journal of Psychosocial Nursing and Mental Health Services* 33, 5: 10–15.

Smith, F. (1995) 'A calculated risk – assessing the desire for death', in *Suicide and the Murderous Self: Hearing it and Bearing it*, conference report. London: Department of Psychotherapy, St George's Hospital.

Smith, K. (1978) *Help for the Bereaved*. London: Duckworth.

Solomon, M.I. (1981) 'Bereavement from suicide', *Psychiatric Nursing*, July–September, 18–19.

Sonneck, G., Etzdorfer, E and Nagel-Huess, S. (1992) 'Subway suicide in Vienna (1980–1990)', in P. Crepet et al. (eds) *Suicidal Behaviour in Europe*. Rome: John Libbey.

Staudacher, C. (1988) *Beyond Grief: A Guide for Recovering from the Death of a Loved One*. London: Souvenir Press.

Stengel, E. (1973) *Suicide and Attempted Suicide*. Harmondsworth: Penguin (revised edition with revisions).

Storr, A. (1989) *Solitude*. London: Flamingo.

Stroebe, M. (1994) 'Helping the bereaved to come to terms with loss: what does bereavement research have to offer?', in *Bereavement and Counselling*, conference proceedings (25 March). London: Department of Mental Health Sciences, St George's Hospital Medical School.

Tekavcic-Grad, O. and Zavasnik, A. (1992) 'Aggression as a natural part of suicide bereavement', *Crisis* 13, 2: 65–9.

Thompson, K.E. and Range, L.M. (1992) 'Bereavement following suicide and other deaths: why support attempts fail', *Omega* 26, 1: 61–70.

Toop, D. (1996) 'The After Life', *Vogue*, November: 190–1, 262.

Valente, S. (1994) 'Psychotherapist reactions to the suicide of a patient', *American Journal of Orthopsychiatry* 64, 4: 614–21.

—— and Saunders, J.M. (1993) 'Adolescent grief after suicide', *Crisis* 14, 1: 16–22, 46.

Van der Wal, J. (1989) 'The aftermath of suicide: a review of empirical evidence', *Omega* 20, 2: 149–71.

Van Dongen, C.J. (1993) 'Social context of postsuicide bereavement', *Death Studies* 17: 125–41.

Vassilas, C.A. and Morgan, H.G. (1993) 'General practitioners' contact with victims of suicide', *British Medical Journal* 307: 221–4.

Vollman, R., Ganzert, A., Picher, L. and Williams, W.V. (1971) 'The reactions of family systems to sudden and unexpected death', *Omega* 2: 101–6.

Wagner, K.G. and Calhoun, L.G. (1991–2) 'Perceptions of social support by suicide survivors and their social networks', *Omega* 24, 1: 61–73

Wallace, S.E. (1977) 'On the atypicality of suicide bereavement', in B.L. Danto and A.H. Kutscher (eds) *Suicide and Bereavement*. New York: MSS Information Corporation.

Wertheimer, A. (1992) Self-help and support groups for people bereaved by suicide. A survey of groups in the UK. Unpublished report.

—— (1996) 'Surviving suicide', *Psychiatry in Practice*, Autumn: 18–20.

Winston's Wish (2001) *Beyond the Rough Rock. Supporting a Child Who has Been Bereaved Through Suicide*. Gloucester: Winston's Wish.

Woolf, L. (1969) *The Journey not the Arrival Matters. An Autobiography of the Years 1939 to 1969*. London: Hogarth Press.

Worden, W.J. (1991) *Grief Counselling and Grief Therapy*. London: Routledge (2nd edn).

Wrobleski, A. (1984–5) 'The Suicide Survivors Grief Group', *Omega* 15, 2: 173–84.

—— (1986) 'Guilt and suicide', *Afterwords*, October.

Zisook, S., Chentsova-Dutton, Y. and Shuchter, S.R. (1998) 'PTSD following bereavement', *Annals of Clinical Psychiatry* 10, 4: 157–63.

Name index

Abernathy, C.B. 67, 126
Alexander, V. 43, 93
Allman, C. 20, 23
Alvarez, A. 5, 11, 12, 62, 63, 69, 70, 225
Andress, V.R. 20
Appel, Y.H. 147
Archer, J. 36, 218, 228
Armson, Simon 9
Asgard, U. 17, 38

Balach, L. 20, 23
Barker, A. 7
Barnett, B.R. 193, 218, 233
Barraclough, B. 11, 18, 38, 71, 80, 83, 87, 88, 100, 115, 116, 123, 125, 136, 182, 187, 188
Barrett, T.W. 18, 22, 23
Barwick, C. 182, 189, 195
Battle, A. 182, 189, 190, 217, 221, 225
Behrens, T. 163
Bell, D. 193
Bernhardt, G.R. 18
Biddle, L. 28, 75, 80, 81, 82–3, 85, 86, 87, 186, 187, 188
Billow, C.J. 189
Black, D. 115
Boakes, J. 20
Bowlby, J. 26, 29, 63, 72, 100, 103, 104, 115, 162, 175
Boyland, M.-B. 20
Branson, M.L. 21, 23
Brent, D. 20, 23, 112, 113, 162
Bricker, P.L. 189, 191
Bridge, J. 23, 112, 113, 162
Brown, H. 20
Brownstein, M. 140
Bruno, A.A. 23

Cain, A.C. 16, 18, 35, 67–8, 95, 101, 116, 117, 121
Calhoun, L.G. 67, 125, 126, 131

Campbell, D. 18–19, 218
Campbell, F.R. 184
Canobbio, R. 23, 112, 113
Carlsson-Bergstrom, M. 17, 38
Carstairs, G.M. 3
Casement, P. 229, 231
Cerel, J. 115
Chambers, D.R. 4, 5, 187
Chentsova-Dutton, Y. 26
Chesser, E. 8
Clark, S.E. 4, 11, 19, 22–3, 24, 25, 26, 27, 30, 44, 46, 48, 63, 67, 70, 90, 91, 96, 104, 106, 107, 136, 137, 150, 152–3, 154, 155, 157, 159, 160, 162, 169, 182, 185, 186, 189, 191, 193, 195, 201, 202, 205, 208, 213, 223, 226
Cleiren, M.P.H.D. 23, 24, 25
Cline, S. 86, 112
Colt, G.H. 17
Compassionate Friends, The 183
Conley, B.H. 43–4, 72
Connolly, J. 162
Constantino, R.E. 23, 189, 191
Cooling, P.J. 189, 191, 195, 202, 205, 208, 213
Cooper, C. 232
Corcoran, P. 4
Corey, D.M. 20
Curphey, T. 17

Dare, C. 29, 105–6
Davenport, Diana 132
Davis, C.G. 66
Department of Health xv–xvi, 3, 57
Diekstra, R.F.W. 23, 24, 25
Doka, K.J. 21, 125
Downey, Anne 43, 110, 128, 146, 150, 176
Dunne, E.J. 15, 25, 31, 117, 118–19, 144, 185, 193, 204, 208, 213, 223, 224–5, 231, 232

Subject index